J.K. LASSER'S™

Estate Planning for Baby Boomers and Retirees

To Joe

Good Fortune

and God's Blessings

Stewart H Welch III

J.K. LASSER'S ™

Estate Planning for
Baby Boomers and Retirees

Stewart H. Welch III

MACMILLAN • USA

J.K. Lasser Editorial and Production

Elliott Eiss, Member of the New York Bar, Editorial Director of the J.K. Lasser Institute™

Gordon Macomber, President, Macmillan Consumer Reference

Lloyd Short, Senior Vice President, Macmillan Consumer Reference

Kathy Nebenhaus, Publisher, Lifestyle Publishing Group

Karin Hirle, Brand Manager

Jennifer Perillo, Managing Editor

Claire Smith, Marketing Manager

Nick Petro, Book Coordinator

George McKeon, Cover Designer

designLab and Holly Wittenberg, Interior Designers

Arun Das, Production Editor

Bill Levy and Eric Brinkman, Layout

Helen Chin, Copyeditor and Indexer

Lisa Nicholas, Proofreader

Stephen Adams and Patricia Douglas, Illustrators

Publisher's Note: *Estate Planning for Baby Boomers and Retirees* is published in recognition of the great need for useful information regarding the income tax laws for the millions of men and women who must fill out returns. We believe the research and interpretation by the J.K. Lasser Institute™ of the nation's tax laws to be authoritative and of help to taxpayers. Reasonable care has been taken in the preparation of the text. Taxpayers are cautioned, however, that this book is sold with the understanding that the publisher and the contributors are not engaged in rendering legal, accounting, or other professional services herein. Taxpayers with specific tax problems are urged to seek the professional advice of a tax accountant, lawyer, or preparer.

The publisher and contributors to this book specifically disclaim any responsibility for any liability, loss, or risk (financial, personal, or otherwise) that may be claimed or incurred as a consequence, directly or indirectly, of the use and/or application of any of the contents of this book.

Macmillan General Reference

A Simon & Schuster Macmillan Company

1633 Broadway

New York, NY 10019

ISBN 0-02-862529-3

Cataloging-in-Publication data available from the Library of Congress

Manufactured in the United States of America

10 9 8 7 6 5 4 3 2 1

Contents

Acknowledgments

This book would have never happened without the help and moral support from many people.

TECHNICAL ASSISTANCE

First and foremost I would like to thank my friend and tax advisor, Bob Holman, CPA. Bob is a senior partner with the accounting firm of Donaldson, Holman and West, PC, in Birmingham, Alabama. I have had the distinct pleasure of working with Bob for more than two decades. He is unquestionably one of the brightest people I have ever met. Bob not only completed a technical review of this book, but he also offered numerous changes and additions. I am very much in his debt.

On the legal front, I received needed assistance from my two friends: Alec Jones, Jr., and Jim Henderson of the law firm Pritchard-McCall and Jones in Birmingham. Kirby Sevier (Maynard, Cooper, and Gale, PC, of Birmingham) is a top estate planning attorney and assisted by helping me locate technical reference guides and has always been available to answer any technical questions I have.

As most of you are aware, life insurance can be a very confusing product to understand. I am fortunate to have had the assistance of two of the country's brightest insurance minds regarding my insurance research. First, I would like to thank my father, Stewart H. Welch, Jr., CLU. My father has been a top professional in the business for more than 50 years. He never ceases to amaze me with his energy and creative ideas. I have truly been blessed to have his guidance throughout my life. Lloyd Wilson, CLU, is another leader in the field of life insurance who gave his time generously to assist me with this book project. Lloyd is one of those caring people who always puts the interest of his clients first, even if it means missing an important sale. I would also like to thank the people at Harrison James for their assistance in running insurance illustrations. Harrison James is an excellent life insurance wholesaler owned by my friend, Clint Janecek.

Another complicated area of finance is charitable giving. I am indebted to Sandra Henningsen and Lon Dufek at Comdel, Inc., Crescendo Planned Gifts Software (Camarillo, California) for their help with calculations regarding charitable contributions. A. Charles Schultz, president of Comdel has developed extensive software for evaluating the benefits of making gifts through various types of trusts. I would also be remiss if I did not thank Tom Harris for introducing me to the people at Comdel. Tom is Church Administrator at Briarwood Church in Birmingham and has been a source of information for me for many years.

THE WELCH GROUP ASSOCIATES

I could not have considered attempting this project without the assistance and moral support of my associates. Gina Starr put in countless hours of developing charts and tables as well as proofing my work and offering constructive advice for changes. She was also invaluable in putting together the list of top professionals that appears in the Appendix. Sheri Robinson is the managing senior associate at The Welch Group. Sheri manages the day-to-day operations and also provided much of the mathematical calculations for this book. She is smart, always greets you with a huge smile, and I count her as one of my greatest business blessings. Chad McWhirter began working for my company in 1993 and has been a valuable resource ever since. For this book project, Chad completed much of the historical research regarding investment portfolios. Other associates I am indebted to include: Isabel Corley, Kristy Lynn, Brandy Hydrick, Laura Archer, and Stan Purvis. Each of these associates has contributed in some way toward the completion of this book and each is a pleasure to work with. Charlotte Isbell is our receptionist and always makes everyone feel well taken care of.

MACMILLAN

I feel very fortunate to have had the opportunity to work with the people at Macmillan. Not only are they very talented but they are very patient. From day one Elliot Eiss (Editorial Director, J.K. Lasser Institute) has offered friendship and encouragement. Jennifer Perillo (Managing Editor, Lifestyle Publishing Group) worked closely with me regarding completion schedules and remains delightful and calm, all the while constantly juggling a very hectic schedule. The busiest of the busy is Kathy Nebenhaus (Publisher, Lifestyle Publishing Group). I thank Kathy for having faith in this project and giving it "the green light." Finally, I want to thank Arun Das (Production Editor) for his patience in working with my staff regarding production issues.

My publisher also provided me with two excellent legal technical advisors: George Smith and Elizabeth Grant of the law firm Robinson and Cole, LLP, in Greenwich, Connecticut. Both did an excellent job of technical review and offered ideas which helped to improve the quality of this project.

THE TOP ADVISORS LIST

I am grateful for the help of two people who assisted me with the development of the state by state listing of top advisors. Tom Nawrocki is senior editor at Worth magazine and headed up the enormous project of the "Nation's Best Financial Advisors" published by Worth each year. The Worth staff puts potential candidates through an extensive screening process in order to identify top financial advisors throughout the United States. Tom is a very professional, friendly sort who saved me many hours of research by his generous offer to use Worth's Best Advisors list. Sally Conlon is the Director for the National Association of Estate Planners and Councils. Sally also reduced my work load by helping me identify CPAs that are also Accredited Estate Planners (AEP).

MY FAMILY

Writing a book of this type is a full-time job. Since running my company is also a full-time job, my family ends up paying a large price for my commitments. The biggest price, by far, was paid by my wife, Kathie. She endured many weeknights and most weekends alone while I wrote for literally six months. Throughout the entire time she remained very supportive and I love her even more for it. I especially want to thank my mother, Sally Welch, for her constant prayers and support. She is a fine person who has been a guiding light all of my life. I also have two wonderful sisters, Jean Watson and Babs Hart, who have always been cheerleaders for all my endeavors.

MY CLIENTS

There is no way to express how grateful I am for the wonderful clients I have the pleasure of serving. Each, in their own way, has contributed to my own learning and therefore to this book.

And finally, I owe a huge debt of gratitude to my longtime friend 'D.E.' Many thanks for all your support and friendship. Your faith in me has given me the confidence to accomplish more than I otherwise could have.

Introduction

Considering the abundance of personal finance books, I have asked myself whether I have something unique or particularly helpful to say. I consider myself fortunate to have worked in the financial services industry since 1973. During this period of time, I have had the opportunity to work with many Baby Boomers and Retirees across this great country. While these two groups would appear to be very different, they share one key characteristic: These groups take pride in both their financial success and in their ability to handle their finances.

Those of us born between 1944 and 1964 represent 80 million Americans of the so-called "Baby Boomer" generation. We represent a sizable economic power and, in fact, control trillions of dollars in assets. In addition to substantial wealth accumulation in our own right, we will inherit an estimated $10 trillion from our parents. For the eldest of the Baby Boomers, retirement is as little as a decade away.

As a Baby Boomer or Retiree you may already have accumulated a sizable amount of assets and feel comfortable handling your investments. However, chances are you haven't paid sufficient attention to your estate plan. This is the reason I wanted to write this book. The purpose of *J.K. Lasser's Estate Planning for Baby Boomers and Retirees* is to make certain that you have taken steps to make sure your estate is in order and that you have a specific strategy in place. Whether you are a Baby Boomer who is just getting your financial feet on the ground or you are a Retiree and millionaire several times over, this book offers important tactics you can use today and in the years to come.

If your parents are living, I encourage you to keep their situation in mind because some of the more advanced strategies may be more appropriate for them than for yourself. You may want to consult with them or loan this book to them. After all, you should have a common family goal of minimizing estate taxes in order to maximize the amount of money that you can transfer to your heirs and charitable organizations.

As a first step in getting your estate plan ready, you will need to assess the adequacy of your current estate plan. What is the value of your total estate? You will learn how to determine your estate "net worth." This is vital because knowing your estate's value will let you define the resources available to your family to provide for their income needs should you die prematurely. You will also be able to determine approximately how much in estate taxes your heirs would owe.

For Baby Boomers, it is also important to determine if you are "on track" toward retirement, i.e., are you accumulating enough investment assets to provide you with a worry-free retirement? Studies indicate that Baby Boomers as a group are only saving one-third of what they need in order to accumulate enough assets to maintain their lifestyles during retirement. In many cases, this "shortfall" will be made up from inheritances. If you find out that you're lagging behind, this book will help you determine how much you need to be investing to get on track and you'll learn how to devise an appropriate investment plan.

For Retirees, I'll show you how much income you can afford to draw from your portfolio so that you can be sure you never run out of money.

Another key aspect of estate planning is, of course, having a will. Research indicates that as many as 80 percent of Americans don't have a will. Fortunately, more than 50 percent of Baby Boomers and Retirees do have wills. If you're in the 50 percent of the population that hasn't yet drawn up a will, you should stop procrastinating. It really matters if you die without a will! In this book, you'll read about the perils of dying without a will—the resulting chaos will surprise you. I know that by the time you complete the related chapters, you'll be thoroughly convinced that you need to have a will. You'll learn how to prepare yourself so that you can minimize the time and expense of working with an attorney.

The use of trusts is a vital part of most estate plans. You can use trusts to protect your children from themselves, to protect you from possible future creditors, or to save on income and estate taxes. These are powerful weapons in the war to protect your assets for yourself as well as future heirs. Many of you carry large amounts of life insurance. Could you reduce taxes by utilizing some type of trust? Absolutely. You'll learn about *the irrevocable life insurance trust, living trust and other types of trust.*

As a Baby Boomer, you may be facing the difficult task of funding your children's education. As a Retiree, you may be willing to help fund the education costs of your grandchildren. You'll learn how to effectively use custodial accounts and minors' trusts.

If you are interested in providing financial support to a religious organization, an educational institution, or a favorite charity, you'll gain insights on the best ways to maximize your donations. Often, gifts to tax-exempt organizations can solve a financial dilemma that you face, such as how to convert low basis non-income producing property into income producing property while avoiding a large tax bill.

If you have accumulated enough assets for your retirement years, you may want to shift your focus to transfer strategies for your children and other heirs. One of the hottest tools in use today is the *family limited partnership.* This form of property ownership will allow you to transfer significant wealth at a fraction of its market value while maintaining control of your property. This technique and the *limited liability corporation* are explained in detail.

The wealth of many Baby Boomers and Retirees is primarily a result of ownership of a family business. Often a major goal is to ensure that the business remains in the family so that it can be continued by future generations of family members. Obstacles to this goal include estate taxes and lack of liquidity. The solution is a well-developed transition plan which is also fully explained in this book.

In today's litigious society, one of the greatest nightmares is a lawsuit that results in financial ruin. Often we feel helpless, cross our fingers, and hope it does not happen to us. A better approach is to be proactive. If you consider yourself a likely target, there are many things you can do to protect your assets. Some solutions are as simple as transferring assets to a spouse who is less "at risk." Other solutions include the use of trusts, family limited partnerships and even more exotic options such as foreign asset protection trusts.

Most people who have accumulated enough assets to have a taxable estate instinctively know that they should take action to avoid estate taxes. Often they do not take appropriate action because of pre-existing psychological roadblocks that they have about money. In Chapter 14, I discuss the different money personality types and show how each type can deal positively with troubling issues.

One thing you are almost certain to need in developing and implementing your estate plan is the assistance of a qualified professional. Finding the right person, someone who is truly qualified, can be a daunting task. It is one of the reasons many Baby Boomers and Retirees fail to establish their estate plan. In an attempt to make this an easier task, I have identified top professional advisors across the country. They are listed on a state-by-state, city-by-city basis in the appendix. Also included in this appendix are tips on how to get the most out of your advisors while minimizing their fees.

As a Baby Boomer or Retiree, your future is bright if you will take the time to plan. Picking up this book is an essential first step. Carefully reading it and implementing the strategies most appropriate to your situation will enable you to take a giant leap toward taking charge of your financial destiny. May God smile on your journey.

Understanding Estate Planning Basics

CHAPTER 1

Why Do You Need Estate Planning?

B efore we can discuss why you need estate planning, you have to understand what estate planning is.

WHAT IS ESTATE PLANNING?

Estate planning is the process of controlling your assets both during your life and after death with three primary objectives in mind. First, you want to ensure that your assets will always be sufficient to provide for your lifestyle needs. Second, you want to make certain that your assets go to the people and/or organizations of your choosing. Finally, you want to minimize the amount of taxes, fees, and court interference. This definition is broad, as well it should be. A properly designed estate plan encompasses the landscape of financial issues:

Investment Planning

Your investment plan should focus on providing adequate assets to meet your retirement needs, the cost of funding education for your children or grandchildren, and other issues such as financial assistance for elderly parents. It should be designed so that expected long-term returns will meet your financial objectives. Your risk tolerance should be examined to ensure that your portfolio is not too aggressive for your personality.

Tax Planning

All aspects of managing your finances should be carried out in the context of tax efficiency. Consider the following question. How can you best use tax-deferred or tax-free investment vehicles? Are there ways to accomplish some of your goals by shifting income from yourself to another family member in a lower tax bracket? Can you make a gift to a charity in such a way that you receive long-term economic benefits? Is it possible to convert ordinary income which is taxed at your highest tax bracket, to long-term capital gains which is taxed at a maximum of 20% (federal)?

Protecting Your Family

How long will you live? Of course, you cannot answer this question, but your estate plan should address the possibility of a premature death as well as the possibility that you will live "too long." Simple solutions to "dying too soon" include the use of life insurance. Issues of "living too long" are often handled through use of trusts, living trusts, or a power of attorney.

Protecting Your Assets

Given our litigious society, if you have accumulated significant assets, your estate plan should include an asset protection plan. Solutions here can include simple strategies such as liability insurance to the more exotic strategies such as using foreign asset protection trusts.

Carrying Out Your Personal Goals and Wishes

Do you have a deep desire to protect our environment? Do you want to provide financial support for your alma mater? How about a relative? Outline all your goals; then design your estate plan to carry out your goals.

Gathering and Drafting Appropriate Documents

A vital part of your estate plan will consist of developing legal documents for the purpose of carrying out your wishes. The most basic of the documents will be your will. Other documents include deeds, mortgages, trusts, and property titles. Part of your estate plan should include gathering and organizing all vital documents. This has two important advantages. First, your documents will be easy for you to locate and retrieve when they need to be reviewed. Second, your survivors are not left searching for documents needed to settle your estate after your death. Believe me, your loved ones will think kindly of you for having done this for them.

Obviously, estate planning is more than just writing your will! Done well, it will not only give you and your family great peace of mind, but it will also help you accumulate wealth faster and more effectively.

THE BENEFITS OF ESTATE PLANNING

Developing your estate plan is perhaps the most important financial step you can take. It creates focus and puts you in charge of many aspects of your finances. Let's look at the benefits to your immediate family.

If you are single your estate plan provides for the orderly transfer of your assets to the people or organizations you desire. You will have minimized the hassle to those people who would assist in settling your estate. If you are married and have children, the issues will usually be more complex, but the benefits of planning will also be more profound. You will want to make certain that your surviving family has immediate access to cash to cover ongoing living expenses while your estate is being settled. While it may be hard to imagine that this would be a problem, I have seen numerous cases where the courts "freeze" assets for weeks or even months, while trying to determine the proper disposition of the estate. The surviving spouse is forced to "apply" to the court for needed cash to pay current living expenses. I am sure you can imagine the additional stress this can cause.

In your estate plan, you may also want to address issues regarding funding for your children's or grandchildren's education. If you are a Baby Boomer with young children, you may want your surviving spouse to have the "option" of not working so that he or she can devote more attention to your children. Raising children in a one-parent household can be quite a challenge.

If your spouse lacks knowledge or experience in financial matters, your estate plan should provide for assistance with financial management such as setting up trusts. Also, your estate plan should consider the consequences of both you and your spouse dying simultaneously. If you have minor or incompetent children, you will want to select someone to manage your assets for their benefit. You do not want to have the court make this decision for you. In this situation, your estate plan should also address when your child will receive your assets free of trust. When children receive substantial assets before they are mature enough to handle the assets properly, the results can be devastating.

I remember a case involving a child movie star. Because he was a minor, his earnings were held in trust until he was legally an adult (age 18 in his state of residence). I am sure you can imagine what happened when he turned 18. Fast cars and late night parties consumed a small fortune in less than 24 months. The last time I checked he was living in a trailer park trying to figure out where he went wrong. Talk about a missed opportunity!

If you are a Baby Boomer with minor children it is critical that you address the issue of who will raise your children if you and your spouse die prematurely. Give very careful thought to your choice of a legal guardian. Remember it is this person's values that are likely to be instilled in your children. In developing your estate plan, you will also want to give consideration to the age and financial condition of a potential guardian. Some guardians may lack the child-rearing skills you feel are necessary. Make sure that your plan does not create an additional financial burden on the guardian.

Do you have a favorite cause, charity, or religious organization? You can use your estate plan to provide assistance either during your life or at your death. This is one of the instances in which our government actually provides you with incentives to do so.

During your lifetime and at your death, your estate plan should focus on how best to reduce taxes and expenses. During your life, there are primarily income tax issues. At death, there are also estate tax issues and administrative fees as well as other expenses to consider. Plan well and you can minimize costs so that more money will pass to your family.

Your estate plan can also be used to provide assistance and guidance to members of your extended family. Consider carefully, for example, if you may need to provide financial support for a parent, sibling, niece, or nephew. If the answer is yes or maybe, there may be solutions that also provide tax benefits to you.

The ultimate benefit of a well-crafted estate plan is that it provides you with a compass for managing your finances. It will lessen not only your own stress, but that of your loved ones as well. It is the appropriate thing for you to do and is worth the time, effort, and expense.

THE NIGHTMARES OF POOR PLANNING

All too often, people procrastinate and neglect their estate planning. The results can be devastating. Take a moment to review the list below and determine if any of the examples could apply to you or your family. If the answer is yes, let this serve as your "wake up call" to get started now!

- You are sued, which results in exceedingly high judgment against you. Your estate plan should include asset protection strategies.

- You become disabled and are unable to handle your finances. Part of an appropriate estate plan includes documents designating who will take control of your finances in the event of your disability.

- You die without naming the guardians of your child or children. This mistake forces the courts to make this decision for you, possibly resulting in your children being raised by someone you would not have chosen.

- Your children inherit money at an age which destroys both their ambition and work ethic. I have seen this happen often. This problem can be solved by setting up a trust that provides for their needs without over-indulging them.

- You own a business or real estate that must be sold at "fire sale" prices in order to pay your estate taxes. I've seen cases where property had to be sold for half its true value because the taxes were due but real estate prices were depressed. You must determine your potential estate tax liability and determine where the cash would come from to pay that liability.

- You or your spouse wind up in a nursing home and the bills consume all of your assets. One potential solution to this problem is to own a long-term care insurance policy.

- You fail to provide for a disabled or special needs child. This results in them becoming a ward of the state. If you have a disabled child you'll need to consider special trust planning.

- Your family ends up paying excessive legal fees and court costs in order to settle your estate. You may not be able to eliminate these costs, but you can significantly reduce them through proper planning.

Each of these "nightmares" has a solution that can be addressed through your estate plan.

THE MYTHS OF ESTATE PLANNING

Are you still not convinced that estate planning is for you? I often find that people have preconceived notions about estate planning that have no basis in reality. Let's examine a few of the more popular versions.

Myth #1: Estate Planning Is for Old People

You have plenty of time to develop your estate plan, right? Wrong. Obviously, you have no idea how much time you have. Many of the best strategies will take months, even years to implement. Unless your family circumstances and finances are incredibly simple, you need to begin developing your estate plan *now*.

Myth #2: Estate Planning Is for the Rich

Be careful to distinguish between your *financial net worth* and your *estate net worth*. Adding life insurance death benefits to your other assets can easily place you in estate tax jeopardy! Additionally, there are many estate planning issues other than taxes. For example, consider the issue of financial management in the event you become incompetent due to an accident or illness.

Myth #3: Estate Planning Focuses on Death

Many people avoid estate planning because it makes them think about death—either their own death or the death of someone they love. I have had many client meetings where one client broke out in tears at the thought of a loved one's death. Obviously, estate planning must deal with death, but many living issues are just as important. For example, what is the best way to fund your child's or grandchild's college education? Do you pay it from cash flow or do you gift them money and use a custodial account or educational trust? What is the best way to protect your hard earned assets from a successful lawsuit? Your estate plan must address an array of living issues as well as death issues.

GUIDELINES FOR ESTABLISHING A SUCCESSFUL ESTATE PLAN

Estate Planning is a process, not an event. The following steps will help you move through that process more efficiently.

Get Organized

Pull all of your vital documents together and organize them so that you or the person(s) who would assist in settling your estate can easily locate each document. For my clients, I developed a Personal Handbook. This is a large portable and expandable book with handles. It has pockets for holding wills, insurance policies, tax returns, etc. along with a table of contents. My clients bring the Personal Handbook in for their annual meeting and my staff updates it. An alternative is to set up a designated file cabinet at your home or office. Essential documents would include:

- Federal Tax Returns (last 7 years)

- State Tax Returns (last 7 years)

- Pay Stubs (2 most recent)

- Financial Statement

- Confirmation Statements (brokerage accounts, mutual funds, etc.)

- Retirement Plan Statements (IRA, Keogh, pension, profit sharing, etc.)

- Insurance Policies (life, disability, property & casualty, health, etc.)

- Amortization Schedules (home, business, property, etc.)

- Business Documents (partnership agreements, corporate papers, etc.)

- Corporate/Partnership Tax Returns

- Wills (both client and spouse)

- Trust Agreements

- Gift Tax Returns

- Employee Benefits Summary

- Notes, Mortgages, Deeds to Real Estate, Termite Bond, Survey, Appraisal

- Bank Account Statements
- Credit Card Statements
- Birth Certificates
- Car Titles
- Marriage Certificates
- Retirement Plan Beneficiary Designations

Determine Your Current Estate Net Worth

This subject will be covered in detail in Chapter 2. It is vital that you know where you are now. I often visit with prospective clients who think they have small estates, and therefore, have little concern for estate planning. They are shocked to find that not only could they potentially owe estate taxes, but that those taxes may run into the tens of thousands of dollars! When you include your life insurance, the dollars add up fast.

Establish Your Estate Planning Goals

We will discuss how to do this in Chapter 3. There are many, many strategies available to accomplish a vast array of potential goals. By establishing them early, you bring order and focus to your estate plan while avoiding the "hit and miss" planning used by most people. Your goals should be divided into lifetime vs. death goals.

Hire Competent Professional Help

You will likely need a team of competent advisors from various fields to assist you in accomplishing your estate planning goals. The list of potential advisors you will need includes attorneys, financial advisors, insurance representatives, accountants, and bankers. Many of these people specialize within their general fields. For example, some attorneys specialize in estate planning. My own practice specializes in a relatively new field called *Wealth Management*. Wealth Management focuses on wealth accumulation and multigenerational wealth transfers. You will find life insurance representatives who specialize in working with business owners and bankers who cater to high net worth clients. Putting together the right advisors and then working with them as a team will pay big dividends in your end results.

Monitor/Review Your Progress

Estate planning is a dynamic process, not a static one. Your circumstances are constantly changing as are our tax laws. You should review your estate plan every year or every other year. This ensures that you will remain on the leading edge of the strategies and techniques available to meet your goals.

CASE STUDY

Proper planning can make a significant difference even in a seemingly simple case. When I first interviewed Tom and Jo Anne Jones, they fit the profile of many of today's Baby Boomers. Tom, age 46, is an executive with a software development company. He is married to Jo Anne, age 42, and they have three children: Donald, age 16, Suzanne, age 12, and Mary, age 10. Tom has always been concerned that his family be well taken care of should he die prematurely. To that end, he had purchased a $1,250,000 term life insurance policy to go along with his group coverage in the amount of $150,000. They had simple wills drawn in which Tom and Jo Anne leave everything to each other. They came to see me because they felt they needed to develop a financial game plan and wondered if their wills were appropriate.

Regarding estate taxes, I was able to assure them that if one of them died, there would be no estate taxes because of the **Unlimited Marital Deduction**.

> **Unlimited Marital Deduction:** The law provides that you can leave an unlimited amount of assets to a surviving spouse free of estate taxes. This has the effect of *postponing* the estate taxes until the death of that surviving spouse.

However, if they *both* died, their taxes could exceed $700,000! They were in disbelief and asked me to show them how that was possible. Let's review a summary of their case facts:

$1,057,000	Assets
− 213,500	Total Liabilities
843,500	Financial Net Worth
+1,250,000	Personal Life Insurance—Tom
+ 150,000	Group Life Insurance—Tom
+ 200,000	Personal Life Insurance—Jo Anne
2,443,500	Taxable Estate (Estate Net Worth)
− 796,065	Federal Estate Tax (1998)
$1,647,435	Net Available for Heirs

(For a detailed Estate Net Worth Statement, see Worksheet 1-1 on p. 13.)

Federal estate taxes consumed $796,065 or 31% of the Jones' estate. "Could this be avoided?" they asked. Absolutely! Using two simple strategies, an Irrevocable Life Insurance Trust and a Credit Shelter Trust, we were able to reduce this potential liability to zero! The specifics of these techniques will be discussed later in this book. Were their case facts unusual? The amount of life insurance was higher than I typically see, but it was not inappropriate. The point is that case facts that appear simplistic on the surface are often found to be much more complex once you complete a detailed review. It is important to identify the issues early so that appropriate strategies can be implemented.

WORKSHEET 1-1

Sample Estate Net Worth Statement—Jones
As of 2/20/XX

Your Name:	Tom Jones	Date of Birth:	4/13/XX
Spouse Name:	Jo Anne Jones	Date of Birth:	2/5/XX

	Ownership			
Assets	**Tom**	**Jo Anne**	**Joint**	**Family Total**
Cash & Cash Equivalents:				
Checking & Savings Account	$	$	$ 25,000	$ 25,000
Other:	$	$	$	$
Personal & Household Property:				
Automobiles	$ 25,000	$	$ 12,000	$ 37,000
Furniture	$	$	$ 20,000	$ 20,000
Jewelry	$	$	$	$
Personal Effects	$	$	$ 8,000	$ 8,000
Art	$	$	$	$
Coin Collections	$	$	$	$
Other:	$	$	$	$
Real Estate (Estimated Current Market Value):				
Residence(s)	$	$	$350,000	$ 350,000

Other Properties:
  Florida Condominium
  (1/2 Interest)
	$	$	$150,000	$ 150,000

	$	$	$	$
Investments (Estimated Current Market Value):				
Individual Stocks	$	$	$	$
Individual Bonds	$	$	$	$
Personal Mutual Funds	$	$	$ 75,000	$ 75,000

Other Investments:
  Real Estate Ltd.
  Partnership
	$ 10,000	$	$	$ 10,000

continued on next page

WORKSHEET 1-1 (CONTINUED)				
	Ownership			
Assets	Tom	Jo Anne	Joint	Family Total
JoAnne's Inheritance from her aunt	$	$ 10,000	$	$ 10,000
	$	$	$	$
Retirement Plans: Tom's IRA	$ 35,000	$	XX	$ 35,000
Jo Anne's IRA	$	$ 12,000	XX	$ 12,000
Tom's 401(k)	$ 175,000	$	XX	$ 175,000
Equity Interest in a Business	$ 150,000	$	XX	$ 150,000
Life Insurance (Face Amount):				
Personal	$1,250,000	$200,000	XX	$1,450,000
Employer Group	$ 150,000	$	XX	$ 150,000
Total Assets	$1,795,000	$222,000	$640,000	$2,657,000

In our next chapter, we will review how our Federal tax system works, develop *your* Estate Net Worth Statement, calculate your potential estate taxes, and outline a broad range of strategies you can use to reduce taxes and implement your estate plan.

	Ownership			
Liabilities	**Tom**	**Jo Anne**	**Joint**	**Family Total**
Short Term Liabilities:				
Credit Cards	$ 2,500	$	$	$ 2,500
Long Term Liabilities:				
Mortgage(s)	$	$	$175,000	$ 175,000
Automobile Loan(s)	$ 9,000	$	$ 12,000	$ 21,000
Other Loans: Home Equity Loan	$	$	$ 15,000	$ 15,000
Miscellaneous Liabilities:				
Unpaid Taxes	$	$	$	$
Estimated Funeral & Administrative Expenses[1]	$	$	$	$
Total Liabilities	$ 11,500	$ 0	$202,000	$ 213,500
Estate Net Worth (Total Assets Less Total Liabilities)	$1,783,500	$222,000	$438,000	$2,443,500

[1] *Funeral and administrative expenses can vary from 2 to 8%. For simplicity, they are ignored in this case study.*

CHAPTER 2

Determining Your Estate Net Worth

Minimizing the amount of estate taxes you will owe should not be your only goal, but it is certainly an important one. Our estate tax system is nothing more than a wealth transfer system whereby the government takes a portion of your wealth and "redistributes" it to the masses. Our lawmakers' original idea was to tax just the very wealthy, but like so many tax programs gone haywire (Social Security, for instance), many middle income Americans now face the possibility of estate taxes. All you need is a home, adequate life insurance, and presto, Uncle Sam's hand is in your back pocket!

Fortunately, Congress has seen fit to provide some relief in the form of the Taxpayer Relief Act of 1997. This new tax law has brought us a hodge-podge of changes, some of which are surprisingly beneficial, particularly in the area of estate planning. One of the most important changes is the increase in the amount of assets you can leave a non-spouse free of tax called the **Applicable Exclusion Amount.** Under the old tax law, this amount was $600,000. Under the Taxpayer Relief Act of 1997, the Applicable Exclusion Amount is scheduled to increase to $1,000,000 by the year 2006. (See Table 2-1 for the "phase-in" schedule.)

> **Applicable Exclusion Amount:** The amount of assets you can leave to someone, other than a spouse, free of estate or gift taxes.

TABLE 2-1
FUTURE APPLICABLE EXCLUSION AMOUNT INCREASES

Year	Exclusion Amount	Increase from Previous Amount
1998	$ 625,000	$ 25,000
1999	$ 650,000	$ 25,000
2000	$ 675,000	$ 25,000
2001	$ 675,000	$ 0
2002	$ 700,000	$ 25,000
2003	$ 700,000	$ 0
2004	$ 850,000	$ 150,000
2005	$ 950,000	$ 100,000
2006	$1,000,000	$ 50,000

I am troubled, however, by the scheduled increases because a full 75% of them are delayed until after 2003. Our Congressional representatives have been quick to congratulate themselves for increasing the exemption to $1,000,000. However, I believe that some future congress facing budget problems will take aim at us "rich" folks and eliminate these promised increases.

UNDERSTANDING THE ESTATE TAX SYSTEM

It seems like everything you do creates another tax: income taxes on your earnings; sales tax on your purchases; property taxes on your real estate holdings; capital gains taxes on your security sales. But taxes because you died? Give me a break! Well, in fact, the government does give you a break of sorts. Here's how the system works:

First, you die. Ouch! Then your **executor** or **executrix** makes a list of all of your assets (called an estate inventory).

> **Executor or Executrix:** The person or institution that is legally responsible for settling an estate. They may also be referred to as the estate representative or administrator. Normally, you appoint them by way of instructions in your will.

The executor or executrix then subtracts all of your liabilities including funeral expenses and the administrative costs of settling your estate (attorneys' fees, court costs, and so on). This net estate is called the **Adjusted Gross Estate.** If you were married and left everything to your spouse, you would receive an Unlimited Marital Deduction, which means that you would owe no taxes at this time. The government is going to wait until your spouse dies to get their estate taxes. If you leave money to qualified charities, you get to deduct that as well. You have now arrived at your **Taxable Estate.**

TABLE 2-2
FEDERAL GIFT AND ESTATE TAX RATE TABLE
(TENTATIVE TAX)

Taxable Estate	Tax Owed	Plus %	On Amount in Excess of:
$ 0 – 10,000	$ 0	18	$ 0
$ 10,001 – 20,000	$ 1,800	20	$ 10,000
$ 20,001 – 40,000	$ 3,800	22	$ 20,000
$ 40,001 – 60,000	$ 8,200	24	$ 40,000
$ 60,001 – 80,000	$ 13,000	26	$ 60,000
$ 80,001 – 100,000	$ 18,200	28	$ 80,000
$ 100,001 – 150,000	$ 23,800	30	$ 100,000
$ 150,001 – 250,000	$ 38,800	32	$ 150,000
$ 250,001 – 500,000	$ 70,800	34	$ 250,000
$ 500,001 – 750,000	$ 155,800	37	$ 500,000
$ 750,001 – 1,000,000	$ 248,300	39	$ 750,000
$ 1,000,001 – 1,250,000	$ 345,800	41	$ 1,000,000
$ 1,250,001 – 1,500,000	$ 448,300	43	$ 1,250,000
$ 1,500,001 – 2,000,000	**$ 555,800**	**45**	**$ 1,500,000**
$ 2,000,001 – 2,500,000	$ 780,800	49	$ 2,000,000
$ 2,500,001 – 3,000,000	$ 1,025,800	53	$ 2,500,000
$ 3,000,001 – 10,000,000	$ 1,290,800	55	$ 3,000,000
$ 10,000,001 – 21,040,000	$ 5,140,800	60	$ 10,000,000
Over $21,040,001	$ 11,764,800	55	$ 21,040,000

Note: These rates were effective as of June 1998 and are subject to change.

Your executor then figures the tentative tax using the IRS Tax Tables (See Table 2-2).

From the tentative tax amount, your executor subtracts the **Unified Federal Gift and Estate Tax Credit**. This is a dollar-for-dollar deduction from the tentative tax amount. (See Table 2-3).

Unified Federal Gift and Estate Tax Credit: The dollar credit amount allowed by the federal government which has the effect of making a certain portion of your estate not subject to taxes.

TABLE 2-3
APPLICABLE FEDERAL GIFT AND ESTATE TAX CREDIT AND EXCLUSION AMOUNTS

Year of Death	Unified Estate Tax Credit	Applicable Exclusion Amount[1]
1998	$ 202,050	$ 625,000
1999	$ 211,300	$ 650,000
2000	$ 220,550	$ 675,000
2001	$ 220,550	$ 675,000
2002	$ 229,800	$ 700,000
2003	$ 229,800	$ 700,000
2004	$ 287,300	$ 850,000
2005	$ 326,300	$ 950,000
2006	$ 345,800	$1,000,000

[1] These are approximate amounts.

If the result is a positive number, that is the amount of taxes that are due. Your executor must then raise the cash to pay the taxes out of your assets, usually within nine months of your death. Once the taxes are paid, your executor distributes the balance of your assets according to your directions under your will. If you do not have a will, your assets will be distributed according to state law (see Chapter 4). This process can take from six months to several years. Sound confusing? Let's walk through an example.

CASE STUDY

John and Sue Smith are Baby Boomers with a mission. They have just moved to a new state and know that they must draw new wills. They want to develop a plan that will minimize taxes and set up trusts for their two daughters in case they die prematurely. Our first objective is to determine their current **Estate Net Worth** as well as to identify how their assets are titled. We do this by completing Worksheet 2-4.

> **Estate Net Worth:** The sum of all of your assets including your share of any jointly owned assets *plus life insurance on your life* minus any debts you owe.

WORKSHEET 2-4

Sample Estate Net Worth Statement—Smith
As of 2/20/XX

Your Name:	John Smith	Date of Birth: 6/29/XX
Spouse Name:	Sue Smith	Date of Birth: 5/20/XX

	Ownership			
Assets	**John**	**Sue**	**Joint**	**Family Total**
Cash & Cash Equivalents:				
Checking & Savings Account	$	$	$ 2,500	$ 2,500
Other:	$	$	$ 7,500	$ 7,500
Personal & Household Property:				
Automobiles	$ 25,000	$ 23,000	$	$ 48,000
Furniture	$	$	$ 19,000	$ 19,000
Jewelry	$ 5,000	$ 20,000	$	$ 25,000
Personal Effects	$ 23,000	$ 19,000	$	$ 42,000
Art	$	$	$ 15,000	$ 15,000

continued on next page

WORKSHEET 2-4 (CONTINUED)			
Ownership			
Assets	**John**	**Sue**	**Joint**	**Family Total**
Coin Collections	$	$	$	$
Other:	$	$	$	$
Real Estate (Estimated Current Market Value):				
Residence(s)	$	$	$350,000	$ 350,000
Other Properties:	$	$	$	$
Investments (Estimated Current Market Value):				
Individual Stocks	$	$	$	$
Individual Bonds	$	$	$	$
Personal Mutual Funds	$	$	$ 50,000	$ 50,000
Other Investments: Ltd. Partnership	$ 5,000	$	$	$ 5,000
Retirement Plans: John's 401(k) & IRA	$ 125,000	$	XX	$ 125,000
Sue's IRA	$	$ 25,000	XX	$ 25,000
Equity Interest in a Business	$	$	XX	$
Life Insurance (Face Amount):				
Personal	$ 750,000	$250,000	XX	$1,000,000
Employer Group	$ 100,000	$	XX	$ 100,000
Total Assets	$1,033,000	$337,000	$444,000	$1,814,000
Liabilities				
Short Term Liabilities:				
Credit Cards	$ 1,500	$ 750	$	$ 2,250
Long Term Liabilities:				
Mortgage(s)	$	$	$190,000	$ 190,000
Automobile Loan(s)	$ 14,000	$ 7,000	$	$ 21,000
Other Loans: Home Equity Loan	$	$	$ 57,000	$ 57,000

continued on next page

Assets	Ownership			Family Total
	John	Sue	Joint	
Miscellaneous Liabilities:				
Unpaid Taxes	$	$	$	$
Estimated Funeral & Administrative Expenses[1] $		$	$	$
Total Liabilities	$ 15,500	$ 7,750	$247,000	$ 270,250
Estate Net Worth (Total Assets Less Total Liabilities)	$1,017,500	$329,250	$197,000	$1,543,750

[1] *Funeral and administrative expenses can vary from 2–8%. For simplicity, they are ignored in this case study.*

Next, we need to determine their potential estate tax liability. For this case study I will assume that John dies first. John has named Sue as the beneficiary of all of his life insurance policies and his retirement plans. Most of their other assets, such as their home and personal property, are titled in both of their names (Joint Tenants with Right of Survivorship). So all of John's assets would be transferred to Sue (see Worksheet 2-5).

WORKSHEET 2-5

Sue's Net Worth Statement After John's Death
As of 2/20/XX
Your Name: Sue Smith   Date of Birth: 5/20/XX

Assets	Ownership Sue
Cash & Cash Equivalents:	
Checking & Savings Account	$ 2,500
Other:	$ 7,500
Other: Proceeds from Life Insurance	$ 850,000
Personal & Household Property:	
Automobiles	$ 48,000
Furniture	$ 19,000

continued on next page

WORKSHEET 2-5 (CONTINUED)	
Assets	**Ownership** **Sue**
Jewelry	$ 25,000
Personal Effects	$ 42,000
Art	$ 15,000
Coin Collections	$
Other:	$
Real Estate (Estimated Current Market Value):	
Residence(s)	$ 350,000
Other Properties:	$
Investments (Estimated Current Market Value):	
Individual Stocks	$
Individual Bonds	$
Personal Mutual Funds	$ 50,000
Other Investments: Ltd. Partnership	$ 5,000
Retirement Plans: 401(k) & IRAs	$ 150,000
Equity Interest in a Business	$
Life Insurance (Face Amount):	
Personal	$ 250,000
Total Assets	**$1,814,000**
Liabilities	
Short Term Liabilities:	
Credit Cards	$ 2,250
Long Term Liabilities:	
Mortgage(s)	$ 190,000
Automobile Loan(s)	$ 21,000
Other Loans: Home Equity Loan	$ 57,000

continued on next page

Assets	Ownership Sue
Miscellaneous Liabilities:	
Unpaid Taxes	$
Estimated Funeral & Administrative Expenses [1]	$
Total Liabilities	$ 270,250
Estate Net Worth (Total Assets Less Total Liabilities)	$1,543,750

[1] *Funeral and administrative expenses can vary from 2–8%. For simplicity, they are ignored in this case study.*

Because of the Unlimited Marital Deduction, there are no estate taxes due at John's death. Our concern would be the tax impact if Sue were to now die prematurely. Let's calculate the tax in this event (calendar year 1998):

Step 1 Determine the total value of Sue's assets $1,814,000

Step 2 Determine Sue's liabilities   - 270,250

Step 3 Subtract your answer in Step 2 from your answer in Step 1 to arrive at her Adjusted Gross Estate $1,543,750

Step 4 Less:

    a) Charitable contributions made through Sue's will   -   0

    b) Unlimited Marital Deduction (N/A for Sue)   -   0

Step 5 This figure represents the Taxable Estate $1,543,750

Step 6 Compute the Gross Federal Estate Tax using Table 2-2. (See highlighted line). Note: The tax is $555,800 on the first $1,500,000 plus 45% on the amount above $1,500,000 or $43,750 for a total of : $ 575,488

Step 7 Subtract the Applicable Credit Amount (See highlighted line of Table 2-3).   -   202,050

Step 8 This is the amount of tax due on Sue's estate. $ 373,438

Not only is this a large tax bill, but it could have been avoided. What is significant is that we have identified a potentially large problem. There are many strategies we can use to substantially reduce or eliminate the Smiths' tax liability.

YOUR ESTATE TAX PICTURE

Now, let's determine the value of *your* estate and *your* potential taxes. Remember, your Estate Net Worth is equal to your Financial Net Worth plus your life insurance death benefits.

WORKSHEET 2-6				
Your Estate Net Worth Statement As of Your Name: Date of Birth: Spouse Name: Date of Birth:				
Assets	**Ownership**			**Family Total**
	You	**Spouse**	**Joint**	
Cash & Cash Equivalents:				
Checking & Savings Account	$	$	$	$
Other:	$	$	$	$
Personal & Household Property:				
Automobiles	$	$	$	$
Furniture	$	$	$	$
Jewelry	$	$	$	$
Personal Effects	$	$	$	$
Art	$	$	$	$
Coin Collections	$	$	$	$
Other:	$	$	$	$
Real Estate (Estimated Current Market Value):				
Residence(s)	$	$	$	$
Other Properties:	$	$	$	$

continued on next page

Assets	Ownership			Family Total
	You	Spouse	Joint	
Investments (Estimated Current Market Value):				
Individual Stocks	$	$	$	$
Individual Bonds	$	$	$	$
Personal Mutual Funds	$	$	$	$
Other Investments:	$	$	$	$
	$	$	$	$
Retirement Plans:	$	$	XX	$
	$	$	XX	$
	$	$	XX	$
Equity Interest in a Business	$	$	XX	$
Life Insurance (Face Amount):				
Personal	$	$	XX	$
Employer Group	$	$	XX	$
Total Assets	**$**	**$**	**$**	**$**
Liabilities				
Short Term Liabilities:				
Credit Cards	$	$	$	$
Long Term Liabilities:				
Mortgage(s)	$	$	$	$
Automobile Loan(s)	$	$	$	$
Other Loans:	$	$	$	$
Miscellaneous Liabilities:				
Unpaid Taxes	$	$	$	$
Estimated Funeral & Administrative Expenses	$	$	$	$
Total Liabilities	**$**	**$**	**$**	**$**
Estate Net Worth (Total Assets Less Total Liabilities)	**$**	**$**	**$**	**$**

Step 1

Add up the value of all your assets using Worksheet 2-6. Note that the dollar figure we are looking for is the **market value**, not what you paid for the asset.

> **Market Value:** The market value represents the value of an asset if it were sold today.

Let's start with the obvious: you will list everything you own solely in your name. You must also include any assets in which you are a joint owner. For example, if you own a hunting lodge with your brother, your one-half interest would be included in your estate. The same is true, for example, if you own your home jointly with your spouse. Some care must be taken in allocating ownership of jointly held property. For example, in the case where you own the hunting lodge with your brother, if you paid for 90% of the purchase price, then 90% of the value would be included in your estate unless you made a gift to your brother. Also, do not overlook any life insurance you own. If the insurance is on your life, remember, it is the **death benefit** that will be included in your estate. If someone owes you money, the value of that note or accounts receivable should be included. Also, do not forget items of personal property like cars, boats, clothing, jewelry, etc.

> **Death Benefit:** The death benefit or "face amount" of a life insurance policy represents the proceeds your beneficiary would receive from the life insurance company upon your death.

Step 2

Now add up all the money you owe including all debts, mortgages, and liens still using Worksheet 2-6. If you have debt on jointly owned property, only your share of that debt counts. You also should include any unpaid property or income taxes as well as the cost of funeral and administrative expenses. Funeral expenses can vary from $2,000 to $10,000 or more. While administrative expenses can vary widely, a good rule of thumb would be five percent of your gross estate.

Step 3

Using Worksheet 2-6, subtract your total liabilities (Step 2) from your total assets (Step 1). The result is your Adjusted Gross Estate.

Step 4

The government allows you two potential deductions.

- The Unlimited Marital Deduction—If you are married, you can leave an unlimited amount of assets to your spouse free of any estate taxes! At first blush, this appears to be the perfect solution to your estate tax dilemma. But, in estate planning you must look beyond this rule for ways to reduce the amount of taxes that your *heirs* will ultimately pay. This will be discussed in detail in Chapter 5.

- Charitable Contributions—If, in your will, you leave money or assets to qualified charitable organizations, you will receive a deduction for estate tax purposes.

Adjusted Gross Estate (From Worksheet 2-6)	$_____
Minus Marital Deduction (Either a "0" if no surviving spouse or 100% of assets left to your surviving spouse.)	-_____ $_____
Minus Charitable Bequests in your will	-_____
Your Taxable Estate	$_____

Step 5

By taking the deductions from Step 4, you have arrived at your Taxable Estate. If you are married and using the marital deduction, you will have effectively postponed your estate taxes until your surviving spouse dies. To better understand the impact of estate taxes, let's assume you and your spouse die simultaneously, or that you are not married. With those assumptions, move on to Step 6.

Step 6

Calculate your Gross Federal Estate Tax. Apply the tax rates from Table 2-2 to determine the Gross Federal Estate Tax. This represents your *tentative* tax.

Step 7

From the Gross Federal Estate Tax, you now get to subtract the Unified Federal Estate Tax Credit or what is more commonly referred to as the Applicable Credit Amount. The Applicable Credit Amount has the effect of allowing you to give a certain amount of your estate to anyone without owing federal estate taxes. The Taxpayer Relief Act of 1997 established a schedule of increases in the Applicable Credit Amount and thus the amount you can give away to anyone tax-free (called the Applicable Exclusion Amount). See Table 2-3 for details. Note that this credit is applied directly dollar-for-dollar against the tentative tax as calculated in Step 6.

YOUR FUTURE ESTATE

If your result in Step 7 is a positive number, that is the tax you would owe and it is time for you to get together with your financial advisor(s) to develop a plan for tax minimization.

If your answer is a negative number, then you currently would not owe any taxes. Even if you owe no taxes now, taxes are likely a part of your future. In addition to federal estate taxes, many states impose their own death or inheritance taxes. Table 2-7 shows future estate values based on various growth rates. Keep these figures in mind as you begin planning. For Baby Boomers, you are likely to be in the middle of your best earning years. In addition to the growth of your current assets, hopefully you are constantly adding new assets through retirement plans, personal investment programs and acquisitions. In fact, these growth rates may be too conservative. You will want to update your estate net worth worksheet annually and gain a sense of your estate's growth rate. This will indicate the kind of planning you will need to consider in the future. It is also important to recognize any potential inheritances that you will receive.

TABLE 2-7
THE FUTURE VALUE OF YOUR ESTATE

Current Estate Value	10 Years	15 Years	20 Years
5% Growth Rate			
500,000	814,000	1,039,000	1,326,000
750,000	1,221,000	1,559,000	1,984,000
1,000,000	1,628,000	2,078,000	2,653,000
2,000,000	3,257,000	4,157,000	5,306,000
3,000,000	4,886,000	6,236,000	7,959,000
7% Growth Rate			
500,000	983,000	1,379,000	1,934,000
750,000	1,475,000	2,069,000	2,902,000
1,000,000	1,967,000	2,759,000	3,869,000
2,000,000	3,934,000	5,518,000	7,739,000
3,000,000	5,901,000	8,277,000	11,609,000
9% Growth Rate			
500,000	1,183,000	1,821,000	2,802,000
750,000	1,775,000	2,731,000	4,203,000
1,000,000	2,367,000	3,642,000	5,604,000
2,000,000	4,734,000	7,284,000	11,208,000
3,000,000	7,102,000	10,927,000	16,813,000

OVERVIEW OF ESTATE PLANNING STRATEGIES

There are many techniques and strategies that can help you achieve your estate planning goals. Some of the more powerful ones include:

- **Wills**—A will forms the cornerstone of most people's estate plan. Wills can provide tremendous flexibility for controlling assets and avoiding taxes.

- **Trusts**—You can use a trust during your lifetime or after your death to help implement your estate game plan. Various types of trust planning will be discussed throughout Section II of this book.

- **Retirement Accounts**—Retirement plans are key to wealth accumulation. In Chapter 3, I will show you ways to increase their effectiveness tenfold.

- **Gifting**—One way to reduce your estate (and thereby, taxes) is to give part of your estate away. Ways to create leverage with a gifting program as well as how to maintain a measure of control over gifted assets will be discussed in Chapter 9.

- **Charities**—There are several strategies such as the Charitable Remainder Trust whereby you can improve your financial circumstances while helping your favorite charity. Take a look at Chapter 10 to gain an understanding of how you can benefit from charitable donations.

- **Family Limited Partnerships**—This strategy can shift assets to family members at a significant discount from the current value. Family limited partnership's are reviewed in Chapter 11.

In this chapter, you learned about our estate tax system and about your specific situation. Before we can begin exploring solutions for you, we need to determine how large an estate you will need in order to support your lifestyle during your retirement years. We will also need to outline your primary estate planning goals. These issues are addressed in the next chapter.

CHAPTER 3

Retire with Dignity

How Much Is Enough?

W hen I begin working with a new client, my first concern is to be sure that their assets will be sufficient to meet their lifestyle income needs for as long as they live. Since many of my younger Baby Boomer clients have not yet accumulated enough assets for this purpose, we must determine the most efficient way for them to accomplish this objective. It may involve setting up a retirement plan or other investment program. Some clients, particularly my Retiree clients, have accumulated significantly more assets than they will need for all of their financial objectives and retirement income needs. In these cases, we can begin focusing on wealth transfer strategies. Until you know whether or not you have enough assets, it is unlikely that you will be willing to implement a truly effective estate plan. In this chapter I will help you determine the amount of assets that you will need in order to provide for your retirement income needs, and I will outline different strategies you can use to improve your wealth accumulation progress. If you are a Retiree, it will be obvious that you can skip some of the steps in this process. However, it will be important to complete this exercise to give you an idea of how much income you can afford to take from your portfolio and how much excess capital you have.

YOUR RETIREMENT REQUIREMENTS

As a Baby Boomer, you are likely entering your peak earning years. If you have not yet accumulated enough money for your retirement, you must now get serious. Let's go through a step-by-step process to determine how much additional capital you need to accumulate for a worry-free retirement. Even if you are certain you have enough money for your retirement, you should still go through this process. By calculating your retirement needs, any "excess" capital can then be used as part of a wealth transfer strategy.

Determining how much capital you will need at retirement is vital to your estate plan. It is also a complicated process, involving many complex calculations and should be done with the assistance of a professional financial advisor. Use your findings in this chapter as a guideline only.

Step 1: Your Assumptions

A word of caution. Many of your assumptions will be little more than educated guesses. Many of these guesses will be wrong. An incorrect assumption can lead to significant errors in the final result. The best solution here is to review your assumptions and expected outcomes often, at least annually. This review-and-refinement process will lead to much better results.

- **Assumption #1: Age at Which You Plan to Retire**

This is the easy one for most people. Most of my clients want the *option* of being able to quit many years before the typical retirement age 65. What they are really searching for is financial *choice* in their life. If their present job becomes too much of a hassle, they want the option of being able, financially speaking, to do something different. The "something different" might be a job that pays a lot less income.

- **Assumption #2: Income Needed at Retirement**

This is a more difficult assumption to make. A rule of thumb is to assume that you will need 80 percent of your pre-retirement income. However, this rule of thumb is not applicable in many individual circumstances. The best way to estimate your future income need is to review current spending patterns and then visualize how expenses will be different at retirement. You will find that many of your current expenses will be dramatically reduced or eliminated at retirement, while other expenses will have increased. For example, the money you spend on children should decrease significantly. (It never completely goes away!) Hopefully, your home mortgage will be fully paid off. Other expenses, such as medical insurance and travel may be much higher than today. To get a clearer picture, use the format in Worksheet 3-1 to compare your current expenses to estimated expenses at

retirement. These retirement expenses should be figured as if you were retiring today. You will adjust the results for inflation later. All expense estimates should be figured on an *annual* basis.

	Estimated Current Expenses	Retirement Expenses (Today's $)	Increasing Expense?
WORKSHEET 3-1 RETIREMENT INCOME WORKSHEET			
Contributions	$ _____	$ _____	Yes No
Home:			
Mortgage	$ _____	$ _____	Yes No
Insurance	$ _____	$ _____	Yes No
Taxes	$ _____	$ _____	Yes No
Maintenance/Repairs	$ _____	$ _____	Yes No
Utilities:			
Electricity/Gas/Water	$ _____	$ _____	Yes No
Phone (Including Toll Charges)	$ _____	$ _____	Yes No
Cable TV	$ _____	$ _____	Yes No
Security System	$ _____	$ _____	Yes No
Insurance:			
Medical	$ _____	$ _____	Yes No
Personal Care	$ _____	$ _____	Yes No
Children:			
Clothing	$ _____	$ _____	Yes No
School Tuition/Expenses	$ _____	$ _____	Yes No
Gifts	$ _____	$ _____	Yes No
Other	$ _____	$ _____	Yes No

continued on next page

WORKSHEET 3-1 (CONTINUED) RETIREMENT INCOME WORKSHEET				
	Estimated Current Expenses	Retirement Expenses (Today's $)	Increasing Expense?	
Debt Payments:				
Autos	$ _____	$ _____	Yes	No
Personal Loans	$ _____	$ _____	Yes	No
Other	$ _____	$ _____	Yes	No
Income Taxes	$ _____	$ _____	Yes	No
Total	$ _____	$ _____		

- **Assumption #3: Pre-Retirement Rate of Return**

Consider what *average rate of return* you expect to earn on your investments prior to retirement. For qualified retirement plan accounts, IRAs, tax deferred annuities, and life insurance policies, the rate you earn will be your *gross* rate of return. For personal investment accounts, you are looking for the *net* rate of return after taxes.

- **Assumption #4: Post Retirement Rate of Return**

Many people manage their investments more aggressively prior to retirement. The assumption is that you can afford to be more aggressive when you still have earned income and are continuing to invest new money each month or year plus you are reinvesting all your interest, dividends and capital gains. Once you retire and start drawing income from your investments, you must take greater care to protect your principal. This logic bears some merit and will be discussed later in this chapter.

- **Assumption #5: Estimated Inflation Rate**

I normally use 3 percent. Other advisors will use rates as high as 6 percent. Historical inflation rates over the last 50 years have averaged 3.3 percent. A recent independent study concluded that the way our government calculates the Consumer Price Index (CPI) overstates the rate of inflation by as much as 1 percent. I will leave it to you to decide what inflation rate is appropriate for your case facts.

Step 2: Determine Your Future Income Need

In Step 1, you went through an exercise to estimate what your retirement income needs would be in terms of *today's* dollars. In this step, you need to convert that income into future dollars based on the inflation rate in assumption 5. To determine the inflation factor, go to Table 3-2. Across the top of the page, identify the inflation rate you chose in your assumptions under Step 1. Moving down the left margin, identify the number that corresponds with the number of years until you intend to retire. The point where the two numbers intersect is your *inflation multiplier*. For example, if your inflation rate was 3 percent and you had 20 years until retirement your inflation multiplier would be 1.81. Having identified your inflation multiplier you should now multiply it times your expected retirement income need from Step 1. The result is income you will need the *first* year you retire. Since inflation will continue to erode the purchasing power of your income, we will have to account for continuing inflation in later calculations.

TABLE 3-2
INFLATION MULTIPLIER CHART

Years Until Retirement	Estimated Inflation Rate							
	1%	2%	3%	4%	5%	6%	7%	8%
1	1.01	1.02	1.03	1.04	1.05	1.06	1.07	1.08
2	1.02	1.04	1.06	1.08	1.10	1.12	1.14	1.17
3	1.03	1.06	1.09	1.12	1.16	1.19	1.23	1.26
4	1.04	1.08	1.13	1.17	1.22	1.26	1.31	1.36
5	1.05	1.10	1.16	1.22	1.28	1.34	1.40	1.47
6	1.06	1.13	1.19	1.27	1.34	1.42	1.50	1.59
7	1.07	1.15	1.23	1.32	1.41	1.50	1.61	1.71
8	1.08	1.17	1.27	1.37	1.48	1.59	1.72	1.85
9	1.09	1.20	1.30	1.42	1.55	1.69	1.84	2.00
10	1.10	1.22	1.34	1.48	1.63	1.79	1.97	2.16
11	1.12	1.24	1.38	1.54	1.71	1.90	2.10	2.33
12	1.13	1.27	1.43	1.60	1.80	2.01	2.25	2.52

continued on next page

TABLE 3-2 (CONTINUED)
INFLATION MULTIPLIER CHART

Years Until Retirement	Estimated Inflation Rate							
	1%	2%	3%	4%	5%	6%	7%	8%
13	1.14	1.29	1.47	1.67	1.89	2.13	2.41	2.72
14	1.15	1.32	1.51	1.73	1.98	2.26	2.58	2.94
15	1.16	1.35	1.56	1.80	2.08	2.40	2.76	3.17
16	1.17	1.37	1.60	1.87	2.18	2.54	2.95	3.43
17	1.18	1.40	1.65	1.95	2.29	2.69	3.16	3.70
18	1.20	1.43	1.70	2.03	2.41	2.85	3.38	4.00
19	1.21	1.46	1.75	2.11	2.53	3.03	3.62	4.32
20	1.22	1.49	1.81	2.19	2.65	3.21	3.87	4.66
21	1.23	1.52	1.86	2.28	2.79	3.40	4.14	5.03
22	1.24	1.55	1.92	2.37	2.93	3.60	4.43	5.44
23	1.26	1.58	1.97	2.46	3.07	3.82	4.74	5.87
24	1.27	1.61	2.03	2.56	3.23	4.05	5.07	6.34
25	1.28	1.64	2.09	2.67	3.39	4.29	5.43	6.85
26	1.30	1.67	2.16	2.77	3.56	4.55	5.81	7.40
27	1.31	1.71	2.22	2.88	3.73	4.82	6.21	7.99
28	1.32	1.74	2.29	3.00	3.92	5.11	6.65	8.63
29	1.33	1.78	2.36	3.12	4.12	5.42	7.11	9.32
30	1.35	1.81	2.43	3.24	4.32	5.74	7.61	10.06

Step 3: Subtract Your Sources of Retirement Income

In Step 2, you determined the total income you would need when you retire. You will need to subtract any income sources you expect to receive at retirement. One source of income will be Social Security. Use Table 3-3 (page 40) to estimate how much Social Security income you will receive.

Another possible source of income would be your company's pension plan. If your company has one, contact your benefits office or plan trustee and ask for the formula for calculating benefits. Often the formula is based on years of service and average wages during your last few years (often five years). While Social Security is indexed for inflation, pension benefits often are not. You will need to take this into account in your final calculations for retirement capital needed. Any other sources of income should be deducted as well. The results of these adjustments will be the income that you need to draw from your investment accounts (including personal investment accounts, IRAs, company 401(k)s, etc.).

Let's look at an example. From Step 2, you determined that your annual retirement income needs to be $120,000 at age 65. You estimate that your Social Security benefit will be $38,000 per year and that your company pension will pay you $29,000 per year. Your results would look as follows:

Retirement Income Need	$120,000
Social Security Benefit	- 38,000
Pension Benefit	- 29,000
Income Needed from Your Investments	$ 53,000

TIP

The Social Security Administration will send you an estimate of your benefits at age 65 if you request it. To receive this information, contact them at 1-800-772-1213. The income estimate does not include inflation, so you will need to use Table 3-2 to calculate the future benefit. I recommend that you use 2 percent inflation because Social Security benefits are not increased except by vote of Congress if the CPI for that year is less than 3 percent.

TABLE 3-3
SOCIAL SECURITY BENEFITS FOR A WORKER EARNING AT OR OVER MAXIMUM SOCIAL SECURITY WAGE BASE

(1997 Estimates)

Age	62	65	70 [1]
Benefit	$13,300	$16,600	$21,700

[1] Age 70 benefit is determined by a percentage increase in the monthly benefit based on the age of the recipient.

Note: These figures are for a worker retiring at age 65 in 1997. To receive an estimate of your future benefits, contact the Social Security Administration at 1-800-772-1213 and ask for Form SSA-7004-SM.

Step 4: Determine Your Investment Account Target

You are now ready to calculate how large of an investment account you must accumulate. Review Table 3-4. The table is broken into 3 groups: Conservative Investors, Moderate Investors, and Aggressive Investors. These profiles were chosen specifically because research indicates that the range of stock allocation in a portfolio that allows the maximum withdrawal rate is between 50 percent and 75 percent. Choose the profile that best fits you. Note that these portfolios are for *post* retirement investment accounts. At the bottom of each portfolio profile is a *withdrawal factor* which is based on 3.5 percent inflation. To choose a different inflation rate, follow the instructions at the bottom of the chart. Divide this factor into your answer in Step 3. Your answer here indicates the total capital you will need to accumulate by retirement to meet your income goals. In our example on page 39, we determined that the income need was $53,000. Choosing the moderate portfolio from Table 3-4, we locate the withdrawal factor of .06. By dividing $53,000 by .06, your result is $883,333. This $833,333 is the amount of capital necessary to produce a lifetime inflation adjusted of $53,000 per year at your retirement. In our example, each year you will withdraw 6 percent (.06) of your account balance. Since the account is expected to earn 9.5 percent, your account balance should be growing *over time*. Short term volatility (bear markets) should be expected. The best way to deal with them is to use all portfolio income plus the principal (as needed) from the debt (bond) portion of your portfolio while you wait for the equity (stock) portion of your portfolio to recover. Once equities rebound, you should then take enough profits to replenish your bonds and bring your portfolio back into balance.

TABLE 3-4
RETIREMENT PORTFOLIO EQUITY (STOCK) ALLOCATION GUIDELINES

	Conservative	Moderate	Aggressive
One year Downside Risk [1]	-8%	-10%	-12%
Historical Returns (5 years)	9%	9.5%	10%
Asset Classes:			
U.S. Large Company	50%	63%	75%
U.S. Intermediate Term Bond	50%	37%	25%
Withdrawal Factor [2]	0.55	.06	.065

[1] *Investment results are not guaranteed. Risks and returns are targets only. Statistics are based on historical data from 1/1/60 through 12/31/97 and include a 1% fee for investment expenses. Downside risks and statistics based on a 95% confidence level.*

[2] *Assumes inflation rate of 3.5%. To calculate use following formula: Expected rate of return - inflation rate × 100 = withdrawal factor. Based on historical research, withdrawal factor should not exceed .065.*

Note: These portfolios are for post retirement investment accounts and should be used only as general guidelines. Your actual retirement portfolio should be diversified into numerous asset classes. Consult with your financial advisor.

Step 5: Determine the Future Value of Your Current Investments

You know how much you must accumulate. Now you will need to determine how far your current investments will go toward meeting your goal. This requires that you estimate the future value of your current investments. You have two choices here. You can assign an average rate of return for all current investments or you can use a different rate of return for each type of investment. For example, if you have $25,000 in a Certificate of Deposit, $75,000 in your company 401(k) plan, and $12,000 in your Whole Life Insurance policy (See Table 3-5), you can either assume an aggregate rate of return or use a different rate of return for each asset. With assets that are this dissimilar, using different rates of return would be preferable, but will require more work. At this stage, do not concern yourself with current and future contributions but only with current balances.

TABLE 3-5
CURRENT INVESTMENT ASSETS

$ 25,000	Certificate of Deposit
$ 75,000	401(k)
$ 12,000	Cash Value Whole Life Policy
$112,000	Total Investments

Using Table 3-6, choose the rate of return that you expect to earn on your investments (top row of table). Next, down the left column of the table, choose the number that represents the number of years until you retire. The point where these two numbers intersect represents your *growth factor*. Multiply this factor times the current value of your investment account(s). Your answer represents the expected value of your investment account(s) the day you retire. If you did not aggregate your investments, you will need to repeat this process for each investment. If the earnings rate you have assumed is not represented on this form, you can use interpolation. For example, if you chose a 9.5 percent earnings rate with 20 years until retirement, your growth factor would be the midpoint between the growth factor for 9 percent (5.60) and 10 percent (6.73). The midpoint between 5.60 and 6.73 equals 6.17, which is the growth factor for a 9.5 percent earnings rate.

TABLE 3-6
GROWTH FACTOR TABLE

Years Until Retire- ment	Expected Return on Investment										
	5%	6%	7%	8%	9%	10%	11%	12%	13%	14%	15%
1	1.05	1.06	1.07	1.08	1.09	1.10	1.11	1.12	1.13	1.14	1.15
2	1.10	1.12	1.14	1.17	1.19	1.21	1.23	1.25	1.28	1.30	1.32
3	1.16	1.19	1.23	1.26	1.30	1.33	1.37	1.40	1.44	1.48	1.52
4	1.22	1.26	1.31	1.36	1.41	1.46	1.52	1.57	1.63	1.69	1.75

continued on next page

Years Until Retirement	Expected Return on Investment										
	5%	6%	7%	8%	9%	10%	11%	12%	13%	14%	15%
5	1.28	1.34	1.40	1.47	1.54	1.61	1.69	1.76	1.84	1.93	2.01
6	1.34	1.42	1.50	1.59	1.68	1.77	1.87	1.97	2.08	2.19	2.31
7	1.41	1.50	1.61	1.71	1.83	1.95	2.08	2.21	2.35	2.50	2.66
8	1.48	1.59	1.72	1.85	1.99	2.14	2.30	2.48	2.66	2.85	3.06
9	1.55	1.69	1.84	2.00	2.17	2.36	2.56	2.77	3.00	3.25	3.52
10	1.63	1.79	1.97	2.16	2.37	2.59	2.84	3.11	3.39	3.71	4.05
11	1.71	1.90	2.10	2.33	2.58	2.85	3.15	3.48	3.84	4.23	4.65
12	1.80	2.01	2.25	2.52	2.81	3.14	3.50	3.90	4.33	4.82	5.35
13	1.89	2.13	2.41	2.72	3.07	3.45	3.88	4.36	4.90	5.49	6.15
14	1.98	2.26	2.58	2.94	3.34	3.80	4.31	4.89	5.53	6.26	7.08
15	2.08	2.40	2.76	3.17	3.64	4.18	4.78	5.47	6.25	7.14	8.14
16	2.18	2.54	2.95	3.43	3.97	4.59	5.31	6.13	7.07	8.14	9.36
17	2.29	2.69	3.16	3.70	4.33	5.05	5.90	6.87	7.99	9.28	10.76
18	2.41	2.85	3.38	4.00	4.72	5.56	6.54	7.69	9.02	10.58	12.38
19	2.53	3.03	3.62	4.32	5.14	6.12	7.26	8.61	10.20	12.06	14.23
20	2.65	3.21	3.87	4.66	5.60	6.73	8.06	9.65	11.52	13.74	16.37
21	2.79	3.40	4.14	5.03	6.11	7.40	8.95	10.80	13.02	15.67	18.82
22	2.93	3.60	4.43	5.44	6.66	8.14	9.93	12.10	14.71	17.86	21.64
23	3.07	3.82	4.74	5.87	7.26	8.95	11.03	13.55	16.63	20.36	24.89
24	3.23	4.05	5.07	6.34	7.91	9.85	12.24	15.18	18.79	23.21	28.63
25	3.39	4.29	5.43	6.85	8.62	10.83	13.59	17.00	21.23	26.46	32.92
26	3.56	4.55	5.81	7.40	9.40	11.92	15.08	19.04	23.99	30.17	37.86
27	3.73	4.82	6.21	7.99	10.25	13.11	16.74	21.32	27.11	34.39	43.54
28	3.92	5.11	6.65	8.63	11.17	14.42	18.58	23.88	30.63	39.20	50.07
29	4.12	5.42	7.11	9.32	12.17	15.86	20.62	26.75	34.62	44.69	57.58
30	4.32	5.74	7.61	10.06	13.27	17.45	22.89	29.96	39.12	50.95	66.21

Let's review another example. Assume you plan to retire in 20 years and that your current investments are as depicted in Table 3-5. Your first investment is a $25,000 Certificate of Deposit (CD). Since this is a taxable investment, you need to determine your rate of return *after* taxes. I have assumed a 28 percent tax bracket for this example resulting in a net rate of return of 5 percent. By going to Table 3-6 and finding the intersection of 5 percent and 20 years you will find your growth factor is 2.65. Note that if you planned to pay all the taxes on your CD with other funds (i.e. you plan to reinvest your interest), you would use the *before* tax rate of return that corresponds with the growth factor in Table 3-6.

Step 6: Determine Your Retirement Account Surplus or Deficit

Just simple arithmetic here. Subtract your answer in Step 5 from your answer in Step 4. If the result is a negative number, congratulations! You will have more money than necessary to meet your retirement income needs (a surplus). If your answer is a positive number, you have a deficit and must continue investing in order to meet your goal. How much will you need to invest? Continue with Steps 7 and 8 to find the answer.

Step 7: Determine Your Monthly Investment Requirements

If your calculations thus far indicate that you will not have accumulated enough money by retirement, you will need to determine how much you need to invest each month in order to meet your goal. If you are currently investing monthly through a 401(k), profit sharing plan, or personal investment plan, you need to determine if it will be enough. Be sure to include any employer matching in your calculations.

At this point, it is important to discuss a fundamental investment concept that you must both understand and implement as part of your wealth accumulation plan. The contributions to your investment plan should be based on a *percentage* of your total income, and therefore, the dollar amount invested should increase as your income rises. Many investment programs automatically do this for you. A good example is a 401(k) program. Typically you contribute, through payroll deduction, a certain percentage of your income, say 6 percent. As your income rises, the dollar amount of your contributions also rises. Hopefully, your income will rise at least as fast as the inflation rate. If you feel this will not be the case, then part of your action plan should be to seek employment where there is more opportunity for you. This may require improving your value through additional education or training.

First, you must decide what is an appropriate *growth rate* on your *contributions*. What percentage do you think you can increase your contributions annually? This number should be at least equal to the rate you assumed for inflation. If you are on your company's fast track and you expect your income to rise sharply over your career span, you may want to use an even higher number. Next, you need to estimate the rate of return you expect to earn on your investments. Remember, that different types of investments will earn different returns. You can either choose an aggregate return for all your investments or do a separate calculation for each. My preference is separate calculations. Using Table 3-7, find the chart represented by the *contributions growth rate* you have chosen. Across the top of that chart, find the *investment earnings rate* you have assumed for your investment account(s). If it is a taxable investment account, do not forget to adjust your expected earnings rate for taxes! Down the left column, find the number that corresponds to the number of years until you plan to retire. Finally, find the point where the number of years until retirement and your investment earnings rate intersect. Multiply this factor times your current *annual* investment contributions. The result is the expected value, at retirement, of your future contributions to your investment account.

TABLE 3-7
GROWTH RATE CALCULATOR

Contribution Growth Rate of 3%

	Investment Earnings Rate			
Years	**6%**	**8%**	**10%**	**12%**
5	5.97	6.20	6.45	6.70
10	14.90	16.30	17.85	19.58
15	27.95	32.28	37.42	43.51
20	46.70	57.10	70.31	87.11
25	73.27	95.09	124.87	165.63
30	110.54	152.71	214.60	305.92

continued on next page

TABLE 3-7 (CONTINUED)
GROWTH RATE CALCULATOR

Contribution Growth Rate of 4%

Investment Earnings Rate			
Years	6%	8%	10%	12%
5	6.08	6.32	6.56	6.82
10	15.53	16.97	18.56	20.32
15	29.78	34.28	39.61	45.91
20	50.80	61.75	75.61	93.19
25	81.30	104.57	136.15	179.18
30	125.00	170.48	236.77	333.96

Contribution Growth Rate of 5%

Investment Earnings Rate			
Years	6%	8%	10%	12%
5	6.19	6.43	6.68	6.94
10	16.20	17.67	19.30	21.10
15	31.76	38.44	41.97	48.49
20	55.38	66.92	81.48	99.90
25	90.55	115.40	148.97	194.48
30	142.15	191.36	262.55	366.26

Contribution Growth Rate of 6%

Investment Earnings Rate			
Years	6%	8%	10%	12%
5	6.31	6.56	6.81	7.07
10	16.90	18.40	20.07	21.92
15	33.91	38.78	44.52	51.28
20	60.51	72.69	88.01	107.32
25	101.22	127.83	163.57	211.80
30	162.55	215.96	292.65	403.61

continued on next page

Contribution Growth Rate of 7%

| Investment Earnings Rate | | | |
Years	6%	8%	10%	12%
5	6.43	6.68	6.93	7.20
10	17.63	19.18	20.89	22.77
15	36.25	41.31	47.27	54.29
20	66.25	79.13	95.26	115.53
25	113.56	142.10	180.24	231.45
30	186.88	245.04	327.90	446.95

Let's review an example of how to use Table 3-7. Assume that you are currently investing $12,000 per year and that you expect to be able to increase your investment contributions by 3 percent per year (the inflation rate). Investments are expected to earn 10 percent and you plan to retire in 20 years. Using Table 3-7, you first find the chart with the contributions growth rate of 3 percent. Next, you find the point of intersection between the investment earnings rate and the years until retirement (70.31). Now simply multiply your investment contributions by this factor.

$$\begin{array}{r} \$ \quad 12{,}000 \\ \times \underline{70.31} \\ \$ \quad 843{,}720 \end{array}$$

Subtract your answer here from your answer in Step 6. If your answer is still a positive number (i.e., a deficit), you will need to consider your options. Maybe your budget would allow you to increase the amount you are investing now. If not, you could increase the *rate of increases* of future contributions. One excellent way to achieve this is to commit half of all pay raises to your investment program. The other half can be used to improve lifestyle.

Another alternative is to invest more aggressively to increase your potential rate of return. Review Table 3-8. History shows that by increasing the percentage of stocks in your portfolio you increase your *long term* rate of return. However, this is a double-edged sword. In the short term, you can expect greater losses when bear markets occur. Note that I said *when,* not *if*. You might pay special attention to the downside risk for each portfolio in Table 3-8.

TABLE 3-8
PORTFOLIOS—SAMPLE ASSET ALLOCATION MIXES

	Low Risk / Low Return			High Risk / High Return	
	#1	#2	#3	#4	#5
1-Year Downside Risks [1]	-3%	-6%	-9%	-12%	-15%
Target Annualized 10-Year Returns [1]	8%	9.5%	10.5%	12%	13+%
Asset Classes					
U.S. Large Company	13%	21%	31%	35%	42%
U.S. Small/ Mid-Size Co.	7%	12%	13%	22%	30%
International Stocks	8%	12%	15%	15%	20%
Real Estate	2%	5%	7%	8%	8%
Short-Term Bonds	32%	17%	9%	2%	0%
Intermediate Bonds	35%	23%	10%	3%	0%
High Yield Bonds	3%	7%	10%	10%	0%
Foreign Bonds	0%	3%	5%	5%	0%
	100%	100%	100%	100%	100%

[1] *No investment results can ever be guaranteed. Risks and returns are targets only, not guarantees. Statistics are based on 95% confidence levels and historical data from 1/1/73–12/31/97. All numbers adjusted 1% for mutual fund expenses.*

If you give your investments more time to work, this may easily solve your problem. Are you willing to postpone your retirement date? While working with clients I find that they usually have an "ideal" retirement age in mind but are perfectly happy to continue working for a few more years if necessary. Finally, you could consider reducing your retirement income goal. Review your estimated expenses from Worksheet 3-1. Are there expense items that could be reduced or eliminated?

It is probably hard for you to make these decisions on your own. Financial advisors are not only skilled in such matters, but they also bring a clarity that is free of emotional bias. You now have the tools to develop your wealth accumulation plan. Good luck!

PRIORITIZING YOUR INVESTMENT DOLLARS

How do you maximize the power of your investment program? You can do so in two ways. The first way has to do with *investment environments* and the second has to do with *asset mix*. The investment environment relates to whether the investment is a retirement account, tax deferred account, or a personal investment account. Each environment has its advantages and disadvantages, but some are better than others, particularly for accumulating money for your retirement. By prioritizing where your investment dollars go, you can significantly enhance your long term accumulation results. Let's start with your best option.

CHOOSING THE BEST INVESTMENT ENVIRONMENTS

Retirement Plans

By far your best method for accumulating money for your retirement is through a retirement plan. This may seem obvious, but you would be surprised at how often I find that people fail to understand this. For example, I was working with a new client who was very concerned about saving for retirement. He contributed 6 percent of his salary to a 401(k) plan, which was being matched 50 percent by his employer. The plan allowed him to contribute up to 15 percent of his pay. When I asked him why he was not investing more money in his 401(k), he said he could not afford to. Upon examining his situation, I found that he was paying several thousand dollars each year toward a whole life insurance policy. We were able to stop paying on the insurance policy and divert those funds into his 401(k). Not only would the "premiums" grow faster in his 401(k), but he got a tax deduction to boot!

This is actually an easy mistake to make. To avoid it, you must review where all your investment dollars are going. To get the most benefit, invest the *maximum* allowable into retirement plans before you invest *any* money in personal investment programs. This is a very important concept. Look at the dramatic differences represented in Table 3-9.

TABLE 3-9
COMPARISON: $800/MO. INVESTMENT IN 401(K) VS. PAY THE TAX ON $800/MO. & INVEST PERSONALLY (12% GROSS RATE OF RETURN ASSUMED)

Retirement	vs.	Personal
$800 per month		$576 per month (after 28% tax)
25 years		25 years
@12%		@10.5% [1]
$1,518,109		$839,875
80% more!!		

[1] *Assumes annual tax load of 1.5%.*

Note: Retirement Plan distributions will be subject to ordinary income taxes (Federal maximum 39.6%). Distributions from the personal investment program will likely be primarily subject to capital gains taxes (Federal maximum 20%). If held until death, the personal account would receive a "stepped-up" cost basis and income taxes would be avoided. If the retirement plan were held until death, a beneficiary (under certain circumstances) could continue to defer a large portion of the gain.

If you are self employed, you should consider starting your own retirement plan. Options available to you include the Simplified Employee Pension Plan (SEP) or the Keogh Plan. To make things a little more complicated, your Keogh Plan comes in four varieties: the Profit Sharing Plan, the Money Purchase Pension Plan, the Paired or Combination Plan and the Defined Benefit Plan. If you have employees, they must be included in your plan. Which one is best for you will depend on your specific circumstances. You should enlist the help of a professional advisor to assist you in setting up one of these plans to make certain you follow the complex plan regulations.

The Taxpayer Relief Act of 1997 provided us with a new type of IRA called the **Roth IRA** as well as new rules for the Traditional IRA. Individual tax filers with Adjusted Gross Income (AGI) of less than $95,000 ($150,000 for joint tax filers), are eligible to contribute up to $2,000 each year to the

Roth IRA as long as he or she has earned income of at least $2,000. A partial contribution is allowed for individual tax filers with AGI between $95,000 and $110,000 ($150,000 and $160,000 for joint tax filers). See Table 3-10 for maximum allowed contributions. While contributions are *not* tax deductible, earnings are tax deferred and withdrawals are tax free if:

- Withdrawals are made at least five years after the Roth IRA was established and

- Withdrawals are made due to death, disability, or after the taxpayer has attained the age of 59 1/2.

Tax free withdrawals of up to $10,000 are allowed to cover the expenses of purchasing your first home.

TABLE 3-10
MAXIMUM ROTH IRA CONTRIBUTIONS

(Assuming earned income at least equal to otherwise contribution amount and no contributions to Traditional IRAs.)

Single Filers		Joint Filers	
Adjusted Gross Income	**Maximum Contribution**	**Adjusted Gross Income**	**Maximum Contribution**
$2,000–$95,000	$2,000	$2,000–$150,000	$2,000
96,500	1,800	151,000	1,800
98,000	1,600	152,000	1,600
99,500	1,400	153,000	1,400
101,000	1,200	154,000	1,200
102,500	1,000	155,000	1,000
104,000	800	156,000	800
105,500	600	157,000	600
107,000	400	158,000	400
108,500	200	159,000	200
110,000 and up	0	160,000 and up	0

Rules for the Traditional IRA also changed under the 1997 Tax Act. Now the spouse of a worker who participates in a company retirement plan is eligible to contribute to a Traditional IRA even if that spouse has no earned income. The rules regarding the phase-out of deductibility of contributions have been relaxed and are shown in Table 3-11.

TABLE 3-11
PHASEOUT OF IRA DEDUCTIONS

Year	Single Taxpayer Phaseout Range	Joint Taxpayers Phaseout Range
Pre-1997 Tax Act	$25,000–35,000	$40,000–50,000
1998	30,000–40,000	50,000–60,000
1999	31,000–41,000	51,000–61,000
2000	32,000–42,000	52,000–62,000
2001	33,000–43,000	53,000–63,000
2002	34,000–44,000	54,000–64,000
2003	40,000–50,000	60,000–70,000
2004	45,000–55,000	65,000–75,000
2005	50,000–60,000	70,000–80,000
2006	50,000–60,000	75,000–85,000
2007	50,000–60,000	80,000–100,000

While you can contribute to both a Traditional IRA and a Roth IRA, your total maximum contribution between the two remains $2,000.

If you are eligible for an IRA, you should invest in one. Are you better off with the Traditional IRA or the Roth IRA? For most people, the Roth IRA will produce better results. However, it is not the "hands down" winner. Again, you will need to do your homework or elicit the aid of a financial advisor. Contributing to a Roth IRA is definitely better than contributing to a *non-deductible* Traditional IRA assuming Congress does not change the law. This is because neither contributions are deductible but future distributions from the Roth IRA will be tax free if you follow the qualifying rules. Also, the Roth IRA is not subject to the **Required Minimum Distribution Rules** which require you to begin systematic withdrawals from retirement plans beginning after you turn age 70 1/2.

Should you convert your existing IRA to a Roth IRA? There is no one right answer for everyone. What is best for you will depend on your particular circumstances. One thing that is clear is that it only makes sense to convert if you can pay the income taxes from proceeds *outside* of your IRA. Your financial advisor can help you "run the numbers" to see what is likely best for you.

Retirement plans do have some disadvantages. First, if you take your money out before age 59 1/2, you will likely owe a 10 percent penalty in addition to ordinary income taxes on the proceeds. More importantly, retirement accounts (excluding Roth IRAs) convert what may have been capital gains (taxed at a maximum rate of 20 percent), to ordinary income taxed at your highest personal tax bracket (currently as high as 39.6 percent Federal). This disadvantage is largely overcome due to the value of the immediate income tax deduction and the tax deferral of income until withdrawn.

Magnify the Power of Your Retirement Plan Tenfold

Receiving an immediate tax deduction and tax deferred growth are two powerful reasons for you to use retirement plans in your investment program. Is there a way to magnify these results? Under certain circumstances, the answer is most definitely yes. The answer lies in who you make your beneficiary. For many reasons, your primary beneficiary should normally be your spouse. However, I often find that people either leave their *contingent beneficiary blank,* or they will name their estate. This can be a big mistake. Let's assume that you have named your spouse as your primary beneficiary and your estate as contingent. If your wife predeceases you, your plan assets will be distributed according to the terms under your will (let's assume it would go to your children). Because your estate is the beneficiary, the income taxes on your retirement plan assets must be paid within five years of your death. In other words, the advantage of tax deferral ends five years after you die. If, on the other hand, you had made your children the contingent beneficiary, they would have the option to continue deferring the majority of the retirement plan assets over their own lifetime. Under these circumstances, the law requires that they begin mandatory distributions within one year of your death. However, the mandatory distributions are based on *their* life expectancy. This results in a reduced mandatory (taxable) distribution thus allowing for a substantial continuation of deferral. Let's look at two examples:

Example #1. Assume that you are age 45 and that you are the named beneficiary under your father's IRA in the amount of $200,000. He dies and you elect to receive only the minimum required distributions. Based on life expectancy tables, your life expectancy is 37 years. For your interest rate assumption you choose 6 percent which results in a required annual distribution of approximately $14,000. When choosing an interest rate assumption, the Internal Revenue Service requires that you choose a "reasonable" rate. Case law indicates that a reasonable range is 6 to 8 percent. For our final assumption, I will assume that you actually earn 10 percent on the portfolio. As a result, you are able to continue to defer all of the $200,000 principal plus approximately $6,000 per year of the growth. Over 37.7 years the account would have grown to over $2.5 million!

Example #2. In our second example, let's assume you (or your father) use this strategy naming your 25-year-old son as the beneficiary. His life expectancy is 57 years. You (or your father) dies and your son now elects to take minimum distributions in the amount of $12,450 per year while deferring any additional growth. If the account earns an average of 10 percent per year, the account value would have grown to over $3.5 million by his age 65. This is in addition to the nearly $500,000 in distributions that he took out over that time period!

Personal Investment Accounts

By now you know that you should put the maximum into your retirement plan(s) before you invest any money personally. The main advantage to a personal investment program is that you have access to your money without penalties if you should need it. Doing so may trigger income taxes, but for investments held for more than 12 months, you will be taxed at the more favorable long term capital gains rate (maximum 20 percent). Note that certain real estate transactions such as depreciation recapture are taxed at a maximum rate of 25 percent.

The primary disadvantage also involves taxes. Namely, your earnings may be subject to *current* taxation. This problem can be reduced by investing in stocks or stock mutual funds and holding them long term. For fixed income investments, you can invest in municipal bonds. The interest income from these bonds is not subject to federal income taxes and in certain cases, is not subject to state, city or county taxes either. However, you should use some caution here. I often see people who have bought municipal securities when they are in a relatively low tax bracket. They would have been better off, after taxes, having bought taxable securities. Remember, it's the *net* "jingle" in your pocket that counts. The formula for comparing taxable verses tax-free investments is:

$$\text{Taxable Yield} = \frac{\text{Tax Free Yield}}{1 - \text{Federal Tax Bracket}}$$

By way of example, if you are in the 28 percent federal tax bracket and you want to compare a tax free bond yielding 4.5 percent to a taxable bond of similar quality and maturity yielding 7 percent, your calculation would be as follows:

$$\text{Taxable Yield} = \frac{.045}{1 - .28} = \frac{.045}{.72} = .0625 \text{ or } 6.25\%$$

From this example, obviously the taxable bond yielding 7 percent is preferred.

It should be noted that all tax free bonds are not entirely tax free. Certain types of municipal bonds are subject to the *Alternative Minimum Tax*. Internal Revenue Service rules require you to first calculate your income taxes the "normal" way, then recalculate them the "alternate" way which includes the interest income from certain municipal bonds. If the alternate method creates a larger tax, that is the tax you must pay. To avoid this potential problem you must either buy municipal bonds that are not subject to the alternative minimum tax or make certain that you will not be subject to the tax. Your tax advisor can help you determine this.

Tax Deferred Investment Programs

Tax deferred investment programs will fall into two main categories: tax deferred annuities and cash value life insurance. The obvious advantage is having your money grow without being subjected to current income taxes. However, the disadvantages are also significant. Let's start by looking at annuities.

Annuities have four main disadvantages. First, most have relatively high expenses associated with their purchase. The average annual expenses for the industry are 2.1 percent per year. Part of the premiums you pay are used to cover mortality charges in the event you choose to have your account converted into a life income. Almost no one does, so this is a waste of money.

The next disadvantage is that an annuity converts what may have been long term capital gains, which are taxed at a maximum rate of 20 percent, to ordinary income where tax rates are as high as 39.6 percent (Federal). For example, if you bought a stock index fund and held it for 20 years, then took your money out, your gains would be taxed at a maximum rate of 20 percent. If, on the other hand, you bought a variable annuity and through the annuity invested in a similar stock index fund, when you take your money out 20 years later, the gain will be subject to *ordinary* income tax rates. Table 3-12 illustrates in dollar terms the disadvantages outlined above.

Another major disadvantage of annuities is limited investment choices. Most have a dozen or fewer choices. Some have many more, but there is a big advantage to being able to choose among the entire universe of mutual funds. By way of analogy, let's assume that you and I each have $100 million to buy a baseball team. (Never mind that this amount wouldn't even buy us a *minor* league team!) There are 20 teams in the league and I give you first choice. Once you choose your team you are stuck with it for the season. Now it's my turn. But instead of choosing a team, I get to choose individual players! Which option would you rather have? I think you can see my point.

The final disadvantage of annuities is that if you had to take your money out before age 59 1/2, you would incur a 10 percent penalty in addition to ordinary income taxes. There are cases where annuities make sense, but they are rare.

TABLE 3-12
COMPARISON: PERSONAL INVESTMENT VS. VARIABLE ANNUITY

	Investor A Index Fund	Investor B Variable Annuity
Gross Rate of Return of 12% before taxes or fees.		
After Tax Contribution	$10,000	$10,000
Net Rate of Return [1]	× 11.06%	× 9.9%
Account Value in 20 Years	$81,499	$66,062
Tax Effect Upon Sale in 30 Years:		
Account Value in 20 Years	$81,499	$66,062
Less Cost Basis [2]	-20,919	-10,000
Taxable Gain	$60,580	$56,062
Capital Gains Tax (20%)	$12,116	$0
Ordinary Income Tax (36%)	$0	$20,182
Net to Investor	$69,383	$45,880
Advantage to Investor	+51%	

[1] *Net rate of return is determined by subtracting fees charged by investment company. For the index fund, the average annual management fee is .4% and yearly dividend income averages 1.5% of principal. Assuming it is taxed at 36%, ordinary income reduces the rate of return .54% if the tax is paid out of the dividends earned. The balance of dividends are reinvested. For the annuity, the industry average fee including mortality expenses is 2.1%.*

[2] *The basis is increased on the personal account due to taxes paid on dividends reinvested. No current tax is paid on the annuity earnings so the basis remains the same.*

Note: If both investors held their accounts until death, Investor A's heirs would receive a "stepped-up" cost basis and avoid all income taxes. Investor B's heirs would be required to pay ordinary income taxes on all gains.

Life Insurance

Life insurance is a fairly complex product, and therefore, is often confusing to the buying public. Let's see if I can de-mystify it a bit. All financial products, including life insurance, are a matter of mathematics. When you buy a cash value life insurance policy, your money (called premiums) goes to the insurance company. A portion of your premium is used to cover the risk of your dying prematurely. This is known as the *mortality charge*. You can think of it as the term insurance charge. Another portion goes to cover the insurance company's overhead, including agents' commissions. The remaining portion is invested by the insurance company for your benefit. The insurance companies have managed to secure some preferential tax treatment. First, the earnings in a cash value policy are tax deferred until withdrawn. If you do withdraw part of your money, it is taxed on a First-In, First-Out basis (FIFO—remember this from Accounting 101?). This means that you pay no taxes until you have withdrawn all the money you contributed. If you never take your money out, but instead, die while the insurance is in force, your investment "gains" are *never* subject to income taxes. While dying is not my idea of a good investment strategy, I am always happy to avoid taxes.

As an investment, life insurance disadvantages center around two big issues: high expenses and limited investment choices. Commissions and expenses can easily consume your first year's entire premium. Many contracts take ten years or longer to "break-even." Some policies are more competitive than this but all contain high expenses compared with direct investments into mutual funds, stocks, or bonds.

As with annuities, your investment options are extremely limited. I should add that cash value life insurance does have an important and appropriate place in estate planning which I will discuss in a future chapter. But if you are using it *primarily* as an investment vehicle, you can likely find better alternatives.

To summarize, if you only have a limited amount of money to invest, you will increase the power of your investment program by prioritizing how those dollars are used. First, you want to invest through retirement plans to the maximum limit the law allows before you invest any money in personal investments. Additionally, you should consider your alternatives carefully before investing in such tax deferred vehicles such as annuities or cash value life insurance.

Improving Investment Results Through Asset Mix

In the last section, we discussed how prioritizing your investment dollars significantly enhances investment accumulation. Another power tool in your investment tool box has to do with choosing your asset mix. Asset mix refers to how you divide your assets between various asset classes. Your decision should be made on two different levels. First is the broad decision of how much money should go into equity investments such as stocks, real estate, etc., verses how much should go into debt investments such as bonds, CDs, and money market accounts. Think of equity investments as the growth or "offensive" element of your portfolio and debt as the "defensive" element of your portfolio. To achieve bigger returns *over the long term,* you should increase the percentage of equity investments in your portfolio. When you do this, you will increase the volatility of your portfolio also. Volatility is a short term problem and is part of the price you pay for higher long term returns. The key to being a successful investor is how well you handle bad market periods (bear markets). When they come, don't panic. Stick to your investment strategy and your patience will eventually be rewarded. Theoretically, your portfolio should be designed to be as conservative as it can be and still get the job done. However, I have found that many clients are willing to invest in more aggressive portfolios than necessary because they are comfortable with higher risks and volatility. I believe this is an appropriate decision as long as you clearly understand how a severe bear market might impact your portfolio. Review the historical risk and return profiles for portfolios illustrated in Table 3-8 (page 48). When you are deciding on your broad asset mix, give careful consideration to your tolerance for potential short term losses. Here "short term" can be defined as 24 months or longer.

Once you have decided on the appropriate broad mix between equities and debt, you are ready for the next level of decision making: **asset allocation**. Asset allocation refers to how you further divide the broad asset classes of debt and equity into their respective sub-classes. Examples for equities include large cap stocks, small cap stocks, international stocks, and real estate. Examples of debt asset classes include CDs, short term bonds, intermediate term bonds, long term bonds, foreign bonds, high yield (junk) bonds, and high quality bonds. The advantages of placing multiple asset classes in a portfolio are that you can reduce volatility and possibly enhance long term returns. In other words, you can have your cake and eat it too! There are computer programs today that allow you to identify the optimal mix of these various asset classes over past time periods. Obviously, the future may turn out to be very different from the past, but studying historical results can provide important insights and is, I believe, beneficial. Table 3-8 portrays various portfolios that have proven to be efficient in the past. There is no exact right answer here, but when you review your own portfolio asset mix, you might want to use one of these examples as a guide for a well diversified portfolio.

Long-Term Care (LTC) Insurance

Long-term care insurance is a complex issue with few perfect answers. What is right for one person will be inappropriate for another. Your best solution is to meet with your financial advisor or someone who specializes in elder care issues. The costs of nursing home care currently ranges from approximately $36,000 to $80,000 per year and will likely triple over the next 20 years, so this is an important issue. When purchasing a policy, consider these guidelines:

- Long-term care insurance is most appropriate for people with assets between $100,000 and $1,500,000 (excluding your home). If your assets are less than $100,000, LTC premiums may be unaffordable and you would quickly become eligible for Medicaid. With assets greater than $1.5 million your can probably afford to self-insure. If you are age 50 today, the cost of a comprehensive LTC policy ranges from about $500 to $1,000 per year for a $150 per day benefit. If you wait to age 70 to buy your policy, this same coverage will cost you $5,000 or more per year.

- Shop for coverage. Coverage provisions can vary widely from policy to policy and company to company. You should be able to tailor a policy to your specific needs and desires. Also, policies available today provide much more complete and liberal coverage than those written just a few short years ago. If you own an older policy, have your agent compare it to a new one. Some companies will allow you to upgrade or exchange your coverage.

- If you are married, you should purchase coverage for both you and your spouse. You do not want to be in a position where the spouse without coverage goes into a nursing home and depletes family assets that may be needed by the healthy spouse to cover his or her living expenses.

- The younger you are, the more important it is to buy an inflation rider. Consider a 5% *compound* inflation rider if you are under age 70. If you are age 70 or older, consider a 5% *simple* inflation rider. Beyond age 75, an inflation rider is probably not a good value.

- Today, approximately 80% of long-term care is received in the home rather than in a nursing care facility. If home care is important to you, be sure your policy includes a rider that covers this benefit.

- Most policies provide a waiver of premium benefit that waives further premium payments once you begin receiving benefits. This benefit usually begins after 90 days of receiving benefits. Many policies waive the premiums only during nursing home stay, not home health care. Since 80% of the care is in the home, it makes sense to be sure your policy waives premiums for home health care as well.

- The likelihood of staying in a nursing home for more than five years is less than 10%. Therefore, the best buy in long-term care insurance is a policy with a five year *benefit period*. Lifetime coverage is available but it is much more expensive.

- If you can afford to self-insure the first 90 days of a nursing home stay, you will reduce your premiums 5% to 10% or more. Be sure to choose a contract that requires you to satisfy your elimination period only once. Since you may go through several phases of need and recovery, you want to avoid having to satisfy the "elimination period" several times.

- The daily costs of nursing home care varies widely depending on where you live. Consult with your advisor regarding the costs in your area. He or she can advise of the appropriate amount of *daily benefit* you should purchase.

- How the insurance companies determine and calculate how benefits are paid can vary widely. The more liberal policies (called *disability income model*) pay full benefits directly to you once you qualify while more restrictive policies (called *reimbursement model*) provide reimbursement of actual expenses incurred directly to the healthcare provider. Some policies calculate "benefits used" based on *the number of days used* (even partial days) while other policies calculate "benefits used" from *the total pool of benefits purchased*. The latter provides potentially more benefits to you. The better contracts pay the benefits directly to you rather than the health care provider. This puts you in a better position to negotiate and control costs as well as the quality of your care.

- As with all insurance products, you will want to make certain that you choose an insurance company that is financially sound. Select a company that is rated AA or better by one of the major rating companies such as Standard and Poor, Moody, or Best. Also, over 130 companies sell LTC policies. Not all of these companies specialize in this type of coverage. Be sure you are buying your LTC policy from one that does. Some of the major players are: UNUM, John Hancock, Metlife, CNA, and GE Capital Assurance.

Estate Planning Benefits of LTC Insurance

If you have an estate of over $1,500,000 you can probably afford to self-insure potential long-term care costs, but that may not be your best estate planning strategy. I have found that one of the biggest reasons people are not willing to give away assets during their lifetime is because of fear of needing those assets if they suffer a catastrophic illness. By purchasing a high quality LTC policy, you are now free to transfer those "reserve" assets, knowing that the risk of paying for a catastrophic illness has now been shifted to your insurance company. Remember, by giving the assets away now, you also give away the future *growth* of those assets which would have increased the estate taxes paid by your heirs had you retained them.

As a Retiree or Baby Boomer, you can expect the cost of nursing home care to continue to rise sharply. Prudence would suggest that this is an issue you need to address with your advisor. Failure to do so may create financial jeopardy in an otherwise sound financial plan.

In this chapter, you determined how much capital you must accumulate in order to have a worry-free retirement. You learned how to make your investment dollars work harder by investing them in the best environment for growth and how to use effective asset allocation to enhance returns and reduce risks. In the next chapter, you will learn the pitfalls of dying without an estate plan. You will also establish appropriate goals for your estate plan.

CHAPTER 4

To Die without an Estate Plan

et's face it, thinking about death is not something most people want to do. It's a depressing topic. The emotional burdens of merely considering it can easily overshadow any financial or legal planning you do. However, not writing your will and failing to do even the most basic estate planning can have disastrous effects on your loved ones and other survivors.

Let's take a closer look at how property is transferred to your heirs if you die without a will. If you die without a will, you are said to die *intestate*. In essence, you have delegated your last wishes to your state legislators. Your "unwritten" will reads something like this:

I, being of sound mind, do hereby direct that the legislators of my state handle my estate as follows:

The state may appoint my surviving spouse as the administrator of my estate or in their infinite wisdom, they may appoint someone completely unknown to my family.

My administrator will be required to post (an expensive) bond to provide "insurance" in case they are incompetent.

My surviving spouse is to receive one half of my estate. The other half is to go to my three year old child.

---

continued on next page

Since my child is a minor, the state may choose my surviving spouse or someone unknown to my family to act as conservator to manage my child's assets. In either case, another (expensive) bond must be purchased annually and the conservator must periodically appear before the court to provide an accounting of how my child's assets have been used. I understand that the court can be pretty "squirrely" about how money is spent. If they disagree with how my conservator has spent money, then my conservator can be held legally liable.

When my child reaches the age of majority (age 18 or 19 in most states), she will receive her inheritance outright and I am going to assume that she is mature enough to handle the money in a manner that would make me proud.

If for some reason my spouse does not survive me (common accident?), I ask the state to decide who would be the best person (or institution) to raise my child. I hope they don't choose my aunt Thelma!

If my surviving spouse remarries and then has the misfortune to predecease her new husband, it's okay that the assets I left her may go to him and not my daughter.

I am happy to pay, from the proceeds of my estate, expensive legal, court, and administrative fees.

Finally, I realize that my poor planning may create large estate taxes which could have been avoided if I hadn't been so darn lazy.

Signed,
Your Loving, But Procrastinating Husband

I hope you find this "will" unacceptable. The intestate laws of each state vary widely so you will need to check with your financial advisor to determine the laws for your state of residence.

PROPERTY TRANSFERS AT DEATH

When you die, your property is going to be transferred to your heirs through one or more of the following distribution channels: probate, direct transfers by title, or living trusts. This is true whether or not you have a will. Each of these transfer methods has both advantages and disadvantages. You need to understand them so that you can intelligently choose the best methods for you. In this chapter, I will cover both probate and direct transfers by title. Transfers through Living Trusts will be covered in a later chapter.

TRANSFERS VIA PROBATE

Probate is the legal process whereby at your death a probate judge oversees the transfer of your property to your rightful heirs. While the probate process can be complicated and confusing, it can be broken down into nine steps.

Step 1: Locate and Interpret the Will

If you have a valid will, assets titled solely in your own name or assets which name your estate as the beneficiary will pass through the probate process. Your will specifies which persons or organizations will receive your property. As mentioned earlier, if you do not have a will, state law will determine who receives your property.

Step 2: Identify Your Estate Representative

If you do not have a will, the court appoints someone to represent your estate. This person is called an administrator (for a man), an administratrix (for a woman), or in some states, a personal representative. This representative is responsible for working with the probate judge and completing the necessary steps to settle your estate and distribute your property to your heirs. In many cases, the court will require your personal representative to post a bond in order to provide some protection for your heirs should he or she be dishonest. This bond is paid for out of your assets. Your personal representative is also entitled to compensation for his or her services. Some states have statutory limits on the amount of compensation a personal representative can receive but most states allow "reasonable" compensation. In all cases, the probate judge must approve the compensation. This is also paid from your assets.

Step 3: Determine Who Your Heirs Are

Your will will specify who your heirs are. If you do not have a will, your rightful heirs will be determined by state law. State laws can vary widely. Check with your local attorney or bank trust officer regarding the laws of your state.

Step 4: Locate and Value All Your Property

This is often the most difficult part of the process. All assets (this means every item of personal property, real estate, business interest, securities, etc.) must be located, inventoried, and valued. It often requires that appraisals be ordered, which takes time and can be very expensive. Appraisals represent an educated guess of value and therefore are subject to the scrutiny and challenge of the court, heirs, and the Internal Revenue Service.

Step 5: Identify Creditors

Your personal representative must publish legal notices of your death so that potential creditors have an opportunity to file a claim against your estate.

Step 6: Resolve Disputes

Whenever money is involved, it's likely that disputes will arise. These problems can come from many sources: disgruntled heirs, creditors, personal representatives, disinherited parties, the Internal Revenue Service. It's the job of the probate judge to see that whatever problems develop get resolved.

Step 7: Pay the Administrative Expenses, Creditors, Debts, Funeral Expenses, Income and Estate Taxes

Everyone must be paid before final disbursements are made to heirs. The estate may or may not be large enough to owe estate taxes. If estate taxes are due, cash must be raised to pay them. Often estates are long on assets but short on cash. The law has special provisions for estates comprised largely of closely held business interest or farm land which allows the estate taxes to be stretched out, reduced, or eliminated.

Step 8: File All Tax Returns

Your estate representative must file your estate tax return as well as a final income tax return.

Step 9: Distribute Property to Heirs

If you have no will and minor children or incompetent heirs are involved, the courts must appoint conservators and may remain involved for years.

Again, like most things, the probate process has its advantages and disadvantages.

Advantages

- Court supervision. It is, after all, a legal process. Your personal representative has a legal and fiduciary responsibility to act on behalf of your legal heirs. The probate judge supervises the process from start to finish. No disbursements are made without ultimate court approval.

- Limited duration. At the beginning of the probate process, legal notices are published in order to alert your creditors that you have died. This "notice" effectively sets a time limit, usually six months, after which no creditor can make a claim against your estate.

- Postmortem planning. Since your estate is a separate taxpaying entity, your representative has the opportunity to do some postmortem planning. Through disclaimers and other strategies, taxes can be postponed, reduced, or in some cases eliminated.

Disadvantages

- Cost. The primary criticism of the probate system is that it is expensive. Depending on the state in which you live, this may or may not be true. Probate costs vary widely from state to state and even from probate judge to probate judge. Many of our states' probate laws officially say that probate costs will be "fair and reasonable." What is fair and reasonable often depends on whether you are the receiver or payer of fees. If you own property in more than one state, you may have to go through probate in those states as well.

- Length of process. The probate process is a slow process, often taking six months to several years. While your heirs can receive interim distributions, they are forced to wait for the ultimate distribution of your estate.

- Public process. The probate process is a public process. Anyone can go down to the courthouse and review a copy of your will, what you owned, and who you owed. Not long after Princess Diana's death, copies of her will were being sold for one dollar each! Some unscrupulous people have made a pretty good living preying on heirs. Many of my clients are very private people, and prefer to avoid public intrusion into their financial affairs and the lives of the people they love.

DIRECT TRANSFERS BY TITLE

One way to avoid the probate process is to set up direct transfers through the titling of your property. Property titles can be very tricky, so you must plan carefully to ensure that you achieve the desired results. How you title your property can have a profound impact on estate taxes and ultimately, your whole estate plan. Typically, couples title all property in joint names. While there is no best way to title property for everyone, individual case facts and goals will determine the best way to title property for you. Let's look at the various ways to title property as well as the advantages and disadvantages of each.

The most common ways of holding title are Fee Simple (also known as Sole Ownership), Joint Tenants with Rights of Survivorship, and Joint Tenants in Common. Some states have special laws that govern Community Property ownership.

Fee Simple Ownership

Under Fee Simple ownership, you have the title totally in your name: "John Smith." Note that this method of ownership does *not* avoid probate.

Advantages

- Fee Simple ownership is easy to establish.

- Fee Simple ownership does not require the signatures of other parties.

- Property titled solely in your name allows you the freedom of total control during your lifetime. You can do with this property as you see fit without interference from other people.

- You have total control over who the property passes to upon your death.

- It can eliminate the income or capital gains tax treatment of appreciated property. If the property has appreciated significantly, then upon your death it will receive a stepped up cost basis and the inheriting party will receive the asset at the fair market value as of the date of your death. (Note: A few states restrict the transfer of "fee simple" real estate without spousal consent.)

Disadvantages

- Upon your death, this property will be subject to the expense and delays of the probate process. If you do not specifically decide who would receive the property and execute an instrument (i.e., a will) that would cause the property to go to a specific person or organization, then those decisions would be determined for you by the current state laws.

- If you become incompetent through some form of disability, then the property would likely be referred to a court process to create a control mechanism. Later, I will discuss how you could avoid this potential problem by signing a *power of attorney.*

- Since the property is held solely in your name, it will be included in your estate and subject to potential estate taxes.

Joint Tenants with Right of Survivorship (JTWRS)

Property held as Joint Tenants with Right of Survivorship would be titled as follows: "John and Sue Smith, Joint Owners with Right of Survivorship."

Under this type of ownership, you cannot transfer the property or make any dispositions of the property without the written permission of the other joint tenant. You are, in effect, joined together in all decisions regarding the disposition of this property.

Upon death, your interest in the property automatically transfers to the surviving tenant(s).

Advantages

While titling by Joint Tenants with Right of Survivorship sounds archaic, it is actually the most common form of ownership for married couples and does have some advantages.

- Such property is not subject to probate until the death of the final joint tenant. For example, if you know that at your death you want your wife to have control and ownership of your residence, this method will ensure that it passes to her immediately without going through the probate process.

- It is easy to set up. It requires no special paperwork.

- It is an inexpensive way to hold title.

Disadvantages

- You lose some control over the property during your lifetime. Remember, your joint tenant must agree with all decisions regarding the property.

- You lose control over who the property ultimately goes to after your death. The joint tenant holder will have the opportunity to decide to whom they wish to leave the property.

- It precludes having the property pass to a credit shelter trust, family trust, or QTIP trust. These concepts will be discussed in detail later in this book.

- Can lead to higher estate taxes if the joint owner is your spouse.

- Eventually property will be subject to probate upon the death of the last surviving tenant.

- Your property may pass to unintended heirs. For example, if your spouse remarries after you die, he/she could change the title to include Joint Tenants with Right of Survivorship with his/her new spouse. If he/she predeceases that new spouse, the property will automatically pass to him/her, not your children.

- Can cause unintended estate tax problems. For example, two brothers go in together to buy a lake home. For simplicity, they decide to title it JTWRS. Upon the death of the first brother, the property automatically passes to the surviving brother. That property, however, is included in the estate of the first brother and is subject to estate taxes without having the property available for sale to raise cash to pay those taxes.

- Leaves property open to the claims of creditors. Take the above example of the brothers who own the lake house. Let's assume that one of them is sued and receives a judgment. Under the titling of Joint Tenancy, that property is subject to the claims of creditors. There could be a forced sale of the property; a situation which the brother (who is not a party to the lawsuit) does not have any control over. This same problem could arise if one of the brothers were to get divorced.

While JTWRS is one of the most common forms of property ownership in America, it is filled with so many pitfalls that anyone owning property under this method of ownership should *carefully* consider all of the ramifications.

Tenants in Common

If you own property as Tenants in Common, it would be listed as follows: "John Smith and Sue Smith, Tenants in Common."

The disposition of the property at your death is similar to what happens during your life. You have the absolute right to determine who your share of the property will go to. If you do not specify who will receive that property in your will, or if you do not have a will, the property will pass according to the state laws where you reside.

Advantages

- An easy way to title property which does not require any special paperwork.

- You have absolute control of your share the property. You can give it away, sell it, and under any method, you can transfer it to someone else. It does not require the signature or permission of the other tenant(s).

- You are free to dispose of the property as you wish through your will.

Disadvantages

- You never have control of the entire property, only your portion or interest in that property.

- You could easily end up with other joint tenants who are incompatible with you.

- Your interest will be included in your estate and, therefore, will be subject to estate taxes.

- The property would be subject to probate and the associated costs and time delays.

- As with Fee Simple property, if you were to become disabled, it would most likely require court intervention in order to handle the control issues unless you have executed a *power of attorney.*

- It is difficult to dispose of fee simple property because a potential buyer will be less likely to purchase an undivided interest in real estate. If someone is interested, they are likely to require a "discount" off the fair market value due to this type of ownership.

Community Property

Nine states have special laws related to what is called community property. These states are Arizona, California, Idaho, Louisiana, Nevada, New Mexico, Texas, Washington, and Wisconsin. In these nine states, the way property is titled is often dictated by state law. The particulars vary by state, so you will need to refer to local professionals for advice if you reside in one of these states. There are some general rules that are observed by all nine states. Some property may be classified as *separate property*. An example of separate property would include property that you owned prior to a marriage or property that you inherited. If you want your separate property to remain as such, the title must be kept in your name and must never be changed. *Community property* is any property that was acquired after the date of marriage or any separate property that was sold or re-titled. Community property operates much like property that is owned by Tenants in Common. You can designate whomever you want as a beneficiary to receive your half when you die. As under Fee Simple titling, your separate property can be disposed of in any manner you wish.

Community property states present special challenges for estate planning. For example, if you and your spouse buy a house together, it is considered community property. If you want your spouse to receive the home when you die, you would have to specifically state this in your will. Otherwise, the property will transfer according to the laws in the state where you live.

OTHER METHODS OF PROPERTY OWNERSHIP

Less common methods of ownership include Life Estates, Revocable Living Trusts, and Irrevocable Trusts.

Life Estates

Life Estates are a way of providing someone the right to enjoy the use of certain property for as long as they live. They are required to maintain the property in good condition and otherwise have no control over the property. At the death of the life owner, the property passes to the beneficiaries of the life estate. This method of transferring and owning property may avoid probate and may provide estate tax benefits as well.

Revocable Living Trusts

As the name implies, Revocable Living Trusts are trusts that you create during your lifetime where you also retain the right to revoke or dismantle the trust. One of the primary advantages of the living trust is that it avoids probate. It is particularly appropriate if you own property in more than one state or your job requires you to move from state to state. With a Revocable Living Trust, you avoid the possibility of having to rewrite your will when you move your residence to a new state. During your lifetime, you can serve as the trustee so that control over your assets is relatively trouble-free. A disadvantage of this method of ownership is that it requires that you re-title all property in the name of the trust which can be time consuming and expensive. (For more about this important method of owning and controlling property, see Chapter 7).

Irrevocable Trusts

Irrevocable Trusts can be established during your life (called inter vivos trusts) or at your death under your will (called testamentary trusts). As a beneficiary of an irrevocable trust, you have no control over the property.

That control has been vested in the *trustee* who is required to follow the instructions written in the trust document. While this may sound restrictive, consider some of the benefits. This type of trust can be used to remove assets from your estate and therefore reduce estate taxes. It can also be used to hold assets for minor children, and in certain states, can protect assets from creditors. (See chapters 6 and 8 for more information about the benefits of irrevocable trusts.)

Payment on Death (POD) Accounts

POD accounts are a special way of owning savings, checking, brokerage accounts, and certificates of deposits. The account holder instructs the financial institution to write on the account a "payable on death" designation. The person(s) named will, by law, receive the account at your death. These accounts, therefore, do not go through probate. This method of titling property is not available in all states.

Beneficiary Designations

Beneficiary designations, while not being a form of title, are another way to avoid the costs, time, and public nature of probate. To accomplish this, you must simply name an individual or organization as the beneficiary of your life insurance, annuity, IRA, or company retirement plan.

As you can see, each of these methods of owning property has both pluses and minuses and must be carefully reviewed in the context of your overall estate plan. Often, the very best method for owning property is through trust. (Trusts will be discussed fully in chapters 6, 7, 8 and 9.)

If you still believe that all this estate planning is too complicated, you're not alone. Over 70 percent of Americans have no will. However, I believe that one simple case study should convince you of the importance of carefully developing your estate plan.

SETTING ESTATE PLANNING GOALS

As you begin to develop your estate plan, it is important for you to prioritize your goals and objectives. Once this is accomplished, you can tailor your plan to meet your specific needs. Below is a list of a number of common goals. Take some time to review these goals and rate them from 1 to 10, with 1 being the most important to you, and 10 being the least important.

CASE STUDY

Ray was a successful salesman, providing for his family with a six-figure income. The family owned a large home and sent their nine-year-old son, William, to a private school. Their lifestyle consumed all their income, so Ray had only a modest savings account. Ray's income was on the rise, so he assumed there would be plenty of opportunity to build up savings and save for retirement later. After all, he was only 42. Then the unthinkable happened. Ray died of a heart attack. The aftermath of his lack of planning will likely be felt by his heirs for the rest of their lives. His estate consisted primarily of the home, which went to his wife Sally by title, and a $1 million life insurance policy. Unfortunately, Ray died without a will and he had named his estate the beneficiary of his life insurance policy. Here's where the financial part of the tragedy begins. Because Ray died without a will, his assets would be distributed according to state law. In the state where he lived, a surviving spouse received one half of the deceased spouse's estate, as did his child. Since William was a minor, the court appointed a legal conservator to watch over his inheritance. Unfortunately, the conservator was unskilled in managing money, so the assets were invested only in CDs and similar "safe" investments. Even more damaging was that the conservator took the position that William's assets could not be used for his support. All support would have to come from Sally. Sally's after-tax income from the $500,000 and Social Security amounted to less than $30,000 per year. The current mortgage payment on their home was $18,000 per year and William's private school tuition amounted to another $4,000 per year. She considered getting a job, but having not worked in the last 10 years, the job market offered her little opportunity. The situation left Sally on the verge of a nervous breakdown. There were very few solutions to her dilemma. She ended up selling the home, moving into an apartment and taking a low-paying job to get extra money in order to keep William in private school.

But this is not the real tragedy here. The real tragedy happened to William. Under state law he was considered an adult when he turned age 19. By that time his account had grown to over $800,000, which he received on his 19th birthday! Unfortunately, William knew nothing about managing money and was going through a stage where he had little use for his mother's advice. Within a couple of years, the money was gone and the relationship between the mother and son was forever damaged.

All of this could have been avoided if Ray had just taken the time to develop his estate plan.

Goals of Your Estate Plan

_____ Providing for your spouse and children.

_____ Protecting assets from creditors and lawsuits.

_____ Making gifts to favorite charities, educational institutions, or religious organizations.

_____ Providing financial help for grandchildren.

_____ Protecting and preserving the family business.

_____ Protecting and preserving real estate holdings.

_____ Minimizing estate and income taxes.

_____ Minimizing administrative expenses and delays in settling your estate.

_____ Providing specific bequests for relatives or other non-family members.

_____ Dividing assets fairly.

_____ Maintaining privacy of your financial affairs.

You will want to refer to this checklist when you begin to implement your estate plan. It is particularly important to discuss your goals and objectives with the financial advisor you choose to help you with your planning. Take your goals along with you when you meet with your financial advisor or the attorney who is advising you on your will.

In this chapter, you have learned the significance of writing a will and determining how your assets will be divided upon your death. Planning is necessary not only to insure that your loved ones are left with property or investments to support them, but also to limit the amount of estate taxes that they will owe on your assets. In the next chapter, you will learn more about how to use a will to accomplish your estate planning goals.

CHAPTER 5

Your Last Will and Testament

The Basic Estate Planning Tool

I n the last chapter, you learned about the many potential pitfalls of dying without a will or of relying on property titles to transfer your property for you. A logical solution is a properly drafted Last Will and Testament (referred to hereafter as "will"). In this chapter, I will discuss the basic structure of a will along with advice on making key decisions concerning guardians, trustees, executors, and trusts.

WHAT IS A WILL?

A will is a legal declaration giving instructions concerning what person(s) or organization(s) are to receive your property after your death. This declaration names the executor or personal representative who will be responsible for settling your estate, the trustee(s) responsible for managing any trusts you created, and the guardian(s) who will care for your minor children.

TYPES OF WILLS

The concept of wills dates back to British law in the mid-1500s. Prior to that time, when a "commoner" died, part of his property automatically reverted to royalty. The Parliament passed a law establishing the *Statute of Wills* which allowed these commoners to leave all of their property to whomever they chose under certain rules and guidelines.

Today, there are many types of wills. While it is instructive to you to know they exist, you should definitely avoid some of them.

Oral or Nuncupative Will

While most states require that wills be in writing, a few states *do* allow oral wills. Oral wills are usually associated with deathbed situations where the testator, in front of witnesses, states his or her final wishes. Typically at least three witnesses are required to be present during the testator's statement and the testator must die within a certain period of time. You want to avoid this approach to estate planning. Why? Because not only are these wills easily contested, but usually they are not well thought-out.

Holographic Will

This is a will that someone makes in his or her own handwriting and is sometimes referred to as a "homemade" will. Only about 15 to 20 states allow holographic wills. Some states allow holographic wills only when the testator is a member of our armed services and is stationed outside of the United States. You remember the old war movies where the infantryman was about to go into a fierce battle and at the last minute handwrites a will leaving everything to his beloved mother or sweetheart. While this solution is better than the oral will, it is still wrought with potential problems and again should be avoided.

Joint Will

A joint will is one document, usually between a husband and wife, in which it is declared that all property passes to the surviving spouse upon the death of the first spouse. The document further indicates where the property must go upon the death of the then remaining spouse. While at first glance a joint will might appear to be a simple and less expensive solution than each spouse having separate wills, it is not. Many states have taken the position that a joint will is in reality a contract between the two parties. This could cause you to lose the benefit of the unlimited marital deduction and thereby cause immediate taxation on a portion of your estate at the first spouse's death. Since avoiding this potential problem is tricky, your legal fees are likely to be *higher* than if you had separate wills prepared. The better solution is to have a separate will for both you and your spouse.

Simple Will

Between spouses this is sometimes referred to as an "I love you" will because it essentially says that you intend to leave everything to your surviving spouse. Obviously, simple wills can be more complicated than that and are often used by non-married people and married people alike to indicate where their property will go when they die. What is implied in the simple will is that your property distributions will be outright distributions and that your estate is uncomplicated and tax planning is not needed. Unfortunately, I have often found that, while the client believes this to be the case, more complex planning is appropriate and necessary.

Testamentary Trust Will

This type of will directs that a *portion* of your property, *all* of your property, or a portion of your property *under certain circumstances* goes to a trust that has been established under your will. There can be many reasons for this type of planning including reducing taxes, providing professional management for heirs, protecting your estate from creditors, and maintaining control over the final disposition of your property.

ADVANTAGES AND DISADVANTAGES OF WILLS

You have probably heard many times that you need a will, but do you really? The answer is almost certainly, yes. While there are many advantages of having a will, there are also several disadvantages.

Advantages

- A will allows you to specifically direct who is going to receive your property at your death. If your will has been correctly drafted and signed, you can be confident that your wishes will be carried out. If you want to specifically exclude someone from receiving your property at your death, you can do so through your will (except that most states do not allow you to totally exclude your spouse).

- Your will can be used as a strategy for reducing estate taxes. There are many ways to use your will to reduce estate taxes including using the unlimited marital deduction, credit shelter trust, and charitable bequest.

- Your will can establish a trust to manage assets for your adult or minor children. Minor children cannot receive assets in their name. Your will allows you to decide who will manage your children's assets, how those assets will be managed, and for how long the assets will be managed.

- Your will is the only way you can nominate who will be responsible for the care of your minor children.

- Your will can reduce certain costs of settling your estate. For example, you can direct that your executor or personal representative will serve without the need to post a bond.

- Through your will, you can leave money or property to your favorite charity, educational institution, or religious organization.

Disadvantages

- Property passing by way of your will must go through probate. As you read in Chapter 4, probate can be both expensive and time-consuming.

- Wills are public documents. You may feel that it is important that your financial affairs not be available for public inspection, but it is a requirement that your will be filed with the court when you die. There are actually Internet sites now that display the wills of famous people (try: http://www.com/legaldocs/newsmakers/wills/). If you find yourself wanting to put this book down and visit the Internet site just mentioned, you will then know exactly why some people want their financial affairs kept private. Worse still, not all onlookers are just curious—some have ill intentions in mind.

- A will that is properly written and signed in one state will likely be valid in all states. However, how your will is *interpreted* can vary widely from state to state, possibly resulting in your wishes not being carried out to your satisfaction. This can be a particular problem if your job causes you to periodically move from one state to another, or if you own property in more than one state. For example, you wrote a will while you lived in Georgia, but you have since moved to Louisiana and did not write a new will. You die while living in Louisiana. Will Georgia law or Louisiana law prevail? The result here could be a major disaster for your loved ones.

- Your will cannot provide for your care in the event that you become incapacitated or incompetent. This issue must be addressed through documents other than your will such as a Power of Attorney or Revocable Living Trust.

- Your will may not control all your property. I have often seen instances in which people feel pretty confident that their affairs are in good order based on their wills, but then discover that much of their property will pass outside of their will because of joint tenancy titles and beneficiary designations.

- Wills can be contested. Sometimes money will bring out the worst in people. This is particularly the case when someone dies and there are disgruntled heirs or people who feel they had a "right" to some portion of assets of the deceased. Often it does not matter if there are valid grounds for the contest or not. Many times the rightful heirs would rather "settle" than risk an expensive and lengthy court battle.

And you thought that you could solve all your estate planning problems by rewriting your will! Actually, it is a little more complicated than that. A properly drafted and executed will is an important part of your estate plan, but many other issues must be considered also. Many of the disadvantages of wills can be resolved by using a Revocable Living Trust which will be discussed in detail in Chapter 7. However, for now, let's discuss the essential elements of a well-crafted will.

INTELLIGENT DECISIONS CONCERNING YOUR WILL'S BASIC PROVISIONS

While there is no perfect formula for drafting a will, certain common provisions should be considered carefully.

Opening Declaration

Your opening declaration should make it clear that this document represents your Last Will and Testament and that it revokes all prior wills. Here's an example:

I, James Dean, a resident of Hollywood, California, being of sound mind and disposing memory, do hereby make, publish and declare this instrument as and for my Last Will and Testament and hereby expressly revoke any and all wills, codicils and other testamentary dispositions heretofore made by me.

Item I: Payment of Debts and Funeral Expenses

This section allows your executor or personal representative to immediately proceed with paying off debts and funeral expenses.

As soon as practical, I direct that my funeral expenses and all my enforceable, secured or unsecured debts be paid in full, or according to the terms of any instrument evidencing such indebtedness, as my executor deems advisable.

This sounds simple and straightforward on the surface, but care should be taken here. The above language excludes the payment of any *un*enforceable debt. Without such language, creditors from a prior bankruptcy may try to enforce a legally discharged debt from your estate. The language, "*. . . paid in full, or according to the language of any instrument . . .*" gives your executor the option to keep in place such debt arrangements as residential mortgages.

Item II: Personal Items

Sometimes referred to as the "specific legacy" clause, this section is where you direct who will receive items of a personal nature such as jewelry, furniture, clothing, automobiles, cash, etc.

I give all my tangible personal property and insurance thereon to my beloved wife, Beatrice Dean, if she survives me. Otherwise, I give said property in equal shares to my children who survive me and to the descendants, per stirpes, of any of my children that do not survive me.

"Insurance" in this section does not refer to life insurance. It refers to insurance proceeds that might be received due to the destruction of property such as by fire or accident. For example, if your death was caused by a boating accident in your boat, your heirs would receive the property insurance proceeds, not the destroyed boat.

This is the most personal section of your will. If you have personal items that you want to go to certain people (called "general bequests"), include them in this section. For example, if you want your stamp collection to go to your son you would indicate so by saying:

I hereby bequeath my stamp collection to go to my son, James Dean, Jr.

You should note that unless you state otherwise, any debt owed on bequeathed property as well as the expense of moving it must be born by the legatee. If you would like to leave a specific amount of money to individuals or charities, you would do so by saying, "*I devise the sum of Twenty-five Thousand dollars to my sister, Jean S. Daily. . . .*" After paying your debts and distributing your personal property, the next $25,000 will go to your sister *before* any other money is distributed to any other heirs (including your spouse).

Item III: Residence(s)

If you are married, you will likely want your home to go to your spouse. This section is included assuming that you own your home in your name solely or under joint tenants in common. (See Chapter 4 for more details concerning how to title property.) Often, homes are owned between spouses as *joint tenants with right of survivorship*. If this is the case, your home will pass by title not by your will.

I devise to my wife, Beatrice Dean, if she survives me, all of my right, title and interest in and to any residences which I own at the time of my death, subject to any mortgages or encumbrances thereon at the time of my death.

Note that in this case, the home was left to the spouse *including* the mortgage, which means the spouse would be required to satisfy the mortgage by either continuing payments or paying it off. If your preference would be for the mortgage to be satisfied from proceeds of your estate then your will would read, "*free of mortgages or encumbrances. . . .*"

Item IV: Division of Residuary Estate

Residuary means "everything that is left." Everything that you have not already given away previously in your will is included in this section.

I give all the rest, residue, and remainder of my estate to my wife, Beatrice Dean, if she survives me. If she does not survive me, my residue shall be divided equally between my children who survive me and to the descendants, per stirpes, of any of my children who predecease me.

Here you should give serious thought about what you would like to do with the balance of your estate. If you are married, do you want it to go outright to your spouse or would it be better to have it go into a trust for his or her benefit? Is your spouse capable of financial management or is management best left to a qualified trustee? You calculated your potential estate taxes in Chapter 2. Should a trust be used to reduce potential estate taxes? How to best utilize trusts under your will will be covered in Chapter 6. If you have minor children, you will need to make provisions here or in another section of your will to provide for trusts, trustees, etc.

Item V: Payment of Taxes

This section outlines how your estate and inheritance taxes will be paid. First, you should estimate the total amount of taxes that you are likely to owe (See Chapter 2). Then, you need to determine how they are to be paid. You have several options including:

- Statutory appointment. In this case, each beneficiary would pay the taxes that his or her bequest generates. The language might read: "*. . . each beneficiary shall bear a pro rata portion of the estate and inheritance taxes due . . .*"

- Off the top. This section would read something like this: "*. . . all estate and inheritance taxes will be paid prior to any distributions from my estate to my heirs . . .*" This has the effect of paying taxes before the residuary estate is distributed. Excluded from this would be any **general bequest** you make.

- From your residuary estate. Here you might say: "*. . . all estate and inheritance taxes will be paid from my residuary estate . . .*" This means that those persons or organizations receiving general bequests from your personal property will do so free of any taxes. Your residuary beneficiary will bear the burden of taxes for your entire estate. Unlike the "off the top" method, here your residuary beneficiaries might end up bearing a disproportionate share of the taxes if one group of beneficiaries is exempt from taxes while another group is not. Be careful to calculate what those taxes are likely to be and be sure that there will be enough cash available to pay them. This can be a particular problem if the residuary estate consists primarily of property that is not liquid, such as real estate.

- Paid from a general bequest. Here you would say: "... *all estate and inheritance taxes to be paid from the general bequest to the American Cancer Foundation* ..." If a general bequest was a large portion of your estate, you might want to have your taxes paid from that bequest to make certain that other persons indicated in your will receive a share of your estate.

Item VI: In Terrorem Clause

If you specifically intend to exclude someone from your will who would normally be included, you would do so in this section. In almost all states, you cannot completely disinherit your spouse. This is not the case with children or other family members. Let's assume that you wish to disinherit your son, David. If your will simply stated that your estate is to be equally divided among your children Dolly Dean, Debbie Dean, and James Dean, Jr., David could contest the will claiming he was left out as an "oversight." This issue is resolved by specifically stating he is to receive nothing from your estate: "... *It is my full intention that my son, David Dean, receive no share or portion of my estate* ..." Some attorneys will take a different approach by specifying that the disinherited person is to receive $1. This indicates that you did not forget them, nor did you think much of them. This method can have a disadvantage. I remember one case where a child received $1 from his parents' estate. The problem was that no one knew where the child was currently living. The executor ended up spending a large amount of money "tracking down" the son so he could receive his $1!

Item VII: Minors Trusts

If you have minor children, this section will establish and outline how assets payable to them will be handled. You have two appropriate choices here:

- Have the assets paid to a custodial account. Here you might say: "*Should any part of my estate become payable to any person(s) under the age of 21, then my executor shall pay such share to my spouse or my child's guardian as custodian under the Uniform Transfer to Minors Acts . . .*" In my opinion, unless you expect it to be a very small amount of money, this approach is not advisable. Under the Uniform Transfer to Minors Act, your child would receive his or her inheritance at the age of majority for your state of residence (age 18 or 19 in most states). Most 19-year-olds are not prepared to handle money. The second alternative is preferable.

- Have the assets paid to a trust. Here you would say: "*. . . should any part of my estate become payable to any person(s) under the age of twenty one, then my executor shall pay such share to a trust for the benefit of said person(s) . . .*" You would then go on to outline the specific terms of the trust.

If you have children, even children who are no longer minors, this is one of the most important sections of your will and deserves considerable thought on your part. First, imagine the worst possible scenario that both you and your spouse die in a common accident. If you are like most people, if there is no surviving spouse, all assets are left to your children. The size of the estate is likely to be large because in addition to your assets, there may be life insurance proceeds payable on both you and your spouse. Your goal should be to make sure your children's needs are met without overwhelming them with money and possibly destroying their ambition and work ethic by providing them with too much money too soon. Remember, neither you nor your spouse will be there to impart your values to your children. You will be counting on your trust documents, your trustees, and your guardians (for minors) to do this for you. It is my opinion that holding assets in trust until mid-adulthood is not such a bad thing. My clients will typically hold children's assets in trust until the child turns age 30 or 35, at which time we will disburse one-third of the trust assets. Final disbursements from the trust usually come five years later. The reasoning behind this strategy is simple. If you give a 21-year-old child a large sum, say $500,000, he or she has two choices: spend it or invest it. If the money is spent, it would likely be spent on something you would not approve of. If your child invests the money, he or she may well lose it because of a lack of investment experience. In most cases, it is better to hold the assets in trust until your children are likely to have gained the maturity and experience necessary to handle large sums of money.

Until that time the trustee is providing for the children's needs with income and, if needed, principal of the trust. This trust can be as flexible or as restrictive as you desire. For example, clients often include provisions allowing the trustee to make disbursements for the down payment on a home or to start a business. Because of the importance of education, clients almost always include provisions for covering all costs of advanced education including college, graduate school, medical school, or law school. Certainly, you will want your trustee to have the right to invade principal to cover the costs of any health issues.

Children who receive too much money too soon often develop a poor system of values. A trustee can never provide the caring guidance of a parent, but a well-drawn trust agreement can provide a guide for carrying out your wishes for your children.

Item VIII: Executors

The executor position is usually one of relatively short duration, although it can last several years. Your executor is charged with the responsibility of settling your estate and distributing your assets to those people or organizations indicated in your will. The language in your document might read something like: *"I hereby appoint my wife, Beatrice Dean, to serve as executrix under this, my Last Will and Testament. In the event that she shall fail to qualify, die, or resign, then I appoint my brother, Robert Dean, as executor hereunder, or if he shall fail to qualify . . ."* One major decision you need to make is whether you should nominate a family member (or close friend) or nominate a professional such as an attorney or bank. My preference is normally to choose a family member or friend. They will often serve for no fee or a nominal fee. They then would retain an attorney or bank trust officer of their choosing to do most of the work. If you nominate a professional, there will be little control over fees that the professional will charge your estate. To allow for the unexpected, you should list a succession of people to serve as your executor should an executor be unable to serve because of his or her death, incapacity, or lack of desire. It is also a good idea to ask your executors if they are willing to serve *before* making your will. If you are married, your spouse is normally a good choice as first executor/executrix. Be sure to include language that your executor will serve without being required to post a bond: "*No executor hereunder shall be required to give bond or to file an inventory or accounting in any court . . .*"

Item IX: Trustees

Choosing your trustee(s) will be among the most important decisions you will make with regard to your estate plan. These are the people charged with the responsibility for carrying out your wishes regarding management of your investments and other assets. They will often serve for years or even decades. Preferably, your choice here is someone with financial experience. A family member is often the best choice. Remember, the trustee has the option to hire professional investment managers to do the work. They could even hire a bank trust department to perform most of the duties normally associated with being a trustee. The advantage of using a family member as trustee is that they are in a position to negotiate fees and change investment managers if they deem appropriate. They also best understand the needs of your family members who are beneficiaries of your trust. As with executors, you need to list a succession of trustees in your will. I normally ask clients to try to list at least three people or more. You can have people serve alone or as co-trustees. Because trusts often last for years, I recommend that after you have selected all the people you can think of as appropriate trustees, you nominate a corporate trustee. *Always* give someone the right to replace your corporate trustee with another corporate trustee. Under most circumstances, I give this right to the majority of the beneficiaries. The language to remove a corporate trustee may read something like: "*Any corporate trustee may be removed by a majority of the adult income beneficiaries and the guardians of any minor beneficiaries . . . to be replaced by a qualified trust company . . .*" I remember one young lady whose parents died leaving her money in trust with a local bank. She tried numerous times to contact her trust officer but he would not return her calls. She sat in my office with tears of frustration as I reviewed her trust document. Her trust contained a clause that allowed her to move the account to another corporate trustee. I picked up the phone and left a message that if she did not receive a phone call from her trust officer in the next 10 minutes, we intended to move the account to another local bank. We got the call and now she is regularly invited to meetings with her trust officer at the bank's executive dining room! The power to move your account creates a lot of leverage.

Under this section or under a separate section, you will list the trustee's powers. This is usually several pages of "boiler plate" language provided by your attorney giving the trustee very broad powers regarding how your money can be invested and managed. You should read through this to be sure you agree with all the terms. You may find that it has been years since your attorney has read it!

This section will also outline how trust assets will be distributed for your adult and minor beneficiaries. When deciding on who are candidates for your trustees, be sure to consider their age. Your parent may have the wisdom you seek in a trustee but will he or she likely be around for the full term of the trust? Make sure at least one or more trustees is young enough to survive the term of the trust.

Item X: Guardians

If you have minor children, there can be no more important decision than who will care for your children in the event you and your spouse die prematurely. Language in your will might read as follows: *If my spouse predeceases me and I leave minor children, I appoint my sister, Jean S. Daily, as the guardian of the persons of said minor children. If she does not qualify to serve or for any reason fails to serve then I appoint my brother Robert Dean. The appointed guardian shall have custody of my minor children and shall serve without bond.* I encourage you to think of people who have similar *values* to you. In the case of guardians, you will definitely want to ask them if they would be willing to serve and you will want to have a succession of at least three. Lives can change dramatically. Someone who agrees to take your children into his or her home should you die today, may not be in a position to do so just a few short years from now.

In many cases, people have the guardian also serve as custodian of the children's assets. I believe these should be separate decisions. The person who is the best choice to raise your children may not be the best choice to handle their money. You should aim for a separate trustee for financial management. It is advisable to try to choose guardians and trustees who would likely work well together. You should consider giving the trustee broad discretion regarding use of children's assets for their benefit. For example, if you have three minor children, you may want the trustee to have the ability to provide the guardian funds to add on to their home or to help pay the costs of family vacations.

Item XI: Simultaneous Death Clause

If you and your spouse are killed in a common accident, this section provides instruction concerning who is presumed to have died first for the purpose of settling your estate. The language can be fairly broad such as: *"If my spouse does not survive me by a period of six (6) months, then my spouse shall be deemed to have predeceased me for the purpose of this will . . ."* Your spouse's will would contain similar language. While this may appear to create a contradiction, it simply allows each separate estate to be carried out as each person had planned.

Item XII: Perpetuities Clause

While the idea of leaving a trust that will perpetuate for many generations of your family is intriguing, it is not permitted under law. This clause prevents the adverse tax consequences from happening by distributing trust assets just prior to the time the law would be violated. Typical language might read: *Notwithstanding anything to the contrary, if any future event shall postpone the vesting of any interest created by this Will beyond the period permitted by law, then at the expiration of such period, the property in each such trust shall immediately be distributed to the primary income beneficiary or beneficiaries of that trust.*

Item XIII: Spendthrift Provision

Some beneficiaries don't want their money in trust, they want it *now*. What's to prevent them from using their trust as collateral for a loan? The spendthrift provision, of course! It might read: *To the extent permitted by law, the interest of any beneficiary in principal or income of any trust under this Will shall not be subject to assignment, alienation, pledge, attachment, or to the claims of creditors of such beneficiary.*

EXECUTING YOUR WILL

After having read through pages upon pages of legalese, you may think that executing your will refers to taking out your gun and filling the document full of holes! However, it refers to the formal legal procedure of signing your will. The signing "ceremony" is witnessed by two or three witnesses depending on your state laws. These witnesses should not be potential beneficiaries in your will. You will be required to state aloud something to the effect that "I declare that this is my Last Will and Testament, I have read it and I understand it." The witnesses must then watch you sign it. They then also sign it. To avoid having to track down the witnesses when you die, you should add a *self-proving affidavit*. This is an attached page in which you and your witnesses again sign which is then notarized.

In order to avoid confusion, you should sign only one original of your will. It is appropriate, though, to have several unsigned copies that will be available for easy reference. Give one to your attorney and keep one in a readily accessible location for yourself. Today, some people are videotaping the will signing ceremony. Not only does this allow you to provide additional "proof" of the signing of your will, but it also allows you to "personalize" it with personal comments to family members. Videotaping your will signing ceremony should be done with care and caution. It may make it easier to contest a videotaped will signing and you will want to follow appropriate signing procedures to insure the validity of your will.

WHERE TO STORE YOUR WILL

Suffice it to say that your will needs to be stored in a safe place. Many people choose to store their wills in their bank safe deposit box. Before you do so, you will need to do a little homework. Many states require that a person's safe deposit box be "sealed" at their death. Since this can cause long delays in the probate process, a safe deposit box, in this case, should not be used. Ask your banker and double check with your attorney. If this is not a problem in your state, be sure your personal representative and several family members know where your safe deposit box is located *and* where you keep the key.

My second choice for your original will would be a secure location at your office or at your attorney's office. Be sure and quiz your attorney about their procedures for storing clients' wills. You'll find that some use fireproof safes and detailed filing records while others do little more than stick them in a desk drawer. Avoid the latter.

If you lose your will or if it is destroyed, be sure to have it replaced as soon as possible. You can take one of your copies to your attorney to be re-drafted. With today's modern technology, your attorney may maintain a copy of your will on his or her word processor; you may be able to "scan" your copy into the computer. If you do re-write your will, don't forget to destroy all of your old copies.

OTHER IMPORTANT DOCUMENTS

Power of Attorney

A *power of attorney* is a vital document that *every* adult should have. This document allows you to appoint another person as your "attorney-in-fact," which gives them the authority to act on your behalf in legal matters should you not have the capacity to do so. A power of attorney can be drafted in several forms. The *springing power of attorney* only becomes effective under certain conditions, usually due to your incapacity. One significant disadvantage of the springing power of attorney is that when someone attempts to use it on your behalf, they may be required to "prove" that you are actually incompetent. This can create both inconvenience and signifi-cant delays. With a *general power of attorney,* you give your attorney-in-fact the authority to act on your behalf at *anytime.* However, if you become incapacitated, this document is null and void. To solve this problem, you can draft a *general and durable power of attorney* which allows your attorney-in-fact to continue acting on your behalf in the event of your inca-pacity. Finally, there is the *limited power of attorney* which allows someone to act on your behalf only under very specific circumstances. The reason might involve the signing of a specific legal agreement by your attorney-in-fact while you are out of the country.

First, you need to decide which power of attorney is most appropriate for your circumstances. Then you need to decide who you would appoint as your attorney-in-fact. If you are married, a natural choice might be your spouse. But you should also have at least one successor attorney-in-fact. It should be noted that if you die, any and all power of attorney documents you have executed become null and void. Also, you should redo this docu-ment every four to five years. Many institutions such as banks are reluctant to accept a power of attorney document that is older than that. These are powerful legal instruments and care should be taken to keep up with who has possession of such documents.

Living Wills and Healthcare Powers

Living wills and *healthcare powers* (also referred to as a *durable power of attorney for health care* or *healthcare proxy*) are documents that indicate to others the level of care you desire should you become severely incapacitated. Many states have passed "living will" legislation which allows you to sign a document requesting that your life not be maintained on life support systems. With medical technology as advanced as it is, someone that is "brain dead" can be kept alive for a long time. The Supreme Court has ruled that you cannot be taken off life support systems without evidence that you considered and desired such action to be taken. As you might imagine, it's pretty hard to give your approval while you are in a coma. The end result can easily be that all of your life savings and assets are used to keep you alive. If this is not your intention, then consider signing a living will.

The living will covers only life support system issues. To give directions regarding quality of life issues you will need a healthcare power. With a healthcare power you appoint someone to make medical decisions on your behalf if you are unable to do so. The kinds of decisions are broad in scope and could include such directives as discontinuing feeding tubes or refusing operations.

Once you have signed these documents, be sure to let the appropriate people know that you have done so and where these documents are kept. As with your power of attorney, these documents should be resigned every four to five years to indicate that they still represent your wishes.

Letter of Instruction

A *letter of instruction,* while not a legal document, is an important part of your estate plan. Its purpose is to make life a little easier for the loved ones you leave behind. Important elements of your letter of instruction include:

- List of people to contact. The "who to contact" typically refers to professional advisors such as your attorney or financial advisor, but it could also refer to lifelong friends and relatives you wish to be contacted. Use Worksheet 5-1 as an attachment to the letter to help you list your professional advisors and others you wish to be contacted.

WORKSHEET 5-1
LETTER OF INSTRUCTION, ATTACHMENT A

PERSONS TO BE NOTIFIED AT YOUR DEATH

Provide the following details for each person to be notified at your death: Relationship Codes: Use these to identify each person. Include *all* codes that apply. For example, if the same individual provides the client with legal, tax, and accounting advice, then enter 3, 4, *and* 5.

1	Friend	6	Banking Advisor
2	Relative	7	Investment Advisor
3	Legal Advisor	8	Insurance Advisor
4	Tax Advisor	9	Financial Advisor
5	Accounting Advisor	10	Other

For relationship codes 7 and 8, use the following letter codes to provide more detail about the type of advice offered. For example, if the same insurance agent provides you with life and health coverage, then enter I and J as the insurance codes for the advisor.

Investment Codes		Insurance Codes	
A Stocks	E Options	I Life	L Property & Casualty
B Bonds	F Real Estate	J Health	M All Coverages
C Mutual Funds	G General	K Disability	
D Commodities	H Other		

Name	Firm	Address	Telephone	Relationship	Codes
1. _____					
2. _____					
3. _____					
4. _____					

Name	Firm	Address	Telephone	Relationship	Codes
5.					
6.					
7.					
8.					
9.					
10.					
11.					
12.					
13.					
14.					
15.					
16.					
17.					
18.					
19.					
20.					

- Your documents. Include a list that gives the location of all of your important documents, papers, insurance policies and the like. Go ahead, make their life easier. They'll say a special prayer for you. To assist you in completing this task, use Worksheet 5-2.

WORKSHEET 5-2

Letter of Instruction, Attachment B
Essential Document Locator
Date_____

It is the sad experience of many families to have to search, often in vain, for important papers and documents requested by various entities and government agencies soon after the death of a family member. By completing this checklist now, you can save your family untold hours of searching and anxiety. It will assist them in locating papers and items you probably had no idea they needed. You may need to contact some government offices to locate some items and you may need to make lists of other assets.

We will list four possible locations. Each asset should be (or should be placed) in one of these areas. Some areas have more than one location. For example, if your will is at your home in your safe, you would circle "B" and write "1." Be sure to note each location of an item if there is more than one.

Locations

A. Safe Deposit Box located at _____Bank , Box # _____

B. Residence - 1) Safe   2) File Cabinet   3) Desk

    4) Other_____

C. Business Office - 1) Safe   2) File Cabinet   3) Desk

    4) Other_____

D. Personal Handbook, which is located_____

E. With Attorney - Name_____ Phone _____

F. Other_____

G. I do not have one of these.

Bank Records

List of all savings/checking accounts	A	B___	C___	D	E	F	G
Bank Statements	A	B___	C___	D	E	F	G
Cancelled Checks	A	B___	C___	D	E	F	G
Checkbooks	A	B___	C___	D	E	F	G
Certificates of Deposit	A	B___	C___	D	E	F	G
Savings Passbook	A	B___	C___	D	E	F	G

continued on next page

Insurance Policies							
Property & Casualty	A	B___	C___	D	E	F	G
Health	A	B___	C___	D	E	F	G
Life, Individual	A	B___	C___	D	E	F	G
Life, Group	A	B___	C___	D	E	F	G
Other Insurances	A	B___	C___	D	E	F	G
Other Death Benefits	A	B___	C___	D	E	F	G
Investments							
Bonds & List of Bonds Owned	A	B___	C___	D	E	F	G
Brokerage Account Records	A	B___	C___	D	E	F	G
Mutual Fund Records	A	B___	C___	D	E	F	G
Partnership Agreements	A	B___	C___	D	E	F	G
List of Partnerships	A	B___	C___	D	E	F	G
Record of Securities	A	B___	C___	D	E	F	G
Stock Certificates	A	B___	C___	D	E	F	G
Stock Option Plans	A	B___	C___	D	E	F	G
T-bills	A	B___	C___	D	E	F	G
Children's Assets							
Savings Accounts	A	B___	C___	D	E	F	G
Brokerage Accounts	A	B___	C___	D	E	F	G
Mutual Fund Records	A	B___	C___	D	E	F	G
Pre-paid College Records	A	B___	C___	D	E	F	G
Trust/Custodial Account Records	A	B___	C___	D	E	F	G
Real Estate							
Titles and Deeds	A	B___	C___	D	E	F	G
Title Insurance Policies	A	B___	C___	D	E	F	G
Mortgages and Notes	A	B___	C___	D	E	F	G

continued on next page

WORKSHEET 5-2 (CONTINUED)

Termite Bond	A	B___	C___	D	E	F	G
Rental Property Records	A	B___	C___	D	E	F	G
Retirement Plans							
Annuity Contracts	A	B___	C___	D	E	F	G
Corporate Plans	A	B___	C___	D	E	F	G
IRA documents	A	B___	C___	D	E	F	G
401(k) Plans	A	B___	C___	D	E	F	G
Pension/Profit-Sharing Plans	A	B___	C___	D	E	F	G
Other	A	B___	C___	D	E	F	G
Beneficiary Designations	A	B___	C___	D	E	F	G
Other Important Records							
Wills	A	B___	C___	D	E	F	G
Trust Documents	A	B___	C___	D	E	F	G
Auto Ownership Records	A	B___	C___	D	E	F	G
Other Vehicle Ownership Records	A	B___	C___	D	E	F	G
Safe Combinations	A	B___	C___	D	E	F	G
Safety Deposit Box Key	A	B___	C___	D	E	F	G
Passports	A	B___	C___	D	E	F	G
Birth Certificates	A	B___	C___	D	E	F	G
Adoption Papers	A	B___	C___	D	E	F	G
Marriage Certificate	A	B___	C___	D	E	F	G
Divorce/Separation Papers	A	B___	C___	D	E	F	G
Military Discharge Papers	A	B___	C___	D	E	F	G
Tax Returns	A	B___	C___	D	E	F	G
Names/Addresses of Family/Friends	A	B___	C___	D	E	F	G
List of Professional/Fraternal Orgs.	A	B___	C___	D	E	F	G
List of Credit Cards w/addr./tel. nos.	A	B___	C___	D	E	F	G
Other:	A	B___	C___	D	E	F	G

• Funeral instructions. While the idea of planning your own funeral may be distasteful, it will save your family time, money, and heartache. Funerals can be quite expensive and your grieving family may not be in the best frame of mind to make appropriate decisions. By taking the time to convey your wishes now, you will provide your loved ones with invaluable help in the event of your death. Use Worksheet 5-3 to assist you with this matter.

WORKSHEET 5-3
LETTER OF INSTRUCTION, ATTACHMENT C

LAST WISHES AND MEMORIAL PLANNING

Funeral Home Desired (Name, address, phone):

_____

_____

Have funeral arrangements been pre-arranged?

Yes   No   With
Whom?_____

Name, number, and location of cemetery plot (if one is owned):

_____

Do you wish to be Cremated? Give instructions:

Yes   No

_____

Notify _____
Phone _____

Are you donating your body or any organs to medical science?

Yes   No

_____

Institution to be notified

_____

Instructions concerning the funeral service (Open/closed casket, songs, type of burial):

_____

continued on next page

WORKSHEET 5-3 (CONTINUED)

_____

_____

_____

Donations in your memory should be sent to:

_____

_____

Clergyman to officiate:

Name _____   Phone _____

Casket Bearers:

Name _____   Phone _____

Name _____   Phone _____

Name _____   Phone _____

Name _____   Phone _____

Name _____   Phone _____

Name _____   Phone _____

- Personal messages. The letter of instruction is a perfect place to leave messages of a personal nature to your family members.

WORKING WITH YOUR ATTORNEY

When it comes to estate planning, attorneys are worth their weight in gold. Speaking of gold, attorneys can be expensive! What they have to sell is their time and expertise. The more organized you are *before* you meet with them, the smaller your bill. In fact, being prepared can save you a *lot* of money. To prepare for your first meeting you should prepare or bring the following:

- Copies and original(s) of your current will.

- A complete list of your assets and liabilities. You should have developed this list in Chapter 2. Use Worksheet 2-6, page 26. Do not rely on your memory regarding whose name your property is in. You should confirm this by checking the actual titles.

- All of your life insurance policies. For group life insurance, bring the certificate if available. Be sure to confirm the beneficiary and owner of each policy.

- For your real estate, bring your deed(s). There will be cases where the deeds need to be transferred to another person such as your spouse in order to reduce taxes.

- Copies of all notes and mortgages that you owe or that are owed to you.

- Copies of any trust agreements in which you are a grantor, beneficiary, or have a power of appointment.

- Employee benefits summary including retirement plans, employee death benefits, stock purchase plans, deferred compensation agreements, and incentive stock options.

- Information regarding any business interest you have.

- Copy of your most recent federal and state income tax return.

- Location and list of general contents of your safe deposit box.

- Lists of advisors with whom you currently work. (See Worksheet 5-1, page 94).

Next is the personal information that your attorney will need about you and your family members:

- For you, your children, and anyone who is a potential beneficiary under your will, list their full name, date of birth, and Social Security number. You should let your attorney know if any of your children are adopted.

- List any prior marriages and any children by a prior marriage. Include any support payments for which you are obligated or which you are the recipient.

- Describe any health issues regarding you or your family members. For example, if you have a physically or mentally challenged child, the attorney will want to discuss possible special trust arrangements to care for that child at your death.

- Provide any appropriate information regarding your parents. Do you expect to ever be required to provide financial support? What do you expect to inherit from them?

The balance of the information your attorney will need relates to the key provisions you want included in your will. This is the section over which most people waste a lot of their attorney's time (and the client's money!) belaboring over who gets the money and who gets the kids. Impress your attorney by having resolved these issues ahead of time. If your attorney brings up an issue you cannot resolve immediately, make a note and move on to the next issue. Resolve the issue at home, then give your attorney a call or drop him/her a note. Remember, attorneys often charge $150 to $500 per hour!

We have discussed many of the key will provisions earlier in this chapter, so you should already have had a chance to give them some thought. They are:

- Personal property. To whom do you want your items of personal property to go? If you are married, most often the personal property is left outright to your spouse.

- General bequests. If you have specific personal items, money, or real property you want to leave to someone, it can be done through a general bequest.

- Disinheritances. If there is someone you intend to disinherit, be sure and let your attorney know.

- Your residence(s). The home often passes by title. Remember "joint tenants with right of survivorship?" If you own yours, you need to decide who you want to leave it to. If you are married, your spouse may be the obvious choice.

- Residue. Sounds disgusting doesn't it? Remember that residue refers to "what's left" after giving away your personal property and home. Who do you want the residue to go to; do you want them to receive it outright, or do you feel they should receive it in trust?

- Executors. The executor is the person responsible for settling your estate. In addition to choosing an executor, you will also need at least one—preferably two—successors.

- Trustees. The trustee(s) will manage your assets for your beneficiaries. Again, you should have one or two successors with the final trustee being a corporate trustee. You should include language that allows the beneficiaries of your trust to replace a corporate trustee with another corporate trustee. This provides a procedure for your beneficiaries to find a trustee with whom they are compatible.

- Guardians. For minor children, you will need to name guardians for their care. This can be one of the most difficult decisions that couples make. Be sure to name as many successor guardians as you think appropriate (the more, the better). Remember, the guardian who will raise your children does not have to be the same person who will manage your assets for the benefit of your children. In many cases, they should not be. You need to make this decision before you meet with your attorney.

- Trusts. Your attorney will discuss with you the advisability of setting up trusts. If you do plan to have a trust for your children, you should decide how you want the trust income distributed, whether you want to empower your trustee with the right to make principal distributions and under what circumstances, and at what age(s) you want the trust dissolved.

- Charitable donations. Do you want to leave any of your estate to charities, religious organizations, or educational institutions? If so, let your attorney know and he/she can discuss the most advantageous strategies. (See Chapter 10.)

Before you begin working with an attorney, you should discuss fees. Most attorneys get paid based on their hourly rate, although some prefer a set fee arrangement. For those who charge hourly, they should be able to give you a reasonable estimate of what your fee will be. Avoid attorneys who do not produce itemized bills. This is a good indication that these attorneys are disorganized and quite likely, when they have to "remember" how much time they have on your case, you could end up being overcharged. Once the attorney gives you an estimate of your fee, require him/her to notify you immediately if it appears that your actual fee will exceed his/her estimate.

WHEN TO REVIEW YOUR ESTATE PLAN

Life has a way of changing rapidly, causing yesterday's well-devised estate plan to become outdated. If any of the following events occur in your life, you should review your plan immediately.

- Marriages. If you marry, you will need to change your will, among other things. The marriage of your children might also cause you to consider changes.

- Births. If you have a child, you should review your wills and other documents. Most wills provide that all children are automatically included whether or not they are specifically named in the will. For sentimental reasons, many parents want each child listed by name. Some situations may call for special attention such as a child with special needs. Also, the birth of a grandchild may cause you to make additional provisions in your plan. For example, you may want to make a general bequest to pay for a pre-funded college education plan.

- Divorces. If you get divorced, you will need to rewrite your will. Virtually all states nullify an ex-spouse's rights under a will. But there are many other considerations including removal of your ex-spouse as executor or trustee, as well as removing your ex-spouse as the beneficiary of your life insurance, retirement plans, and other employee benefit plans.

- Inheritances. If you or a family member inherits a large sum of money, you may want to change your plan.

- Deaths. If a spouse or child dies, you need to review and consider changing your plan. You will need to do likewise if an executor, guardian, or trustee dies.

- Career changes. A simple change of career may necessitate changes to your plan. For example, your new job may offer substantially more or less life insurance. If you have business interests that change significantly, your plan should again be reviewed.

- Moves out of state. As we have discussed before, the laws of different states can vary widely resulting in undesirable interpretations of your will.

- Changes to the tax law. Congress seems compelled to make significant changes in the law every couple of years. This often results not in better laws, but busier lawyers. Just look at the list of more recent major tax law changes:

Taxpayer Relief Act of 1997

Small Business Job Protection Act of 1996

Health Insurance Portability and Accountability Act of 1996

Personal Responsibility and Work Opportunity Reconciliation Act of 1996

Tax Simplification and Technical Corrections Act of 1993

The Revenue Reconciliation Act of 1993

The Revenue Act of 1992

- Changes in estate values. If the value of your estate rises or falls significantly, you should review your estate plan. It is a good idea to update your Estate Net Worth Statement each year (see Chapter 2).

These are just some of the major events that would cause you to review your estate plan. Even if you feel your facts have not changed at all, you should review your estate plan every three to five years at the very least. If you do decide that changes are appropriate, then you have two choices. For relatively minor changes, you can have your attorney draw a **codicil** to your existing will. A codicil is, in effect, an amendment to a specific section or item in your will. The codicil must be witnessed under the same procedure as your will was. Your other alternative is to rewrite your entire will. While this may seem like overkill, many attorneys prefer this method because it reduces the chance of conflicting language and instructions in your will. You can imagine the potential for trouble if over the years you add several codicils. Often your attorney will maintain a copy of your will in his/her word processor so that the cost of redoing the will is not significantly different than drawing a codicil. If you do rewrite your will, be sure to destroy your old original(s) and all copies.

In this chapter, you have learned how important it is to understand the impact of your decisions about the disposal of your property and assets upon your death. We have discussed the necessity for carefully planning how you want to own property and to whom you want to leave it. You should also remember that writing a will is not a once-in-a-lifetime event. You should review your will every three to five years, or even sooner if major life events have occurred.

In the next chapter, you will learn about the various types of trusts that can be used to protect your property and help you leave it in the most practical ways from an estate and tax viewpoint.

Using Trusts in Your Estate Plan

CHAPTER 6

Using Trusts in Your Estate Plan

I n Chapter 5, we reviewed the key elements that should be considered in all wills. At what point should you consider more complex estate planning? Additional planning is appropriate if you feel it is desirable to maintain some control over your property after you die. In this situation, establishing one or more trusts under your will may be advisable. Also, if you are married and the total of your and your spouse's estate, (including life insurance) exceeds the *applicable exclusion amount* (see page 17), you need to consider a more complex will. As you recall from the last chapter, two important tax strategies may be available to you.

The first strategy, available only if you are married to a U.S. citizen, is called the **unlimited marital deduction** (or simply the "marital deduction"). Under federal tax laws, you may give an unlimited amount of assets to your spouse without incurring gift or estate taxes. These gifts can either be during your lifetime or at your death. This means that Bill Gates, reportedly the richest person in the world, could give or leave his entire fortune to his wife and not a dime of federal estate taxes would be due. However, when she dies, the tax man will be dancing at her funeral! I will discuss strategies associated with the marital deduction later in this chapter.

The second strategy relates to the **applicable exclusion amount**. The rules here changed with the passage of the Taxpayer Relief Act of 1997. This section of the law allows you to give a certain amount of your assets to someone *other* than your spouse, either during your lifetime or at your death, free of federal gift or estate taxes. This "other" can be a *trust* called the **Credit Shelter Trust**.

CASE STUDY

It is the year 2006. David and Diane are married and have one child, Amy. Their combined estates equal $2,000,000. They remember from an estate planning seminar they attended, that joint property is bad and that they should "equalize" their assets as much as possible. They have divided their assets so that they each own $1,000,000 in their separate names. They currently have simple wills in which they leave all their assets to each other upon their demise. Here's what their current tax situation looks like:

DAVID HAS A SIMPLE WILL AND DIES LEAVING AN ESTATE OF $1,000,000 OUTRIGHT TO DIANE:

David's Gross Estate	$1,000,000
Less Unlimited Marital Deduction	- 1,000,000
Taxable Estate	$ 0
Estate Tax at David's Death	$ 0
Assets Passing to Diane	$1,000,000
Diane's Gross Estate:	
Diane's Separate Estate	$1,000,000
Received From David's Estate	+1,000,000
	$2,000,000

TENTATIVE TAX CALCULATION AT DIANE'S DEATH:

Tax on $2,000,000 (per table 2.2 on page 19)	$ 780,800
Less Applicable Credit Amount (per table 2.3 page 20)	- 345,800
Estate Tax at Diane's Death	$ 435,000
Net Estate Available for Heirs	$1,565,000

Now $1,565,000 is nothing to sneeze at, but let's see what we can do by utilizing a Credit Shelter Trust Will.

DAVID HAS A CREDIT SHELTER TRUST WILL AND DIES WITH AN ESTATE OF $1,000,000:

David's Gross Estate	$1,000,000
Assets Passing Directly to Diane	- 0
Assets Passing to Credit Shelter Trust	- 1,000,000
Taxable Estate	$1,000,000
Estate Tax	$ 345,800
Less Applicable Credit Amount	- 345,800
Net Tax at David's Death	$ 0
Diane's Own Separate Estate	$1,000,000
David's Assets Passing Directly to Diane	$ 0
Diane's Gross Estate	$1,000,000
Less Unlimited Marital Deduction	- 0
Diane's Taxable Estate	$1,000,000
Tentative Tax Calculation on Diane's Death	$ 345,800
Less Applicable Credit Amount	- 345,800
Estate Tax at Diane's Death	$ 0
Net Estate Available to Heirs	$2,000,000

By utilizing a Credit Shelter Trust Will, we were able to eliminate David and Diane's federal estate taxes and preserve the maximum amount of assets for their daughter Amy. For a graphic description of the simple will vs. the Credit Shelter Trust Will see the two figures on p. 113. Rarely are the facts this straightforward. Usually, you must shift assets from one spouse to another. Some assets are easy to move, while other assets may be impossible to move. However, if done correctly, you can achieve dramatic tax savings. You can also meet other goals including providing professional management of assets and protecting your assets from the potential future creditors of your surviving spouse. It should be noted that the Credit Shelter Trust Will often is structured to provide your surviving spouse with all the income from the trust as well as the principal for

continued on next page

certain specific reasons. Legally, these "reasons" are referred to as *ascertainable standards* and include distributions for health, maintenance, education, and support. This definition is sufficiently broad to cover most reasonable requests for additional money. In addition, the law permits what is referred to as the "five and five power." This rule would permit your spouse to take a distribution from the trust each year equal to five percent of its total value or $5,000, whichever is greater. Your surviving spouse can also serve as the trustee or co-trustee of the trust.

THE CREDIT SHELTER TRUST WILL

The purpose of the Credit Shelter Trust Will is to take advantage of the *Applicable Exclusion Amount* and thus reduce the estate taxes that would be due at the last to die between you and your spouse. Your Credit Shelter Trust Will can be set up for the specific purpose of benefiting your spouse and/or anyone else you desire. For example, for 1999, you could avoid federal estate taxes on up to $650,000 by placing that amount in your Credit Shelter Trust Will. This exclusion amount is scheduled to increase to $1,000,000 by the year 2006. Both you and your spouse can *each* use this exclusion, so if you plan well, the two of you could have combined estates of up to $2,000,000 (year 2006) and owe no federal estate taxes. This is partially a "use it or lose it" proposition, so it's important to plan appropriately.

In working with clients, I will sometimes recommend a provision that I call the *remarriage provision*. Some clients are primarily concerned with their surviving spouse's income needs only as long as he or she remains unmarried. If the surviving spouse remarries, the clients would prefer that the assets from their Credit Shelter Trust benefit their children or some other beneficiary. To resolve this issue, a provision is included which states that if the surviving spouse remarries, his or her benefits under the Credit Shelter Trust shall cease. Several years ago, I observed an interesting twist involving this remarriage provision. In this particular case, the surviving spouse remarried, thus forfeiting her interest in her deceased husband's Credit Shelter Trust. Her second marriage failed within two months. Instead of getting a divorce, she got an annulment which, in effect, revived her status as a surviving spouse as well as her interest in the Credit Shelter Trust.

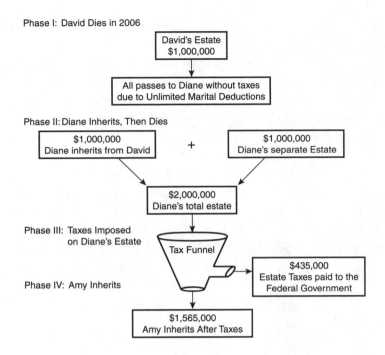

Phase I: David Dies in 2006

David's Estate
$1,000,000

All passes to Diane without taxes
due to Unlimited Marital Deductions

Phase II: Diane Inherits, Then Dies

$1,000,000
Diane inherits from David

$+$

$1,000,000
Diane's separate Estate

$2,000,000
Diane's total estate

Phase III: Taxes Imposed
on Diane's Estate

Tax Funnel

$435,000
Estate Taxes paid to the
Federal Government

Phase IV: Amy Inherits

$1,565,000
Amy Inherits After Taxes

Simple Will

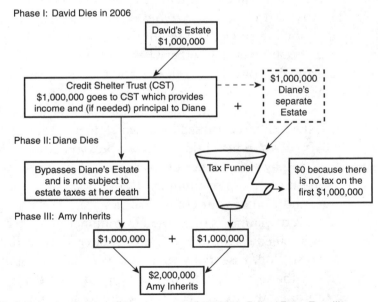

Phase I: David Dies in 2006

David's Estate
$1,000,000

Credit Shelter Trust (CST)
$1,000,000 goes to CST which provides
income and (if needed) principal to Diane

$1,000,000
Diane's
separate
Estate

$+$

Phase II: Diane Dies

Bypasses Diane's Estate
and is not subject to
estate taxes at her death

Tax Funnel

$0 because there
is no tax on the
first $1,000,000

Phase III: Amy Inherits

$1,000,000 $+$ $1,000,000

$2,000,000
Amy Inherits

Perfect planning. David and Diane have saved $435,000 in Federal Estate Taxes!!!

Credit Shelter Trust Will

Another provision you may want to consider as part of your Credit Shelter Trust Will is the *income sprinkling provision.* This provision allows the trustee to pay trust income to trust beneficiaries *other* than the surviving spouse, typically the children. Often, the assets left to the surviving spouse outside of the Credit Shelter Trust, when added to the surviving spouse's own assets are expected to be more than sufficient for his or her lifestyle needs. In these cases, if you *require* the Credit Shelter Trust to pay the surviving spouse all of the trust income, you will effectively increase the estate taxes paid by the surviving spouse's estate and reduce the inheritance received by your heirs. This is because your surviving spouse, not needing the trust income, will "stack" it up in his or her estate only to be taxed later. Not only is the income taxed, but the *growth* on the income is taxed as well. This sprinkling provision can be an effective tool which allows your trustee to distribute income to your family members who have the greatest needs.

DISCLAIMERS

A **disclaimer** is the refusal to accept property that has been given to you either by gift or through someone's will. It may sound strange that anyone would refuse an inheritance, but there can be very good reasons for doing so. The most typical reason is to avoid or at least postpone estate taxes. Let's say that you are single, and in your will, you leave all your estate to your sister if she survives you, otherwise you leave everything to her children. When you die, your sister is elderly and has a large estate of her own. She has no need for your money, so if she does receive it, it will be added to her estate and taxed at her death. Instead, she disclaims it. In the eyes of the law it is as if she has "predeceased" you which means that under the terms of your will, it passes to her children. It will be a long time before they are likely to have to pay estate taxes on your money. It should be noted that disclaimers are not an "all or nothing" thing. Your sister could have disclaimed only a portion of your estate. She can even disclaim specific items of your estate. A disclaimer is often used in conjunction with a Credit Shelter Trust and is called a **Disclaimer Credit Shelter Trust Will** (or simply a Disclaimer Trust Will). Essentially what you have here is a simple will with an "option" by the surviving heir(s) to convert to a trust type will in order to reduce future estate taxes. Let's revisit our first example with David,

Diane, and Amy. Suppose that when David and Diane first wrote their wills, they had a much smaller estate. They were, however optimistic about their financial future and they wanted their will to reflect that optimism. To accommodate them, their attorney prepared their will with disclaimers in mind. David's will was set up so that if Diane disclaimed any portion, that portion would go into a Credit Shelter Trust that was set up to provide Diane with income (and principal for certain reasons). Diane now has the *option* of sending money to the Disclaimer Credit Shelter Trust or receiving the money outright. This strategy allows her to do postmortem planning. If it is tax beneficial to do so, she disclaims the appropriate amount of money to a trust that is set up to benefit her! Graphically, the Disclaimer Credit Shelter Trust Will is depicted in the figure below.

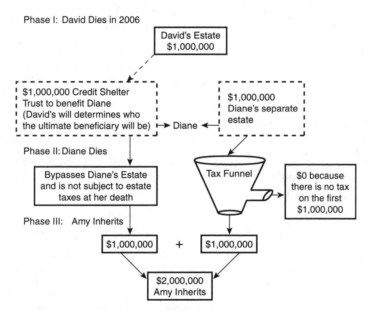

Simple Will with Disclaimer Credit Shelter Trust Option

Certain criteria must be met for the disclaimed property to bypass the disclaiming heir's estate for estate tax purposes. First, the disclaimer must be irrevocable and unqualified. Second, it must be in writing. Third, you must not have accepted any interest in, or received any benefit from, the disclaimed property. Fourth, you must disclaim the property within nine months from the time you were eligible to receive it. Finally, you must have no say as to whom the disclaimed property goes.

MARITAL TRUSTS

Marital trusts will generally fall into one of three types: the General Power of Appointment Trust, the QTIP trust, and the QDOT trust. The purpose of each is to allow you to exercise some control over how your assets will be handled after your death. Which trust you choose will depend on the *degree* of control you wish to exercise.

General Power of Appointment Trust

There may be situations in which it is not desirable to leave assets outright to your spouse. For example, if your spouse has little experience in managing money, you may want to remove that burden from him or her by establishing a trust run by a professional money manager. The **General Power of Appointment Trust** allows you to place certain controls on the assets that you leave to your spouse while continuing to qualify those assets for the unlimited marital deduction. In order for this trust to qualify for the unlimited marital deduction, and therefore not be taxed at your death, your spouse must receive *all* the income from the trust at least annually. Also, as the name implies, your spouse must be given a *general power of appointment* that allows him or her to determine what person(s) or organization(s) receive the trust property at his or her death. Other than these two requirements, the trust can be very flexible or very restrictive. You can give your spouse the power to terminate the trust, although most are irrevocable. You can give the trustee the power to distribute principal "at his or her discretion." This makes certain that there will be access to trust principal for appropriate needs. At the opposite end of the spectrum, you can structure the trust so that your spouse receives only the income during his or her lifetime. As with the Credit Shelter Trust and Disclaimer Trust, you can appoint your spouse as the trustee, the co-trustee, or you can have someone else serve as trustee. Often the General Power of Appointment Trust is used in conjunction with the Credit Shelter Trust and graphically would look as depicted in the figure on p. 117. For this example, I have assumed that David's estate equals $2,000,000 and Diane's estate equals $0.

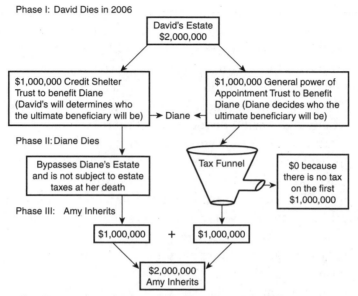

Two Trust Will Utilizing a General Power of Appointment Trust and a Credit Shelter Trust

Notice that the use of the marital trust does not affect estate taxes. At your spouse's death, all the assets in the marital trust plus any of your spouse's separate property will be included in his or her estate for federal estate tax purposes. A disadvantage of the General Power of Appointment Trust is that your spouse can determine who will eventually receive your property. If you would like to place more restrictions on the assets you leave your spouse, consider the benefits of the QTIP trust.

The QTIP Trust

QTIP is short for Qualified Terminable Interest Property. Under a QTIP trust, *you* decide who will ultimately receive your property at your spouse's death. This determination is specifically indicated in your will. As with the marital trust, to qualify for the unlimited marital deduction, your spouse must receive *all* the income from the trust at least annually. People often use QTIP trusts in cases of second marriages. Consider this example: Richard and Yvonne recently married. They both have children from prior marriages and both have brought assets into the marriage. Richard's total estate is $1,500,000 and Yvonne's assets total $800,000. Their goals are twofold. When the first of them dies, they would like their assets to be available as a source of income for the surviving spouse during that spouse's lifetime. At that spouse's death, they want to make certain that their assets go to their children. Their attorney recommends a QTIP trust. Under the provisions of the QTIP trust, if Richard dies first, his assets would go into the trust and pay Yvonne all the income as long as she lives. Because Yvonne is receiving all the income, Richard's property passing into the trust qualifies for the unlimited marital deduction and thereby avoids taxation at his death. The trust does *not* give Yvonne a general power of appointment and states that at her death the trust assets go to his children. Yvonne's will is a "mirror" of Richard's will. As a result of this planning, both of their goals have been met. The surviving spouse has the income from the deceased spouse's estate and the deceased spouse is certain that his or her estate eventually passes to his or her children.

The QTIP trust is an important planning technique. Think of what might happen without the QTIP trust. Richard dies and leaves all of his assets to Yvonne with the presumption that she will take care of his children. Yvonne remarries and over time loses touch with Richard's children. Her will already leaves all of her property to her children. When Yvonne dies, Richard's children receive nothing. If Richard dies without a will, the laws of intestacy in his state of residence direct that one half of his property passes to Yvonne and the other half passes to his children. Yvonne later leaves her portion to her children. As with the General Power of Appointment Trust, the QTIP trust is often used in conjunction with the Credit Shelter Trust. Graphically, this planning strategy is depicted in the figure on p. 119.

Notice what has happened in this figure. At Yvonne's death the assets from the QTIP trust ($500,000) which will go to Richard's children *plus* Yvonne's own separate assets ($800,000) which will go to her children, are added together for estate tax purposes. The result is that Yvonne's estate owes $124,000 in federal estate taxes. The question is, will these taxes come from Richard's assets (the QTIP trust) or from Yvonne's assets? The law provides that any additional taxes caused by a QTIP trust shall be paid from the QTIP trust unless directed otherwise by the surviving spouse. You need to take special care here. Boilerplate language in many wills provides that *"all estate taxes are to be paid from the residuary estate."* This oversight could result in all estate taxes of Yvonne's estate ($124,000) being

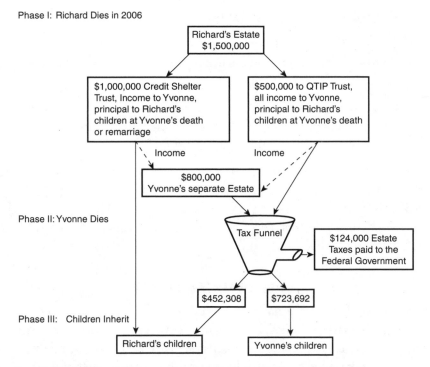

Phase I: Richard Dies in 2006

Richard's Estate
$1,500,000

$1,000,000 Credit Shelter Trust, Income to Yvonne, principal to Richard's children at Yvonne's death or remarriage

$500,000 to QTIP Trust, all income to Yvonne, principal to Richard's children at Yvonne's death

Income

Income

$800,000
Yvonne's separate Estate

Phase II: Yvonne Dies

Tax Funnel

$124,000 Estate Taxes paid to the Federal Government

$452,308

$723,692

Phase III: Children Inherit

Richard's children

Yvonne's children

Two Trust Will Utilizing a QTIP Trust and a Credit Shelter Trust

paid from her children's share! To resolve this problem, both Richard and Yvonne should have provisions in their wills requiring that any taxes caused by a QTIP trust will be paid from the QTIP trust assets.

Qualified Domestic Trust (QDOT)

If your spouse is not a United States citizen, you are not eligible for the unlimited marital deduction. (Congress reasoned that a non-U.S. citizen spouse might leave the United States in order to avoid U.S. taxes.) Currently, the maximum that you can transfer to a non-U.S. citizen spouse free of gift or estate taxes is $100,000 in any calendar year. In order to resolve this potentially unfair treatment, Congress passed a law allowing an unlimited marital deduction for property that is transferred to a **Qualified Domestic Trust (QDOT)**. Requirements of a QDOT include:

- All income from the trust must be paid to the surviving spouse at least annually.

- The trust must be irrevocable.

- Certain IRS regulations must be included in the trust agreement that have the effect of ensuring that trust assets will not escape U.S. taxes.

- Generally, at least one of your trustees must be either a U.S. citizen or a U.S. corporation *at all times*. Be sure that your trust document has language that assures this result.

Certain foreign countries do not recognize either trusts or non-citizen trustees which, in effect, would prohibit you from establishing a QDOT. To address this problem, Congress has provided for the Treasury Department to make exceptions under certain conditions. If this is the case for you, consult with an attorney that specializes in such matters.

SPENDTHRIFT TRUST

A **Spendthrift Trust**, originally intended as a way to protect people that tend to squander their money, is appropriate under numerous circumstances. Essentially, this trust provides the trustee with very strict guidelines as to how much and under what conditions money can be distributed to your beneficiary(s). The language in the trust forbids using the trust assets or the trust income as collateral or pledge for any type of loan. If a lender accepts any interest in the trust as a pledge, that pledge is not valid even if the loan is provable. The trustee can simply refuse to disperse funds to the creditor and the creditor will have no recourse against the trust or trustee. Spendthrift Trusts are normally set up for the lifetime of the beneficiary(s). Another circumstance where a Spendthrift Trust can prove useful is where a beneficiary, due to his or her profession, is a likely candidate for a lawsuit. The classic examples would include the doctor or commercial building contractor. Say your daughter is a physician and is concerned about being subject to a large malpractice judgment. Instead of giving your daughter her inheritance outright, you give it to her by way of a Spendthrift Trust. By doing so, those assets will be protected from all creditors in most states. In most states, it is not possible for you to receive this creditor protection by placing your *own* assets in a Spendthrift Trust. A Spendthrift Trust is also appropriate if you have a beneficiary who is incompetent.

STANDBY TRUST

If you were to become incompetent because of an accident or sickness, who would handle your financial affairs on your behalf? Would you want them to have specific instructions? If the answer to the first question is "I don't know" and/or the answer to the second question is "yes," then you might want to consider a **Standby Trust** (sometimes referred to as a *unfunded revocable trust* or *living trust*). This trust will state who will be your trustee and outline instructions for how trust assets are to be handled. The trust would remain unfunded until there was a "triggering" event, such as your incompetence. Your Standby Trust will be used in conjunction with a durable power of attorney that has specific language allowing your assets to be transferred to your trust under the conditions that you specify.

OTHER TRUSTS

With the exception of the Standby Trust just discussed, all the trusts that we have reviewed in this chapter have been *testamentary trusts*. That is, they are trusts that you created under your will. *Inter vivos trusts* are trusts that you create during your lifetime and can also be an important part of your estate planning arsenal. They include the Revocable Living Trust, the Irrevocable Insurance Trust, the 2503(c) Trust which is sometimes referred to as the Qualified Minors Trust, and various charitable trusts. In Chapter 7, I will discuss the details of the Revocable Living Trust. Charitable trusts will be covered in Chapter 10. The Irrevocable Insurance Trusts will be covered in Chapter 8 and the 2503(c) Trust will be discussed in Chapter 9.

CHAPTER 7

The Revocable Living Trust

As its name implies, a Revocable Living Trust is one that you establish during your lifetime. The Revocable Living Trust can be an excellent estate planning device in the right circumstances. Some attorneys say Revocable Living Trusts are essential, while others suggest they should rarely be used. The real answer lies somewhere in the middle.

In the typical Revocable Living Trust, you set up the trust and make yourself the trustee. You then re-title your property in the name of the trust. Once this is completed, you manage your property pretty much as you always have. One of the key ingredients in the Revocable Living Trust is that you will name a successor trustee in the event of your death or incompetence. People often think of the Revocable Living Trust as a will substitute. This is only partially true. As you will find out, there are both significant advantages and disadvantages to the Revocable Living Trust. By examining them fully, you will be in better position to determine if a Living Trust is appropriate for you.

ADVANTAGES

- Probate. The most often cited reason for setting up a Revocable Living Trust is to avoid the probate process. As we discussed in Chapter 4, probate can be an expensive and time-consuming process. Any property that you transfer to your Revocable Living Trust will avoid the probate process altogether. This means you avoid some expenses and lengthy delays. Some opponents of Revocable Living Trusts suggest that these advantages are overstated because probate is not expensive in most states. While this is in fact the case in many states, the issue of time delays is significant. Even the simplest of estates may take at least six months to settle.

- Privacy. Because property placed in a Revocable Living Trust is not subject to probate, your records are not made public. Many of my clients prefer to keep their financial matters out of the public eye. If this is your objective, a Revocable Living Trust is an excellent tool.

- Avoids delays. As already mentioned, at your death there are no time delays incurred in transferring assets to heirs. The assets are already in your trust and the only thing that changes is your trustee. The trustee is someone whom you have selected.

- Incompetence. Your Revocable Living Trust can provide for a quick transfer of management of your assets should you become incompetent due to an accident or illness. In these circumstances, without a Revocable Living Trust or at least a durable power of attorney, the courts would appoint a conservator to manage your property for your benefit. This takes time and can be expensive.

- Easily established. A Revocable Living Trust is easy to establish. Any attorney versed in estate planning should be able to set up one. There are even "do-it-yourself" books that take you step by step through the process. However, I highly recommend that you have a lawyer establish your Revocable Living Trust because of the many complex issues and provisions involved.

- Changes. It is easy to make changes to your Revocable Living Trust. Trusts, unlike wills, generally do not require much administrative formality in either the initial setup or amendments. You simply decide what changes you want to make, write them down, and have two witnesses attest to your signature on the amendments. Again, it is best to do so with the assistance of an attorney.

- Contest. Another key advantage to trusts is that they are very difficult for anyone to contest. We have already discussed how easily a will can be contested.

- Consolidation of control. There is some benefit to consolidating your assets under one management system. This is especially important if you choose to have someone other than yourself act as trustee. With a Revocable Living Trust, you have the opportunity to "observe the trustee in action."

- Low maintenance costs. A Revocable Living Trust is treated much the same as outright ownership of property for tax purposes. If you are your own trustee, there will not be any additional taxes, tax returns, or other costs associated with your Revocable Living Trust.

- Estate tax savings. Using a Revocable Living Trust does not restrict any of your potential estate tax savings strategies. Every technique for reducing taxes that I discuss in this book can be used in conjunction with a Revocable Living Trust.

- Legal across state lines. If you die and you own real or tangible personal property in more than one state, chances are your will would have to be probated in each of those states. A Revocable Living Trust is a perfect solution for this situation. Remember, the property in your Revocable Living Trust is not subject to probate at all. If your work causes you to move from state to state, your Revocable Living Trust removes the necessity of having to draw a new will every time you change your state of residence.

DISADVANTAGES

- Costs. Opponents of the Revocable Living Trust often cite the cost of drafting the document as well as the cost of transferring property into the trust as one of the main reasons to avoid them. You will actually need to draft two documents: first, the Revocable Living Trust and secondly, a will. The purpose of the will is to direct any assets that you failed to place in your Revocable Living Trust be sent to your trust at your death. In addition to the expense of drawing two documents, you also will incur the expenses of transferring the title to your property into your trust. For example, you would need to transfer the deed to your home which would include some filing fees and possibly attorneys' fees. The same applies to car titles, bank accounts, investment accounts, etc. While it is true that the initial cost of setting up your Revocable Living Trust will likely be higher than the costs of preparing a will, over the long run, the costs are likely to be similar. For example, if you utilize a will for your planning instead of the Revocable Living Trust, your executor would still incur the expense of transferring your property to your heirs. In one sense it may be cheaper to pay the cost now. This is because you are in control, can negotiate fees, and can do much of the work yourself. As a separate matter, if someone other than yourself is the trustee of your Revocable Living Trust, some states may require that trustee to file an annual income tax return.

- Time and trouble. A legitimate disadvantage of the Living Trust is that some time and effort must be made to move your property into your trust. You must locate all your property deeds and titles as well as write letters to your banks, brokerage firms, employee benefits office in order to move all your property into your trust. Not only that, but every time you purchase property or open a new bank account, you must remember to make your trust the owner. Obviously, if you plan to use the Revocable Living Trust as your basic estate planning device, you cannot procrastinate or you may forget to move some property into the trust. Remember, at some point someone must do this work. If you don't do it, you are leaving it to someone else to do it for you.

- Taxes. Some states have "homestead" laws that provide for a reduction of property taxes on your home. If your Revocable Living Trust, not you, owns your home, you may lose the homestead exemption which will cause an increase in your property taxes. If you are married, one possible solution to this problem is to title your home as "joint tenants with right of survivorship."

  The Taxpayer Relief Act of 1997 provides that the first $250,000 ($500,000 for married couples) of profit from the sale of your home is not subject to taxes. Having your Revocable Living Trust "own" your home will not affect this valuable benefit.

- Divorce. If you get a divorce, your Revocable Living Trust will not automatically remove your ex-spouse as a potential beneficiary. To remove your spouse, you must amend your trust. In the case of wills, divorce does automatically remove your ex-spouse as a potential beneficiary.

HOW A LIVING TRUST OPERATES

Trust laws do vary from state to state so you should seek the counsel of an experienced trusts and estates attorney. In setting up your Revocable Living Trust you will need to go through much of the same process as you would in setting up a will as described in Chapter 5. You will have to make decisions concerning trustees, guardians, when income and principal are to be distributed and under what conditions. These issues relate to what you want to happen to your property after your death. Furthermore, you will need to decide how you want your trust to operate during your lifetime. Some of the more important "living" decisions include:

Choosing the Trustee

Are you going to be your own trustee during your lifetime or are you going to appoint someone else? Most people make themselves the trustee of their trust. As your own trustee, you are able to operate your trust in much the same manner as you do now without a trust. The key difference is that you would have to sign your name as "John Smith, trustee." Some people prefer to leave the administrative details of handling their finances to someone else. This "someone else" is often a professional trustee such as a bank trust officer. If you fall into this category, you would choose a trustee, pay them an ongoing fee and they would do as much administrative work as you request. This could include such tasks as depositing a monthly check in your checking account, paying your bills, doing your tax returns, and investing your money. A professional trustee can make life easy for you but as you might imagine, they can be quite expensive. One major advantage of hiring a professional trustee during your lifetime is that you get to see how competent they are. If they do not perform satisfactorily, you are free to seek out someone else before you die.

Revocable vs. Irrevocable

Do you want your trust to be revocable or irrevocable? Most people set their trust up as a revocable trust which provides for maximum flexibility.

With a revocable trust, you can make changes anytime, move property into and out of your trust as you desire, or abandon the trust altogether. Reasons for using an irrevocable trust include providing a level of protection against creditors or creating tax benefits by removing assets (and the growth of those assets) from your estate. Under the irrevocable trust, the trust maker must give up all control.

Funded vs. Unfunded

With your Revocable Living Trust, you have the option of fully funding your trust, partially funding your trust, or leaving your trust unfunded until you die or become incompetent. Some people even leave their trusts unfunded until just before they die. The idea here is that unless your death comes suddenly, you will have time to transfer your property when you actually become ill. However, I believe that the best method is to fully fund your trust at the time that it is established. This may be a little more trouble initially, but will provide you with greater control and certainty of desired results.

One Trust or Two?

If you are married, should you use one trust for both you and your spouse or should you set up a separate trust? In most cases, you and your spouse should each have a separate trust. This is particularly true if you have reasons to keep property separated as may be the case with a second marriage. Remember, the act of placing your property into your Living Trust does not eliminate the need for estate tax reduction strategies or prohibit you from directing that your property goes to certain person(s).

Incompetence Provision

One of the most important characteristics of the Revocable Living Trust is that it can provide instructions for your care should you become incompetent due to sickness or accident. You should include trust language that indicates the level of care you desire and who your successor trustee will be in the event you become incompetent. In addition, it is advisable to include a separate durable power of attorney that gives someone you trust the power to transfer into your trust property you own that is not titled in your trust. In your trust agreement, you can be as explicit as you wish concerning the type and level of care you desire during your disability. For example, you could specify that you wanted hospice care versus a nursing home. Or you could specify which nursing home(s) would be acceptable.

Wills

A Revocable Living Trust is sometimes referred to as a will substitute. Is it really? The answer is yes *if* you transfer *all* your property into your trust. That's a mighty big "if." In my experience, people are rarely successful in transferring 100 percent of their property into their trust. First of all, certain property such as jewelry, clothes, furniture, stamp collections, guns, and other personal property is almost impossible to "title" at all. Secondly, you have what I call "the forget and procrastination factor." As you acquire new property, you must title each asset in the name of your trust. This requires some extra effort and you just might not do it. To resolve this potential problem, you need to have a will in addition to your Revocable Living Trust. This will is often described as a "pour over" will because it instructs your personal representative to "pour" any of your remaining assets over into your trust. This is not a complex will and should not add much additional expense to the cost of setting up your Revocable Living Trust. If you have minor children, you will list your choice of guardians here.

TRANSFERRING PROPERTY INTO
YOUR REVOCABLE LIVING TRUST

The greatest challenge for you in setting up your Revocable Living Trust will likely be transferring the title to your property to the name of your trust. This task is actually more time consuming than it is difficult. However, under certain circumstances, re-titling property in the name of your trust can cause problems. In some states you are required to file your trust agreement with the court if you transfer the title to real estate into a trust. Some transfer agents will require a copy of your trust agreement in order to transfer title of your securities. Your bank may require a copy of your trust if you put your safe box in the name of your trust. This is to make sure that you, as the trustee, have the authority to transact these transfers. You could simply supply these people or institutions with a copy of your trust document, but one of the main features of your Revocable Living Trust is that it keeps your financial affairs private. Passing your trust document all over town hardly meets this objective. There are two effective solutions to this problem. The first is called an **affidavit of trust.** This is a notarized statement indicating:

- The name of the trust.
- The names of the trustees.
- The trust powers.
- Pertinent provisions of the trust including revocability, successor trustees and signature page.

This affidavit of trust provides proof that your trust is legitimate and that you have the authority as trustee to transact business on behalf of your trust.

The second solution to this problem is called a **nominee partnership.** Some institutions are more comfortable dealing with partnerships rather than trusts. A nominee partnership *controls* rather than owns property. The partners of the nominee partnership are usually the same as the trustees of your trust. The idea of a nominee partnership may sound strange, but businesses and financial institutions have used this form for decades.

Transferring property into your Living Trust need not be an expensive process. Let your attorney know that you would like to do as much of the "leg work" as possible. Together, you can then divide the work according to who can best complete each job. Your attorney will also be able to alert you to any potential tax or other problems. Much of the work assigned to you can then be completed with the aid of your other advisors such as your banker, investment advisor, insurance agent, and employee benefits specialist.

Your attorney, however, should review all of the final transfers. You want to make certain that one professional accepts overall responsibility for the implementation of your plan. If mistakes are made, this person can be held accountable. This responsibility should be spelled out in your engagement letter with your attorney so that there is no misunderstanding as to the scope of his or her responsibility. Use the following sample engagement letter for hiring your attorney:

Dear (your attorney's name),

I enjoyed meeting with you today and look forward to working with you on establishing and funding my Revocable Living Trust. As per our conversation, you will be responsible for transferring titles to the following property into my trust:

_____

_____

_____

_____

I will be responsible for transferring title and beneficiaries of all my other property. Once completed, I am asking that you review all property transfers to insure that they have been properly completed.

You have indicated that you expect to have ___ hours in completing this project and that you expect your total fee to be $____ to $____. Please notify me immediately if it appears that your time or fees will exceed these estimates.

Further, you have indicated that you expect to complete the drafting of my trust agreement and the property transfers that you are responsible for by ____. Time is of the essence, so I appreciate your attention to this matter.

Sincerely,
Your name

You need to become organized before you meet with your attorney. Complete the following checklist and bring it along with the evidence of title for all your assets. (For example, bring the deed to your home and car title with you.)

You and Your Family:

_____   Your full name

_____   Date of birth

_____ Social Security number

_____ Spouse's full name

_____ Spouse's Social Security number

_____ Spouse's Date of birth

_____ Each Child's full name

_____ Each Child's Date of birth

_____ Each Child's Social Security number

Your Trustee:

_____ Trustee's name

_____ Co-trustee's name

_____ First successor trustee

_____ Second successor trustee

_____ Third successor trustee

Your Property & How It's Titled:

_____ Residence

_____ Other real estate

_____ All bank accounts

_____ Brokerage accounts

_____ Individual stock certificates

_____ Individual bonds

_____ Vehicles, boats, campers, etc.

_____ Other-list untitled assets

Your Beneficiaries:

_____ Life insurance

_____ Disability income insurance

_____ IRAs

_____ Retirement plans

_____ Annuities

This list is not intended to be all-inclusive, but the list you take to your attorney should be. You should also be prepared to make decisions on all of the issues we discussed in Chapter 5. These issues include how income is to be distributed to your heirs and under what conditions the trust principal is to be distributed. This preparation will save your attorney time, and thereby reduce your legal fees.

TYPES OF PROPERTY LIKELY TO BE TRANSFERRED

Real Estate
Ownership in real estate is evidenced by a deed. To change the ownership, you will need to have a new deed prepared and filed with the court. While it is possible to do this yourself, this is the one area that you would be well served to enlist the aid of your attorney. Most real estate mortgages have a "due on sale" clause that requires you to pay off your mortgage in full if the property is sold or transferred out of your name. Since you are transferring your property from yourself to yourself via your trust, this "due on sale" provision should not apply. It would be best if you contact your mortgage company ahead of time to determine if it requires any special procedures for the transfer. If the property you are transferring is your residence and your county has homestead laws, you should also contact your county clerk's office and determine if it has any special procedures in order to maintain your homestead exemption.

Bank Accounts and Bank Money Market Accounts
Changing title of your bank accounts should be a relatively straightforward matter that you can handle yourself. Simply contact your bank and ask about the procedure. In most cases the bank will require little more than a copy of your affidavit of trust.

Brokerage Accounts
In order to transfer the title of your brokerage accounts, you will likely need to close out your current account and open a new one in the name of

your trust. Your broker will be able to do this for you based on a letter of instruction and your affidavit of trust. Once your new account is opened, your broker will then "journal" the securities from your current account to your new account. This procedure will not trigger an income tax event.

Individual Stock Certificates and Individual Bonds
If you hold stock certificates or bonds that have not been left in your brokerage account, there are two ways to transfer the titles to your trust. Most brokers will assist you for no fee. In other cases, they will charge a small fee for each certificate or bond. Alternatively, you can deal directly with the issuer of the certificate or bond. This will be more challenging and may be more expensive than getting your broker's help.

Life and Disability Insurance
Your insurance agent will be a big help to you here. With a letter of instruction, she or he will do much, if not all of the work for you. Ask the agent to complete your ownership and beneficiary forms for you rather than sending blank forms for you to fill out. These forms can be confusing to those who have never completed them. You should not be charged for this service. Note that in many cases it will be advisable to have your life insurance owned by an irrevocable trust rather than your Revocable Living Trust. This subject will be discussed in the next chapter.

Vehicles, Motorcycles, Boats
The laws for transferring title to these types of properties vary widely from state to state so you will need to consult with your attorney and possibly, local state agencies for advice. For this type of property, you will typically receive a "certificate of title" that indicates that you are the owner. This certificate often has a section that allows you to transfer the title to someone else. An alternative is to dispose of this property through the "pour-over" provision in your will.

IRAs and Other Retirement Accounts
You will need to be especially careful in dealing with your IRAs and retirement accounts. First, the law does not allow you to transfer ownership of retirement accounts and changing your beneficiary to your trust could create adverse income and estate tax consequences. Also, qualified retirement

plans such as 401(k) plans, profit sharing plans, and defined contribution plans do not allow you to remove your spouse as the beneficiary unless he or she signs a release giving his or her permission. You will definitely want to consult with your attorney or financial advisor regarding these changes.

Annuities

As with retirement accounts, annuities must be handled with care. If you are married and your spouse is the beneficiary, there is no immediate income tax due upon your death. If someone other than your spouse is your beneficiary, then that individual will have to pay income tax on the gain within five years of your death. One possible solution is to make your spouse the primary beneficiary and your living trust the contingent beneficiary. Be sure and discuss this with your professional advisor.

Property Having No Title

Much of your personal property will not have evidence of title. Property that falls into this category includes: jewelry; furniture; furs; coin, stamp, and art collections; and clothes. This property can be handled in one of three ways.

- You can use your pour-over will to "sweep" all untitled property into your trust. The disadvantage here is that this property will go through probate. But because your will leaves the property to your trust, the ultimate distribution of this property will remain private.

- Your trust can state that all "other" property is deemed to be owned by your trust. This may solve the problem but could be contested.

- Through your trust agreement or through your will, you could make a specific bequest of certain untitled property.

Jointly Held Property

Another area that deserves special attention is transferring property that you own jointly with someone else. Negative gift, income tax, and estate tax consequences can occur if the transfer is handled improperly. This is especially true if you own property with someone other than your spouse. Consult your attorney before proceeding.

REVOCABLE LIVING TRUST MYTHS

Some myths concerning Revocable Living Trusts continue to prevail today. While a Revocable Living Trust can solve many of your estate planning problems, it does not solve them all. The following list contains the most prevalent myths along with the realities.

Myth #1: A Revocable Living Trust Will Protect My Assets From Creditors

A Revocable Living Trust provides no protection from creditors. Part of the reason is that the trust is revocable. If it were irrevocable, some creditor protection might be available, but of course, you would lose control over your property.

Myth #2: A Revocable Living Trust Will Save Taxes

The act of creating a Revocable Living Trust does nothing to reduce your tax burden. However, all of the estate tax saving strategies available to you under traditional will planning are also available to you with your Revocable Living Trust. By including appropriate language in your trust, you can reduce estate taxes.

Myth #3: If I Have a Revocable Living Trust, I Do Not Need a Will

As I mentioned earlier in this chapter, you will still need to have a will drawn in addition to your Revocable Living Trust. Its purpose is to direct any property not already owned by your Revocable Living Trust to your Revocable Living Trust and to name guardians for any minor children. You won't need a complex or expensive will, but it *is* necessary.

Myth #4: All My Property Will Ultimately End Up in My Revocable Living Trust

Some people believe that because their Revocable Living Trust is set up to handle all their property, eventually all their property will end up in their trust. Nothing could be further from the truth. Property held *joint tenants with right of survivorship* will pass by title no matter what your trust says. The same is true for beneficiary designations of life insurance, retirement plans, and annuities. You must play an active role in seeing that your property ends up in your trust.

Myth #5: When I Die, My Revocable Living Trust Will Prevent Delays Typically Associated with Probate

It is true that the time delays at your death are likely to be much less than that of probate, but some delays will take place. Your trustee must still complete many of the administrative duties of an executor including the preparation and filing of your estate tax return, payment of debts, creditor notices, etc. The process is more difficult in some states than others, so check with your attorney. If time delays are likely to be a problem in your state, you will need to make certain that your spouse will have sufficient assets to meet living expenses until trust assets are released.

Myth #6: A Revocable Living Trust Eliminates the Cost of Probate

Again, this is only partially true. Many of the tasks normally performed by an executor must now be completed by your trustee. Depending on your state of residence and choice of trustee, the cost savings can be significant or minimal. A Revocable Living Trust *does* put you in a better position to control costs at your death.

It is your responsibility to develop the complete list of your assets. You should use your checklist to make sure that all property has been properly handled. Be sure to have your attorney review *all* of the property transfers and beneficiary changes. You should have your attorney acknowledge in writing that he or she has reviewed each transfer and that it has been properly completed. Be sure to keep a record of all this correspondence. If there is ever a problem, you or your family members will be able to return to your attorney and have him or her correct the problem.

TRANSACTING BUSINESS WITH YOUR TRUST

Once you have set up your trust and transferred your property into it, you will now have to transact your business in a slightly new way. If you buy property, be sure to buy it in the name of your trust. Your purchases will be made in your name as trustee. This may take a little getting used to, but you will get the hang of it. One exception is your checking account. It is not necessary that the name of your trust be listed on your checks or that you sign your checks as trustee. When you decide to sell property you will do so as trustee. Be sure to keep a copy of your affidavit of trust or nominee partnership papers close at hand. In most cases you will not need them, but if you do, having them handy will save time and frustration.

A Revocable Living Trust is an excellent tool for the right person. While the Revocable Living Trust has many advantages over traditional will planning, I believe that the four most important ones are:

- If you have substantial assets and are concerned about keeping your financial affairs private or just want to save your family the headache of probate.

- If you want a well-defined mechanism in place to take care of you in the event you become incapacitated.

- If you own property in multiple states, and want to avoid multiple probate proceedings.

- If your job causes you to move from state to state, you don't want to incur the expense of having to draw a new will every time you move.

Life insurance can play an important role in your estate plan. Many people depend on life insurance to provide their families with needed income and cash should they die prematurely. In addition, it is often used to provide cash to pay estate taxes so other assets will not have to be sold. Finally, it can be used to leverage your estate for the benefit of your heirs. I will discuss these as well as many other life insurance issues in our next chapter.

CHAPTER 8

Using Life Insurance in Your Estate Plan

L ife insurance serves three important purposes in your estate plan. If you have not accumulated enough financial assets to provide financial independence for yourself and your family, life insurance provides a means of replacing income should the family income earner die prematurely. Secondly, if you have accumulated enough assets to be financially independent, then life insurance can be used as a source of cash to pay estate taxes. Finally, life insurance can be used as a way to leverage the size of your estate. I will cover each of these issues in this chapter as well as discuss the various types of life insurance policies; under what circumstances each is appropriate; and the amount of life insurance you will need.

LIFE INSURANCE BASICS

Before I discuss the best use of life insurance in your estate plan, let's first review the basics of how life insurance works and the various types of policies offered.

Life insurance is certainly one of the most confusing financial products sold today. The variation in products is so vast that it is very difficult to compare one product to another. While life insurance policies come in many shapes and sizes, all life insurance falls into one of two categories: Term insurance or Cash Value insurance. **Term Insurance** is pure insurance. You pay a premium that covers you for a certain period of time. If you die during that period of time, your beneficiary collects the face amount of the policy. If you do not die, you do not get any money back and you must "renew" the insurance by paying an additional premium if you want the coverage to continue. **Cash Value Insurance** is nothing more than term insurance with a savings feature. In addition to the term premium, called mortality reserves, you give the insurance company extra money which it "invests" for you. Later, that savings can be accessed through loans or in some cases, withdrawals. At the time of your death, your beneficiary receives the term insurance plus the "savings account."

To fully understand all your life insurance options, what follows is a more detailed look at the various term and cash value policies.

Term Insurance

Term insurance plans are typically sold as either annual renewable term insurance or level term insurance. With **annual renewable term insurance**, each year your insurance company sends you a bill that is higher than the prior year. This is because each year as you get older, you are statistically more likely to die. With **level term insurance**, the insurance company "levelizes" the premium for a stated period of time, typically 5, 10, 15 or 20 years. The longer the term period, the higher your premiums will be. At the end of the stated period, you have a guaranteed right to renew the policy regardless of your health condition, but for a significantly higher premium. Some companies offer a lower renewal rate if you are willing to provide proof that you are still in good health by taking a physical exam. Look at Table 8-1 for comparable premiums.

Cash Value Insurance

As with term insurance, there are also various types of cash value insurance. Several of the more popular products include:

- **Whole Life**. This product represents the traditional cash value type of insurance. With whole life insurance, you commit to a fixed premium that includes the term insurance charge plus the savings feature. The insurance company takes the savings portion of your premium and invests it for you as part of their general assets. These general assets include real estate, commercial mortgages, bonds, and to a limited extent, stocks. You receive a guaranteed rate of return (usually 4% to 4.5%) and, in many cases, dividends that are declared by the Board of Directors.

TABLE 8-1
$1,000,000 TERM LIFE INSURANCE FOR MALE, AGE 45

Year	Annual Renewable Term	10-Year Level Term	15-Year Level Term	20-Year Level Term
1	$840	$1,120	$1,390	$1,710
2	$870	$1,120	$1,390	$1,710
3	$940	$1,120	$1,390	$1,710
4	$1,020	$1,120	$1,390	$1,710
5	$1,110	$1,120	$1,390	$1,710
6	$1,200	$1,120	$1,390	$1,710
7	$1,290	$1,120	$1,390	$1,710
8	$6,430	$1,120	$1,390	$1,710
9	$7,070	$1,120	$1,390	$1,710
10	$7,770	$1,120	$1,390	$1,710
11	$8,540	$3,180*	$1,390	$1,710
12	$9,380	$3,180	$1,390	$1,710
13	$10,290	$3,180	$1,390	$1,710
14	$11,270	$3,180	$1,390	$1,710
15	$12,320	$3,180	$1,390	$1,710
16	$13,440	$3,180	$5,010*	$1,710
17	$14,630	$3,180	$5,010	$1,710
18	$15,890	$3,180	$5,010	$1,710
19	$17,230	$3,180	$5,010	$1,710
20	$18,670	$3,180	$5,010	$1,710
Totals	$160,200	$43,000	$45,900	$34,200

Note: Assumes insured provides proof of good health with an updated physical. If not, premium becomes significantly higher.

- **Universal Life.** Universal Life became popular in the 1980s when interest rates were very high. With this type of policy, your savings are invested in interest sensitive investments such as certificates of deposit, commercial paper, and bonds. You are notified periodically of the interest earned on your savings. Unlike whole life policies, however, you pay flexible, rather than fixed premiums. You must pay an amount that covers the term insurance premiums, but the insurance company allows you to vary the amount you contribute toward the savings program.

- **Variable Life.** Variable Life is one of the newest types of life insurance. As mutual funds became increasingly popular, the insurance companies developed a life insurance product that uses mutual funds. You must pay your term insurance charge but you can then direct your savings into various mutual funds offered by the insurance company. The company typically offers a variety of choices such as stock funds, bond funds, money market funds, and guaranteed interest rate contracts which are similar to certificates of deposit. You make the decision which funds to invest in and you are allowed to make changes from time to time.

- **Survivorship Life.** This product was developed specifically for the estate planning marketplace. Survivorship life covers two lives, but does not pay a death benefit until the last person dies. Assuming that the two people are a husband and wife, the policy death benefit becomes available at just the time when it is needed to pay the estate taxes. Statistically, the odds of the insurance company having to pay a claim early are very low. As a result, the mortality charges for these policies are very low.

USING LIFE INSURANCE TO REPLACE INCOME

One of the primary reasons to purchase life insurance is to provide a source of income for your family should you die prematurely. Your basic assumption here is that you have people that are dependent on you for their financial support. If you don't have someone dependent upon you for his or her financial support, you do not need life insurance as an income replacement device. Many people misunderstand this concept and end up buying life insurance they do not need.

Life Insurance for Income Earners

Everyone does not need life insurance. Use the guidelines below to help you decide if life insurance is appropriate for you or your family members.

- You are single without children. Most single people have no dependents and, therefore, have no need for life insurance.

- You are married without children. If both you and your spouse work, in all likelihood neither is financially dependent upon the other. Again, no life insurance is necessary. If one spouse is unemployed, you may need some life insurance to provide a "bridge of income" until the other person can acquire the training necessary to get a good job. You may also need life insurance to cover a portion of joint debts that are being paid from both incomes, such as a mortgage.

- You are married with young children. Now, you have dependents and should consider your life insurance needs carefully. You should buy enough insurance to maintain a similar lifestyle for your surviving family.

- Insurance on children. Unless your child is a movie star, it is unlikely that you or anyone else is dependent on them for financial support.

HOW MUCH LIFE INSURANCE DO YOU NEED?

Ask 10 people and you are likely to get 10 different answers. First, if you are married and have no children, you only need enough life insurance to pay off any joint debts. If, on the other hand, you have children, your need for life insurance increases substantially. Use the following three-step process to determine your life insurance needs:

Step 1

If you are the sole income provider, multiply your annual income by .80. (Note: If both you and your spouse work, combine both incomes and multiply by .80.) This results in reducing your income by 20%. The reason you do this is because there is one less spender in the household (you!).

Step 2

Divide your answer in Step 1 by the rate of return you would reasonably expect to earn on the life insurance proceeds once they are invested. Your answer here indicates how much money you will need in order to continue the necessary income stream to your surviving family.

Step 3

Subtract any savings or investments you already have from your answer in Step 2. This is the amount of life insurance you should own.

CASE STUDY 1

John and Mary Smith have two children. John earns $150,000 a year and Mary stays home to raise the children. The couple assumes that they could earn 7.5 percent on investments; they have $125,000 in personal investments and $400,000 in their retirement plans.

STEP 1

John's Income	$ 150,000
"One Less Spender" Factor	× .80
Adjusted Income Need	$ 120,000

STEP 2

Adjusted Income Need	$ 120,000
Divided by Expected Rate of Return	÷ 7.5%
	$1,600,000

This amount of money invested at 7.5 percent will provide the needed $120,000 per year for Mary and the children.

STEP 3

Capital Needed	$1,600,000
Minus Current Savings and Investments	- 525,000
John's Life Insurance Need	$1,075,000

CASE STUDY 2

If both John and Mary work, the example changes. Assume their total income is $165,000, but John's earnings are $80,000 and Mary's earnings are $85,000. To see how much life insurance John needs, complete the following calculation.

STEP 1

Multiply the family income of $165,000 by .80. This equals $132,000. Again, the survivor's income need is reduced because John is no longer a spender. Since Mary plans to continue working, subtract her income also. $132,000 - $85,000 = $47,000. This $47,000 represents the income that needs to be replaced upon John's death.

STEP 2

Divide $47,000 by their expected rate of return (7.5 percent). $47,000 ÷ .075 = $626,667.

STEP 3

Subtract their current investments ($525,000) from $626,667. This equals $101,667. This is the amount of life insurance needed on John.

NOTE: Since the family also depends on Mary's income, you now need to complete this exercise for her and to find how much life insurance Mary needs!

Now calculate *your* insurance needs using Worksheet 8-2 (page 146).

The answer arrived at using this three-step process should only be used as a rule of thumb. Then you should personalize the solution to your particular situation. For example, you may want to increase the amount of insurance to help cover the costs of funding college expenses for your children. Or, you may want additional insurance which would be used to pay off some of your debts. If your goal is to provide a *lifetime* income for your dependents, additional insurance will be needed to offset the ravages of inflation.

WORKSHEET 8-2	
LIFE INSURANCE NEEDS WORKSHEET	
Step 1	
Your Annual Family Income	$
Discount Factor	× .80
Total Income Needed by Surviving Family	$
Subtract Surviving Spouse's Annual Income	-
Surviving Family Income Need From Outside Sources	$
Step 2	
Divide By Your Estimated ROR on Invested Assets	÷
Total Amount of Money Needed to Provide for Survivors	$
Step 3	
Subtract Your Current Savings and Investments	-
Equals Total Life Insurance Needed	$

Our government provides a Social Security Survivors Benefit to help surviving spouses with small children. To determine the level of income for which you are eligible, call the Social Security Administration (1-800-772-1213) and request the form entitled "Record of Earnings and Estimate of Benefits Statement." After you complete this form and return it to the Social Security Administration, you will get a summary of your benefits. View these benefits as "extra" money and not as part of your calculation for life insurance needs. Remember, these benefits end when your youngest child reaches age 18.

WHAT TYPE OF LIFE INSURANCE IS BEST FOR YOU?

If your primary purpose is to provide your family with a source of income should you die prematurely, then level term insurance is your best bet. This assumes that you have a wealth accumulation plan in place as outlined in Chapter 3. In working with my clients, I normally recommend either 15-year or 20-year level term policies. This is because I have implemented a wealth accumulation plan that is expected to achieve total financial independence by the end of that period. For example, let's say that you determined in Chapter 3 that you need to accumulate $3,000,000 of investment capital to be financially independent. Once you have accumulated that sum, you no longer need life insurance as a source of income for your family. It is possible that you might need "permanent" cash value life insurance for *other* reasons, such as estate liquidity. Remember, since term insurance is convertible to cash value insurance without having to pass a new physical exam, you have left your options open.

INSURANCE ON A HOMEMAKER

If you have young children, replacing the services of a homemaker can be quite expensive. Ask yourself this question: If my homemaker spouse were to die, could I afford to pay someone to perform those services out of my current income? You may be lucky enough to have a family member who could step in and provide childcare services. In such a case, no life insurance would be necessary. On the other hand, if you decide life insurance on a homemaker is necessary, a $100,000 to $250,000 term policy should provide adequate coverage. By buying a 10- to 15-year level term insurance policy, you will provide coverage until the children are old enough to assist with their own care.

INSURANCE ON ADULT CHILDREN

If you have adult children that have started their own families, you might consider buying insurance on their lives to provide protection for their families. I am sure you can remember how tight cash flow was when you first started your family. This is a situation where you have the cash and they have the need. From a selfish point of view, if you had a breadwinner son-in-law die without enough life insurance, you might feel compelled to step in with financial support for your daughter and grandchildren. Believe me, paying the premiums on a large term life policy for your son-in-law is a lot more palatable than financially supporting a second family! The latter could have a serious negative impact on your own retirement and estate plan.

HOW TO GET THE BEST DEAL ON TERM LIFE INSURANCE

Fortunately for the consumer, term insurance is a very competitive product. In terms of planning and budgeting, 10-, 15- or 20-year level term is advised. That way you have a predictable premium for a fixed period of time. There are several companies that specialize in helping consumers shop for the best rates:

- Wholesale Insurance Network (800) 808-5810

- Insurance Clearing House (800) 522-2827

- Insurance Information Inc. (800) 472-5800

To get the best deal, first decide how much life insurance you need and what kind of term insurance best fits your circumstances. For example, if you decide that you need $750,000 of 15-year level term life insurance, call one or two of the companies listed above. If you have a local agent, ask him or her for a quote. A simple comparison will make sure you get the best deal. Personally, I prefer to work with a local agent. For the most part, these are hardworking people and deserve the commissions that they receive.

INSURANCE WARNINGS!

Not all insurance is good insurance and not all insurance companies are good companies. A few warnings are in order here.

Financial Strength

Make sure the company you use is financially strong. Accept only a company that is rated AA or better by one of the three major rating services: AM Best Co., Standard & Poor's, or Moody's. Request this information at the same time you request your premium quotes.

Mortgage Life Insurance

If you borrowed money to buy your home, you undoubtedly have received offers to buy mortgage life insurance. This particular type of policy is a decreasing term insurance policy that provides enough insurance to pay off your mortgage if you die before your mortgage is paid off. While you may want to have enough life insurance to pay off your mortgage if you die, these policies represent poor values. Consider the following comparison. A client of mine had a $200,000, 15-year mortgage. Through his mortgage company, he received an offer for mortgage life insurance costing about

$141.40 per month. However, a 15-year *level* term life insurance policy for $200,000 only costs $36 per month. That amounts to savings of almost 400 percent! Mortgage Life insurance is a deal you can afford to pass up.

Credit Life Insurance

Credit life is similar to mortgage life except that it is used to pay off non-real estate loans such as car, appliance, and furniture loans. Here is a typical scenario. You're about to finalize the loan when the banker asks, "You do want this car loan to be paid off if you die, don't you?" You then sign a credit life insurance application without reviewing the cost. Premiums for credit life can be up to 10 times higher than normal policies. It will probably not surprise you to find out that your banker often receives incentive compensation for selling these policies.

USING LIFE INSURANCE FOR ESTATE LIQUIDITY

If you have accumulated enough assets to be financially independent, then your estate is almost certainly large enough to face possible estate taxes. If this is the case, you need to determine where your heirs will get the cash to pay your estate taxes. Let's review three extreme case examples.

CASE STUDY 1

Dave and Cindy Adams are retirees who have a total estate valued at $5,000,000. They have implemented all the typical estate reduction strategies such as the Credit Shelter Trust. Their financial advisor estimates that they still have an estate tax liability of approximately $1,500,000. They are trying to decide if they should buy life insurance to cover their tax liability. A review of their assets indicates that they own $3,000,000 in real estate and business interests and $2,000,000 in stocks and bonds. One solution to their tax problem would be for their executor to sell $1,500,000 of securities to pay the taxes and distribute the remaining estate to the Adams family heirs. This solution would not require the purchase of any life insurance.

CASE STUDY 2

For case scenario number two, let's use the same facts but change the asset mix a bit. In this case, the Adams' estate consists of $3,000,000 of real estate and business interests plus $2,000,000 in stocks and bonds. However, this time the stocks and bonds are all in various retirement plans. If the executor were to take $1,500,000 from the retirement plan to pay the taxes, he would immediately trigger *income taxes* on the money. To pay the added income tax, he would need to sell more securities from the retirement plan thus triggering even more income tax. In this case, a better choice is to use life insurance to provide cash to pay the taxes so that the retirement plan assets can continue to be deferred as long as possible.

CASE STUDY 3

In our final scenario, we will continue to use the Adams' family facts, but this time the bulk of their estate is made up of illiquid real estate. A forced sale of the real estate would likely result in fire sale prices. Clearly, the best choice here would be life insurance.

HOW MUCH IS ENOUGH?

In our last scenario the Adams family had an estate tax problem of $1,500,000 with no liquid assets available to pay the tax. How much life insurance do they need to solve their problem? An obvious answer is $1,500,000, of course. Wrong! Dave and Cindy Adams are both alive today and the odds of at least one of them remaining alive for years to come is very good. This being the case, their estate is likely to continue to grow as will their tax problem. Initially, it appeared that the solution was simple, but clearly, this needs to be well thought-out. You must review your overall estate planning strategy and perform some estate growth projections. These projections will give you a much better sense of how much insurance you will ultimately need. For example, assume in this case that the Adams have established a Family Limited Partnership (see chapter 11) and place all their real estate in it. They have a large number of children and grandchildren. Based on discounted annual gifts to all family members, they project that over the next 10 years they can give away enough partnership interests to reduce their estate tax liability to zero. They have solved their long-term problem and therefore should consider term life insurance to solve their short-term need. If they did not have a large number of children or were unwilling to make family gifts, then their future life insurance need could easily exceed $3,000,000. Again, you must take the time to run realistic projections.

WHAT TYPE OF LIFE INSURANCE IS BEST FOR ESTATE LIQUIDITY?

The life insurance that is tailor-made for paying estate taxes is **survivorship life insurance**. It is also often referred to as *second to die* insurance. As described earlier in this chapter, this type of insurance is written on two lives, usually a husband and wife, and pays off when the last insured dies. This just happens to be the time when the estate taxes are due. Survivorship life is a cash value policy, not a term life policy. This "permanent" type policy is appropriate because you want to be certain it remains in force as long as you or your spouse is living. You could not guarantee that with term life insurance. Survivorship life is available as whole life, universal life, or variable life. The whole life version will contain more guarantees, but will likely carry the highest premium. If you are somewhat adventuresome, you might want to consider the variable life version. Regardless of your choice, you do not want to buy this type of insurance "mail order." You will definitely need a qualified agent who is knowledgeable about this product and estate planning. I recommend that you only consider an agent with at least 10 years of experience in the field and who has obtained the Chartered Life Underwriter (CLU) designation. A good place to find one is by contacting the president of the nearest Estate Planning Council. You can get the name and number of the local chapter president nearest you by calling the National Association of Estate Planners and Councils at (610) 526-1389 or by fax at (610) 525-1224.

As with all life insurance, you want to make certain that you are dealing with a financially strong company. Remember, you are counting on them to provide the cash to pay your estate taxes 15, 20, even 30 or 40 years into the future. Stick with a company that is rated AA or higher by the major rating services.

In the case of our friends, the Adams, let's assume that they determined that they needed $3,000,000 of survivorship life to pay their future estate taxes. So they find an agent, take the necessary physical exams, pay the premium, and they are set, right? Actually, they have created a major problem for their heirs and unwittingly made their estate tax problem worse. The reason is that now the life insurance policy is also part of their estate, and therefore, the insurance death proceeds will be subject to the estate tax. To resolve this problem they need to consider the *irrevocable life insurance trust*.

THE IRREVOCABLE LIFE INSURANCE TRUST

The primary reason for establishing an irrevocable life insurance trust is to save estate taxes. These trusts are not just for survivorship life policies, but are appropriate for all kinds of life insurance. Here's how they work:

Step 1

You have your attorney draw up the trust. It will usually have the same or similar provisions as your Credit Shelter Trust (Chapter 6). Typically, it provides that the income goes to your spouse along with access to principal for certain reasons. At your spouse's death, the trust either continues for the benefit of your children or the trust terminates and trust principal is distributed to them outright.

Step 2

Once the trust is established, you make a gift to the trust in the amount of the premium of your life insurance policy(s).

Step 3

The trustee sends all beneficiaries a written notice that they have a right to withdraw the money that you have just contributed to the trust. This notice is technically referred to as a **Crummey notice**. It is not so named because it is "crummy" to get a notice stating that there's money available for you that everyone expects you to decline. Rather, the name comes from a 1968 court case *Crummey vs. Commissioner*, which Mr. Crummey won. This notice will give your beneficiaries a time period in which to request a distribution. The time period is typically 30 days. If they do not request a distribution within the time period, their ability to take a distribution expires. Since it is your intent that the money be used for payment of life insurance premiums, your assumption is that no beneficiary will request a distribution. In working with my clients, I normally request that each beneficiary sign a letter indicating that they waive the right to take a distribution. This provides proof for the Internal Revenue Service that the letters were actually sent. The effect of giving the beneficiaries the right to withdraw money now creates a gift of a "present interest" to the trust and thus qualifies your premium contributions for your Annual Gift Tax Exclusion.

Step 4

Once all beneficiaries have declined their right to take a distribution, or the time period for exercising that right has expired, the trustee pays the life insurance premium.

Step 5

When you die, the trust is funded via the death benefit proceeds and the trustee uses the money to provide financial support for your beneficiaries. The death benefits are not part of your estate and therefore no estate taxes are due.

In order to consolidate the number of trusts a family has, I will sometimes recommend that the Credit Shelter Trust pour over into the irrevocable insurance trust at the death of the grantor.

Irrevocable life insurance trusts are an excellent strategy for reducing estate taxes. Let's look at an example of this strategy in action.

CASE STUDY 4

The year is 2006. Bill and Barbara Millhouse are married and have four children. In addition to their $2,000,000 net worth, Bill owns a $1,500,000 term life insurance policy on his life payable to Barbara. For illustration purposes, I will assume that Bill dies first (in year 2006) and that all of the assets are in his name. They have basic wills that utilize the Credit Shelter Trust. Without an irrevocable life insurance trust, the Millhouse's estate tax situation would appear as depicted in the figure below.

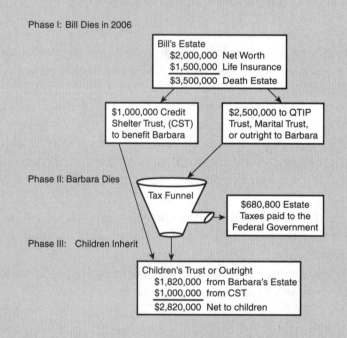

Phase I: Bill Dies in 2006

Bill's Estate
$2,000,000 Net Worth
$1,500,000 Life Insurance
$3,500,000 Death Estate

$1,000,000 Credit Shelter Trust, (CST) to benefit Barbara

$2,500,000 to QTIP Trust, Marital Trust, or outright to Barbara

Phase II: Barbara Dies

Tax Funnel

$680,800 Estate Taxes paid to the Federal Government

Phase III: Children Inherit

Children's Trust or Outright
$1,820,000 from Barbara's Estate
$1,000,000 from CST
$2,820,000 Net to children

Millhouse Estate Plan without Irrevocable Life Insurance Trust

If on the other hand, Bill established an irrevocable life insurance trust that was the owner and beneficiary of his life insurance policy, the estate taxes would have been zero. Take a look at the figure on the next page to see how this works.

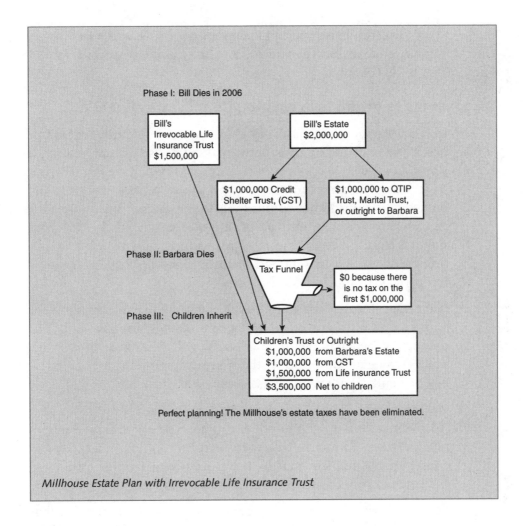

Phase I: Bill Dies in 2006

Bill's Irrevocable Life Insurance Trust $1,500,000

Bill's Estate $2,000,000

$1,000,000 Credit Shelter Trust, (CST)

$1,000,000 to QTIP Trust, Marital Trust, or outright to Barbara

Phase II: Barbara Dies

Tax Funnel

$0 because there is no tax on the first $1,000,000

Phase III: Children Inherit

Children's Trust or Outright
$1,000,000 from Barbara's Estate
$1,000,000 from CST
$1,500,000 from Life insurance Trust
$3,500,000 Net to children

Perfect planning! The Millhouse's estate taxes have been eliminated.

Millhouse Estate Plan with Irrevocable Life Insurance Trust

GETTING YOUR LIFE INSURANCE INTO YOUR TRUST

If you move existing life insurance policies into your trust and die during the first three years of that transfer, the insurance proceeds will be included in your estate. This is exactly what you are trying to avoid. The only way to solve this problem is to live the three years or use *new* insurance. When using new insurance, you must first establish your irrevocable life insurance trust, then have the trustee apply for the life insurance policy on your life. Your trustee will be both the owner and beneficiary of the policy. By following this procedure, you will have never had an *incident of ownership* in the policy. The result is that the insurance proceeds will never be included in your estate as long as you follow the Crummey procedures outlined earlier in this chapter.

Disadvantages of the Irrevocable Life Insurance Trust

- Irrevocable. Once the trust is established, it cannot be changed. Life has a way of changing constantly, making decisions that you made a few short years ago inappropriate today. If you have funded your trust with term life insurance, you can simply write a new trust and buy new term insurance to put in it. If you are not insurable, or if you used cash value life insurance, you may be stuck with your original trust. Since the trust is irrevocable, you will want to give thoughtful consideration to all the provisions and have your attorney provide as much flexibility as possible.

- Gift tax problems. Care must be taken when you make gifts to your trust that you do not create gift tax problems unknowingly. The number of beneficiaries of your trust will determine how much money you can contribute without creating gift taxes. Your attorney or financial advisor can assist you with this.

- Crummey procedures. In order to be certain that your gifts are considered gifts of a present interest, you must strictly follow the notification rules. Failure to follow these rules could have adverse tax consequences. Implementation is not particularly time-consuming, but you and your trustee must be consistent in your follow-through.

- Separate entity. Your trust is a separate tax-paying entity. If it has income, it must file a tax return and pay taxes. Your trustee must also apply for, and receive, a tax identification number. If your trust does have income, but the income is "passed through" to your beneficiaries, then that income is taxed to the beneficiaries, not the trust.

- Expense. This is a trust that you will definitely want drawn by a qualified attorney. Depending on your attorney and how complicated your trust is, your fee could range from a few hundred dollars to several thousand dollars. However, this expense is small when compared to the potential estate tax savings.

USING LIFE INSURANCE TO LEVERAGE YOUR ESTATE

Thus far, I have touted the estate tax savings benefits of the irrevocable life insurance trust, but you can also use this type of trust to leverage the *size* of your estate. The purpose is not to cover your estate taxes, but rather to create a much larger estate for your heirs. This type of irrevocable trust is often referred to as a **Dynasty Trust**. The procedures for setting up your dynasty trust are the same as we have discussed for the irrevocable life insurance trust.

How Much Is Enough?

The amount of life insurance to place in your dynasty trust is typically determined in one of three ways. The first method is for you to decide how large a premium commitment you are comfortable making. Then you would have your life insurance agent determine how much life insurance the premium will buy. For example, you decide that you are willing to commit to a $10,000 per year premium. You then have your life agent determine how much life insurance that $10,000 premium will buy with a competitive company.

The second method is for you to predetermine the amount of insurance you want in your dynasty trust. Say you have three children and want to make sure they each receive a $1,000,000 inheritance. You would have your insurance agent shop for a competitive $3,000,000 life policy.

The final method of determining how much life insurance to place in your dynasty trust is to make gifts based on the maximum you can give without incurring gift taxes. The maximum you can contribute to your trust without paying gift taxes is defined by two constraints:

- Annually, the maximum you can contribute is based on the Annual Gift Tax Exclusion. For 1998 the maximum tax-free gift is $10,000 per beneficiary. If you are married and you and your spouse join in the gift, you can give up to $20,000 per beneficiary. These dollar limits increase annually based on the consumer price index beginning in 1999.

- The second constraint is your lifetime Applicable Exclusion Amount, which we discussed in Chapter 2. For 1999, the Applicable Exclusion Amount is $650,000. However, this exclusion increases to $1,000,000 in 2006.

The combination of your Annual Gift Tax Exclusion and lifetime Applicable Exclusion Amount leaves plenty of room for large premiums and correspondingly large amounts of life insurance.

WHAT TYPE OF INSURANCE IS BEST FOR YOUR DYNASTY TRUST?

Term Insurance

If your spouse would need the income from the insurance proceeds at your death, and you want to minimize your initial premiums, then term life insurance should be considered. Using term insurance is a short-term solution only. The reason is that if you live to anything close to life expectancy, term insurance will become too expensive. Make sure that the term insurance that you *do* buy is convertible to permanent cash value life insurance without further evidence of insurability. Later, when you can afford to pay the higher premiums of a cash value policy, you will be guaranteed the right to do so. Note that some term life plans are not convertible during their last few years. Avoid these plans.

Cash Value Insurance

If your spouse would need the income from the insurance proceeds at your death and you can afford the premiums, then you should purchase a traditional cash value life insurance policy such as whole life, universal life, or variable life.

Survivorship Life Insurance

If your assets outside of your dynasty trust are sufficient to provide adequate financial support for your surviving spouse and family, then you can maximize the leverage by using a survivorship life insurance policy. This is because comparable premiums for survivorship life will purchase 50% to 100% more death benefit than traditional cash value life insurance.

Comparative premiums and cash values for each type of policy for a male age 45 are shown in Table 8-5.

TABLE 8-5
$1,000,000 LIFE INSURANCE PREMIUM COMPARISON FOR MALE, AGE 45

20 Year Level Term

Year	Premium	Cash Value	Death Benefit
1	$1,710	$0	$1,000,000
5	$1,710	$0	$1,000,000
10	$1,710	$0	$1,000,000
20	$1,710	$0	$1,000,000

Whole Life

Year	Premium	Cash Value	Death Benefit
1	$18,580	$0	$1,000,000
5	$18,580	$61,105	$1,020,586
10	$18,580	$196,397	$1,085,051
20	$18,580	$643,341	$1,428,379

Universal Life

Year	Premium	Cash Value	Death Benefit
1	$13,206	$0	$1,000,000
5	$13,206	$45,776	$1,065,193
10	$13,206	$138,970	$1,147,600
20	$13,206	$389,864	$1,389,864

Variable Life

Year	Premium	Cash Value	Death Benefit
1	$7,326	$0	$1,000,000
5	$7,326	$21,814	$1,027,527
10	$7,326	$68,017	$1,055,344
20	$7,326	$189,670	$1,189,670

continued on next page

TABLE 8-5 (CONTINUED)
$1,000,000 LIFE INSURANCE PREMIUM COMPARISON FOR MALE, AGE 45

Survivorship Life

Year	Premium	Cash Value	Death Benefit
1	$11,700	$0	$1,000,000
5	$11,700	$48,746	$1,001,415
10	$11,700	$132,633	$1,032,222
20	$11,700	$447,487	$1,283,700

Note: Premiums and cash values based on current mortality costs and current dividends/interest and are not guaranteed. For variable life policy, a 12% gross rate of return is assumed.

ABOUT YOUR CASH VALUES

I am sure you noticed the significant amount of cash value build-up in the policies illustrated in Table 8-5. Since this is an irrevocable trust, do you give up the access to all that cash? What if you have an emergency, and really need your cash value? The answer lies in a technically drafted clause called a **limited power of appointment**. This clause in your trust allows the holder of the power to make trust distributions anytime to you (the grantor) or others (presumably children) designated in the trust. It would be typical for your spouse to be the holder of this trust power. It should be noted that the power holder cannot be forced to make distributions. Distributions must be at his or her sole discretion. This provision allows you some access to your cash values during your lifetime. As an added bonus, in most situations these cash values would be insulated from your creditors and potential lawsuits.

THE JOINT DYNASTY TRUST

Your dynasty trust can include life insurance policies on the lives of people other than yourself. Most typically, the "other" is your spouse. If neither of you needs the life insurance proceeds at the death of the other, placing your policies into your Dynasty Trust can be an excellent strategy. The result is the transfer of a large asset (the life insurance death benefits) to future generations of heirs free of income and estate taxes.

DYNASTY PLANNING WITHOUT A TRUST

While a trust is often used in dynasty planning, it is not a requirement. Non-trust dynasty planning is most often used in conjunction with annual gifts to children. The typical situation looks something like this: You decide that you want to make annual gifts to your adult children, but are concerned that they might squander the money. An excellent solution is to have them apply for and own a life insurance policy on your life. You then gift them an amount of money each year equal to the life insurance premiums. At your death, they receive the death proceeds free of both income and estate taxes. You could accomplish the same result using life policies that you already own, but existing insurance would be included in your estate if you died during the first three years from the date of transfer. Remember, if you want to maximize the leverage of premiums paid, the best type policy for this purpose is the survivorship life insurance policy.

ONE FINAL BENEFIT OF DYNASTY PLANNING

By establishing a dynasty trust or plan, you have, in effect, provided a substantial inheritance for your children or other heirs. This allows you the freedom to "spend" all your other assets in order to maximize your retirement lifestyle. Too often, I find retirees are denying themselves the style of retirement they deserve so that they can "leave an inheritance for their children." Dynasty planning allows you to "die broke" without guilt.

As you can see, life insurance can be a powerful tool in developing your strategic estate plan. I should remind you that my practice is "fee only," so I have no particular interest in recommending life insurance to my clients unless it is appropriate to their case facts. Many of the ideas discussed in this chapter revolve around gifting money for paying life insurance premiums. Reducing your estate through gifting programs is a basic, yet important estate planning strategy. In the next chapter, I will cover this issue in more detail.

CHAPTER 9

Smart Strategies for Gifting Assets to Family Members

O
ne of the most basic ways to reduce estate taxes is to give away your assets. Still, many people are reluctant to do this, fearing that they might need those assets at some future date. The best way to overcome these fears is to understand how much assets you'll need in the future. To do this, review Chapter 3 and complete the analysis of the capital required for your retirement. Knowing that you have substantially more assets than you need for your retirement years should make you more confident about giving away assets today. In this chapter, I will examine the most popular strategies for gifting assets to family members.

THE ANNUAL GIFT TAX EXCLUSION

Giving away your assets may seem like a simple process—one that doesn't require interference from the government. After all, it is your property and you should be able to do with it as you please. There was a time in our history when this was the case. The result was deathbed gifts of all one's property in order to avoid estate taxes. (After all, we as Americans can be quite ingenious at learning how to avoid taxes!) However, newer laws have changed the nature of the game and you must follow the new rules if you're going to successfully minimize your taxes. The rules for annual gifting are as follows:

- In any calendar year you are allowed to give away up to $10,000 each, to as many people as you desire without triggering any gift taxes. The gifts can be in cash or property. Beginning with calendar year 1999, this $10,000 annual exclusion will be indexed for inflation.

- If you are married, you may give away up to $20,000 per year to as many people as you desire. This assumes that your spouse consents to make the gifts with you. This is called a "split gift." Again, this amount will be adjusted for inflation annually beginning in 1999.

- Your gift must be a gift of "present" interest versus a gift of a future interest. For example, assume that you deeded your 25-year-old son a piece of land, but the deed said he would not receive the title until his 30th birthday. This would be considered a gift of *future* interest and would not be eligible for the Annual Gift Tax Exclusion.

- Gifts to spouses who are U.S. citizens are unlimited.

- If your gift results in a gift tax, you—not the receiver of the gift—are responsible for paying the tax. The gift tax return (Form 709) and the taxes on gifts in excess of the Annual Gift Tax Exclusion can be handled in one of two ways. You can pay the tax on the gift on or before the time your income tax return is due (April 15th or later if you file an extension) *or* you can use a portion of your *Applicable Credit Amount* for any federal gift tax due. If you remember from earlier discussions in this book, the federal tax law allows you give to whomever you wish, either during your lifetime or at your death, an amount equal to the lifetime Applicable Exclusion Amount free of federal estate taxes. See Table 9-1 for the current schedule.

UNINTENDED GIFTS

It is possible to make a gift to someone without realizing what you have done. The result can create unintended tax consequences. Let's look at some typical examples:

- You add your child's name to your savings or checking account. This is considered a gift the moment your child makes a withdrawal.

If the withdrawal exceeds the allowed Annual Gift Tax Exclusion it will be considered a taxable gift.

- You want to be certain that a particular person receives a specific piece of real estate at your death. Your solution is to add his or her name to the deed. When the deed is executed, you have just made a gift for gift tax purposes.

- You decide to buy a security such as a stock, bond, or limited partnership interest and do so in both your name and someone else's name. As soon as you designate the joint owner, a gift is deemed to have occurred.

Under each of the preceding examples where you created a joint ownership arrangement, at your death the entire value of the property is included in your estate. This is because you provided all of the financial consideration. If this is not your intended result, you can attempt to resolve the problem by making qualified gifts and filing a gift tax return.

- If you guarantee a loan for someone else, you could end up being deemed to have made a gift for gift tax purposes. Assume that your child wants to start a business with start-up costs of $95,000. Your child has no money or collateral with which to obtain a loan from the bank. You agree to guarantee the loan at the bank. Based on the 1984 Supreme Court case *Dickman vs. United States,* the Internal Revenue Service concluded that the act of guaranteeing a loan created a gift. The amount of the gift was to be based on the difference between the value of the loan the child could have received on his or her own versus the deal they received with your help. You can imagine the difficulty of arriving at an appropriate figure for gift tax purposes. Since this ruling, the Internal Revenue Service has indicated that no gift is imputed unless there is an actual default on the loan which requires you to satisfy the debt for the benefit of your child. If this occurs, you are deemed to have made a gift for the full unpaid balance of the loan less any repayments to you by your child.

Providing loan guarantees can also create negative estate tax results. When you die, your loan guarantee becomes an obligation of your estate. As such, it might not qualify for the unlimited marital deduction and could disqualify a QTIP election. The Internal Revenue Service has issued both favorable and unfavorable private letter rulings on this subject. If you're involved in this type of situation, proceed with caution and get assistance from a competent legal advisor.

FILING A GIFT TAX RETURN

Gifts that you make to someone for less than $10,000 do not require the filing of a federal gift tax return. If you and your spouse jointly make a gift, you are required to file a federal gift tax return (Form 709). This is true even if the combined gift is less than $20,000 and no gift tax is due. All gifts greater than $10,000 require the filing of a federal gift tax return. If your state of residence has a gift tax, you may also have to file a state gift tax return.

THE APPLICABLE EXCLUSION AMOUNT

In addition to the annual exclusion, you are also allowed a lifetime Applicable Exclusion Amount. This lifetime exclusion represents the amount of money or property that you can give to persons other than your spouse free of gift or estate taxes. If these gifts are not made during your lifetime, they can be used at the time of your death. The amount of these lifetime gifts is scheduled to increase to $1,000,000 in the year 2006. For the schedule of increases see Table 9-1.

TABLE 9-1
FUTURE APPLICABLE EXCLUSION AMOUNT INCREASES

Year	Exclusion Amount	Increase from Previous Amount
1998	$ 625,000	$ 25,000
1999	$ 650,000	$ 25,000
2000	$ 675,000	$ 25,000
2001	$ 675,000	$ 0
2002	$ 700,000	$ 25,000
2003	$ 700,000	$ 0
2004	$ 850,000	$ 150,000
2005	$ 950,000	$ 100,000
2006	$ 1,000,000	$ 50,000

While most people wait to use their lifetime applicable exclusion amount at death, it can be advantageous to use it during your life. If you own an asset that you expect to appreciate rapidly, you can remove the asset plus the *appreciation* of that asset from your future estate by giving it away now. Let's assume that you own 100 acres of farmland on the outskirts of town that is valued at $400,000 today. Your town is growing rapidly and the growth is all headed in your direction. If the growth continues, you speculate that your land value could increase tenfold or better. You decide to use part of your lifetime applicable exclusion amount and gift the property to your children via a trust. It turns out that your estimates were low and the land ends up being valued at $10,000,000. By giving the property to your children, you saved over $5,000,000 in federal estate taxes that would have been imposed at your death.

OUTRIGHT GIFTS

Based on an evaluation of your estate, you determine that you have excess assets, and can therefore afford to begin a gifting program for your children. Now that you have made this decision, what is the best way to maximize the "power" of your gifts? The answer is to evaluate the different assets that you own that are available to give away. Here is a review of the pros and cons of several different possibilities:

Outright Gifts of Cash

Perhaps the easiest gift to make is cash. You simply write a check to your child or other donee. The recipient receives the money and does with it as he or she pleases. The advantage is that it is easy: you simply write a check. The disadvantage is that your child may spend the money unwisely. I have seen many cases where children become "dependent" on the annual gifts from their parents. Another disadvantage is that the money you give could become subject to either a divorce proceeding or a creditor's claim.

Outright Gifts of Appreciating Property

The value of giving away property that is expected to appreciate rapidly is that you are also giving away the *future growth*. Say you give your child $10,000 worth of stock in a start-up company that you expect to appreciate significantly. As it turns out, you were correct and the stock appreciates on average 15 percent per year over the next 25 years. By making a gift of

$10,000 today, you have removed an asset that would have grown to $329,000 in the future.

Outright Gifts of Appreciated Property

Some people choose to give away assets that have already appreciated substantially. If you expect the asset to continue to appreciate rapidly in the future, then you will receive some of the same benefits mentioned above. Gifting appreciated property can also be a disadvantage. If you had held the property until you died, you would have received a "stepped up" cost basis. If you then passed the property to your child, he or she could sell the property and pay no capital gains or income taxes.

Gifts of appreciated property would *also* be subject to divorce proceedings and creditor claims.

Roth IRAs

It may seem strange that I am discussing Roth IRAs under the section of giving assets to your children, but one of the true power plays is to give your children the money to make a Roth IRA contribution. Assume that your 19-year-old daughter or granddaughter works summers to earn extra spending money. Her total earnings are $2,500. You give her $2,000 so she can make a contribution to a Roth IRA. Her contribution to the Roth IRA is not deductible, but because of her low tax bracket this is unimportant. The true value of the Roth IRA is *tax free growth*. The earnings will *never* be taxed if she follows certain rules:

- If she waits until after she turns age 59 1/2, withdrawals would be tax free.

- If she were to become disabled, withdrawals are tax free.

- If she uses the money for a "qualified" purpose, there will be no tax on withdrawals. A qualified purpose includes withdrawals of up to $10,000 in acquisition costs for her first home.

- Another qualified purpose is withdrawals for tuition payments of qualified higher education expenses of your daughter, her spouse or children.

- Generally, no tax-free withdrawals are allowed during the five taxable year period beginning with the first taxable year for which the contribution was made.

While a $2,000 contribution does not seem significant, the results can be quite dramatic. Let's assume that your daughter invests in a stock mutual fund that earns on average 12 percent and she does not touch it until she is age 75. Your measly $2,000 gift has turned into $1,140,878! This is the type of gift you will want to make each year. As an added bonus, since it is a retirement account, she is less likely to squander the money.

WHEN THE DONEE IS A MINOR

If you have decided to begin making gifts to your children or grandchildren but they are minors, you will need to make special preparations. While the law does allow minors to receive property in their name, no state allows them to sign legally binding contracts, so future dealings involving their property can be difficult. Practical choices to managing minor children's property include custodial accounts or minor's trusts. Let's examine each approach.

Custodial Accounts

Most often, assets are transferred to minors under either the Uniform Gifts to Minors Act (UGMA) or the Uniform Transfers to Minors Act (UTMA) depending on which Act your state has adopted. The forerunner of these was the Uniform Gifts to Minors Act which allowed an adult (the custodian) to act on the behalf of a minor concerning the minor's property. Under this Act, the custodian can invest the child's money in bank accounts, securities, annuities, and life insurance. The Uniform Transfers to Minors Act expanded the types of investments to include real estate and tangible personal property.

Advantages of Custodial Accounts

- Easy to set up and transfer property. To set up a custodial account all you need to do is open the account by listing the name of the child and custodian as follows: "John B. Smith (the name of the custodian) as Custodian f/b/o (for the benefit of) Sara J. Smith (the name of the child) under the Alabama (your state) Uniform Gifts (or Transfers) to Minors Act." Transferring title to existing property is equally as easy.

- No additional documents or agreements are required so the costs to set up custodial accounts are minimal.

- Custodians are not required to post any bonds and are not required to provide any reporting to the courts.

- The custodian is allowed broad powers to transact business on behalf of the minor child.

- The gifted assets as well as the future appreciation of the assets may be removed from your estate.

- The assets can be used for the health, education, maintenance, and support of your child.

- Transfers to custodial accounts are treated as gifts of "present" interests, and therefore qualify for the Annual Gift Tax Exclusion.

Disadvantages of Custodial Accounts

- The gifts are irrevocable. Once you have made a gift, you cannot change your mind later and take the property back.

- Your child will get legal control of the property no later than his or her 21st birthday. The Uniform Gifts to Minors Act requires transfer of the property at the age of majority for your state of residence, usually age 18 or 19. Under the Uniform Transfers to Minors Act, some states allow the transferor to select when the child receives the property outright between the ages of 18 and 21. Other states set the age of legal transfer at age 21. If you have a choice in your state, I prefer the Uniform Transfers to Minors Act with age 21 as the legal age of transfer. The obvious concern here is that children between ages 18 to 21 may not be mature enough to handle money without parental supervision.

- The assets you have gifted your child may become part of your estate for estate tax purposes. This is exactly the result you are trying to avoid. Here is how this can happen. No states allow minors to draw a will. If a minor child dies, the laws of intestacy of your state of residence will determine to whom the child's estate will go. In virtually every state, a minor child's property reverts to the parents. The only way to avoid this pitfall is to establish a trust.

There is a second way that property you have given your child can end up being part of your estate. If you act as both the transferor and custodian and you die before your child reaches the age of majority (as defined under UGMA or UTMA), property you gave your child will be included in your estate for estate tax purposes. One solution to this problem is to have your spouse act as the custodian. However, this too can be a problem in some states if your spouse is legally obligated to support your minor child and state law does not preclude the use of custodial funds for this purpose. Consult competent legal advice before proceeding. A better strategy would be to choose another family member or friend to act as custodian. By so doing, you have effectively resolved this problem.

- Your child can sue the custodian. This may sound far-fetched, but it does happen. Once your child reaches the age of majority as defined under UGMA or UTMA, he or she has the legal right to request an accounting of how his or her money has been handled. If it has been handled improperly in the eyes of the courts, the custodian could be held personally liable.

- Income from the custodial account may be taxed to you or your child at your tax rate. If your child is under the age of 14 and receives unearned income in excess of $1,500 (for 1998 and indexed each year for inflation), that excess income will be taxed at your highest marginal tax rate. This is what is commonly referred to as the "kiddie tax." Once the child turns age 14, all income is then taxed at the child's tax bracket.

If you prefer to exercise more control over your gifts to your children than allowed under custodial accounts, then you will need to consider either a 2503(b) Trust or a 2503(c) Trust. These are both minor's trusts and are named after the applicable Internal Revenue Code section.

2503(b) Trust

The primary advantage of this trust is that the trustee is never required to distribute principal to your child. The trustee must, however, distribute all the income on at least an annual basis. Gifts to the trust do qualify for the Annual Gift Tax Exclusion, but only as related to the present value of the future income stream. For example, you contribute $10,000 to a trust for your 5-year-old daughter. The Internal Revenue Service interest rate assumption is 8 percent. Considering these facts, the value of your gift was $9,702 which qualifies for the $10,000 Annual Gift Tax Exclusion (calendar year 1998). $298 is considered a gift of a future interest and you must either pay gift taxes on this amount or use part of your lifetime Applicable Exclusion Amount. This trust can also be structured to allow the trustee to distribute principal under certain conditions. This type of trust requires the filing of an annual gift tax return in any year that a gift is made. The trustee must also apply for and receive a tax identification number. A separate trust must be set up for each beneficiary.

2503(c) Trust

I have found that, because of greater flexibility and control, clients are more willing to consider the 2503(c) Trust arrangement. This type of trust allows the trustee to either distribute or accumulate trust income. The trust document can also allow the trustee to make distributions of trust corpus for predetermined reasons or at the trustee's discretion. Any income not distributed will be taxed to the trust. Income distributed to your child will be taxed at your child's tax bracket if your child is age 14 or older. The "kiddie tax" rules apply for children under the age of 14.

The primary disadvantage of the 2503(c) Trust is that your child has a legal right to all trust assets when he or she turns age 21. This is a result that many of my clients wish to avoid. The best solution is to incorporate a "Crummey Power" in your trust document. This is the same concept we discussed in Chapter 8 regarding the Irrevocable Life Insurance Trust. When your child reaches age 21, your trustee would send your child a notice of his or her right to take title to all trust assets. If he or she fails to exercise his or her right within a certain time period (usually 30 days), the child's right to take possession of the trust assets will expire. The trust then continues to be managed for your child's benefit until your child reaches a certain age which you choose. As with the custodial accounts and the 2503(b) trust, this trust is irrevocable. Once you have made the gifts, you cannot get your assets back. Gifts to the trust do qualify for the Annual Gift Tax Exclusion.

OTHER TAX FREE GIFTS

In addition to your annual and lifetime gift tax exclusions, you receive an unlimited annual exclusion for the payment of a donee's medical expenses or tuition. I have seen this particularly useful where one of my Retiree clients is already making maximum annual gifts to grandchildren. They can then pay the tuition costs or medical costs of the grandchild without incurring gift taxes. For these payments to qualify for the unlimited annual exclusion, they must be made *directly* to the qualifying educational institution or medical provider. These payments are not tax deductible by the donor or donee.

One gift that qualifies for the annual exclusion but is still includable in your estate is a gift of life insurance within three years of your death. In this case, all of the life insurance proceeds would be included in your estate for estate tax purposes. For example, you decide that you want to remove your $250,000 term life insurance policy from your estate by transferring the ownership to your adult son. You do so, but die within three years of the gift. The result is that the $250,000 of life insurance proceeds will be included as part of your estate for the purpose of calculating your estate taxes.

FAMILY GIFTS UTILIZING TRUSTS

Thus far we have primarily discussed outright gifts to family members. There can also be significant advantages to making gifts to family members through the use of trusts. Two primary benefits include control issues and the possibility of receiving substantial valuation discounts for such gifts. Some of the more often used trusts include the Grantor Retained Annuity Trust, the Grantor Retained Unitrust, and the Qualified Personal Residence Trust.

Grantor Retained Annuity Trust

A Grantor Retained Annuity Trust (GRAT) allows you to make a substantial gift to a child (or anyone) at a significant reduction or elimination of gift taxes while you retain an income interest for a stated period of time.

Because your beneficiary is only receiving "what's left" at the end of the trust term, his or her interest is considered a *future* interest and not a present interest. Here's how this works:

- You, the grantor, establish an irrevocable trust in which you retain a fixed income interest. This fixed income can either be based on a fixed dollar amount or a fixed percent based on the initial asset value transferred.

- You determine the number of years the trust will last. The trust period can be any period of time. The longer the period of time, the smaller the amount of the gift to your beneficiaries is in the eyes of the Internal Revenue Service.

- You determine who the remainder beneficiaries will be (typically your children or grandchildren).

- You transfer assets into your GRAT.

- You receive the designated income stream for the designated term of the trust.

- At the end of the trust term, the remaining assets revert to your beneficiaries. This reversion can either be outright or in trust.

When you transfer assets into your trust, you have made a gift for gift tax purposes. To determine the value of your gift, you subtract the present value of your future stream of income from the value of your original contribution to your GRAT.

Advantages

- The primary advantage of a GRAT is that it allows you to give away a large asset while paying little or no gift taxes.

- The gift, while being a gift of a future interest, represents the immediate transfer of an asset. As a result, any *appreciation* of that asset will accrue to the benefit of your beneficiaries and will not be included in your estate.

- As grantor, you retain the income from the trust during the term of the trust.

- You can act as the trustee of your GRAT if the trust is properly drafted.

Disadvantages

- One of the primary disadvantages of the GRAT is that if you die during the term of the trust, the assets revert back to your estate for estate tax purposes. For planning purposes, you will want to choose a trust term that you are likely to survive.

- A GRAT is an irrevocable trust, and therefore, you have permanently given up the right to your principal.

- The GRAT is a grantor trust, and as such, all income is taxed to the grantor (you) whether or not it is paid to the grantor.

- Your beneficiaries' interest in the trust is a future interest, and therefore, does not qualify for the Annual Gift Tax Exclusion. Your only alternatives are to pay the gift taxes associated with the gift or use a portion of your lifetime Applicable Exclusion Amount.

- The income that you receive is a fixed income, and therefore, may not adequately offset the future ravages of inflation.

Grantor Retained Unitrust

The Grantor Retained Unitrust (GRUT), while very similar to the GRAT, has several significant differences. The key distinction has to do with how your income is determined. As discussed previously, with a GRAT you receive a fixed income. Under a GRUT, the income you receive is variable. Say that you (at age 50) place $500,000 into a GRUT and elect a 7 percent income. The first year your income would be $35,000. If next year, the account grew to $550,000 your income would be 7 percent of the new balance, or $38,500. If, however, the account decreased to $450,000 your income would only be $31,500. If the assets that you are transferring to your trust are likely to appreciate at a greater rate than your withdrawal rate and you want an increasing income, then you should consider a GRUT.

Look at Table 9-2 for an example of how the mathematics can work for a GRAT versus a GRUT.

TABLE 9-2
BENEFITS COMPARISON OF GRAT VS. GRUT

ASSUMPTIONS: $500,000 CONTRIBUTION, 20 YEAR TERM, 7% WITHDRAWAL RATE, 9% RETURN ON INVESTMENTS

GRAT: $145,000 Present Value of Gift			GRUT: $155,995 Present Value of Gift		
Year	Annual Distribution to Donor	Value of Remainder Interest	Year	Annual Distribution to Donor	Value of Remainder Interest
1	$35,000	$ 0	1	$38,150	$ 0
2	$35,000	$ 0	2	$38,673	$ 0
3	$35,000	$ 0	3	$39,202	$ 0
4	$35,000	$ 0	4	$39,740	$ 0
5	$35,000	$ 0	5	$40,284	$ 0
6	$35,000	$ 0	6	$40,836	$ 0
7	$35,000	$ 0	7	$41,395	$ 0
8	$35,000	$ 0	8	$41,962	$ 0
9	$35,000	$ 0	9	$42,537	$ 0
10	$35,000	$ 0	10	$43,120	$ 0
11	$35,000	$ 0	11	$43,711	$ 0
12	$35,000	$ 0	12	$44,310	$ 0
13	$35,000	$ 0	13	$44,917	$ 0
14	$35,000	$ 0	14	$45,532	$ 0
15	$35,000	$ 0	15	$46,156	$ 0
16	$35,000	$ 0	16	$46,788	$ 0
17	$35,000	$ 0	17	$47,429	$ 0
18	$35,000	$ 0	18	$48,079	$ 0
19	$35,000	$ 0	19	$48,738	$ 0

continued on next page

Year	Annual Distribution to Donor	Value of Remainder Interest	Year	Annual Distribution to Donor	Value of Remainder Interest
20	$ 35,000	$ 0	20	$ 49,405	$ 0
21	$ 0	$1,011,601	21	$ 0	$656,385
	$700,000	$1,011,601		$870,964	$656,385

Calculations courtesy of Comdel, Inc., Crescendo Planned Gifts Marketing Software
Charles Schultz, President/Author 800-858-9154

QUALIFIED PERSONAL RESIDENCE TRUST

When someone is trying to reduce the size of their estate in order to reduce taxes, the notion of gifting their residence rarely comes to mind. If done properly, the gifting of a residence can have significant tax benefits without limiting one's use of the residence. One of the best methods to do this is called a Qualified Personal Residence Trust (QPRT).

In working with clients who have taxable estates, I have often found that they are much more willing to give away their residence if they have the right to continue to live there, rather than giving away their securities or cash, which often represent their security against unknown financial circumstances such as an illness. In other cases, the residence may be one of the only available assets to give.

How to Set Up a QPRT

- Under a Qualified Personal Residence Trust, an individual, known as a grantor, irrevocably transfers his or her primary or secondary residence to a trust for a fixed period of time, say 10 to 15 years.

- During the term of the trust, the grantor retains the right to use and occupy the personal residence on an unrestricted basis.

- At the end of the term, the residence then passes to the designated beneficiaries known as remaindermen (usually your children).

- At the end of the term, the grantor then leases the residence back from the remaindermen. These lease payments do not interfere with his or her ability to make annual gifts each year.

Tax Treatment

Since the remaindermen will not receive the gift for 10 to 15 years, you are allowed a discount based on the present value of that future gift. The amount of the discount is determined by Internal Revenue Service tables. This allows you to significantly discount the value of the gift. Let's take the example of John and Sue Smith. John, age 67 and Sue, age 64, have a total estate exceeding $3,000,000. Of that, approximately $1,000,000 is in real estate consisting of their primary home and their vacation home. Their primary residence has a market value of $450,000. They have a strong desire to keep the home and a strong desire to reduce their taxes as their estate continues to grow. John and Sue decide to establish a QPRT and transfer their residence into the trust for 15 years. At the end of that time, the home will be transferred to their two adult children. Since the gift of the property to the trust is irrevocable, it creates a completed gift for gift tax purposes. Because the beneficiaries will not receive the property until the end of the 15 year period of time, it is a gift of future interest rather than a gift of present interest. Therefore, it qualifies for a discount. For federal gift tax purposes, the value of the gift, based on IRS discount tables, is only $95,000. They will use a portion of their lifetime Applicable Exclusion Amount to pay the gift taxes due.

For the Smiths, life has changed very little. They continue to live in their home just as they always have. At the end of the 15 year period, when the property does revert to their children, they will establish a lease that requires that they pay rent to the children, which further reduces their estate. It should be noted that these rental payments do not limit their Annual Gift Tax Exclusion.

Advantages

There are many advantages to setting up a Qualified Personal Residence Trust. Among them are:

- In many cases, it is more palatable to give away your residence rather than cash or securities in order to reduce estate taxes. By holding onto your stocks, bonds, and cash, you can feel more secure about handling a significant financial emergency if one should occur. However, by giving away the house while retaining the right to live in it, you have not changed your lifestyle, even though you have made a significant move toward reducing the value of your current and future estate.

- You have effectively removed a large asset from your estate at a significant discount from its current value. The Smiths were able to give away an asset worth $450,000 for $95,000.

- You remove the *growth* of your residence from your estate. If the Smiths' home continued to appreciate over the next 15 years at 5 percent, it would be worth $935,000. By giving their home away now, they saved the taxes on the additional $485,000 of appreciation.

- You have entirely avoided probate on your residence because it is passing to your heirs through the trust instead of under your will.

- At the end of the trust term, you are allowed to increase your annual gifting by paying rent to your heirs. These payments will not be included as part of your allowable Annual Gift Tax Exclusion.

Disadvantages

There are also several disadvantages to a Qualified Personal Residence Trust:

- If you die during the term of the trust, the value of the personal residence will be included in your estate for estate tax purposes. While this result is not what you hoped for, it is not as bad as it seems. The property would receive a "stepped-up" cost basis and any Applicable Credit Amount that has been used would be retrieved. In other words, for federal estate tax purposes, it is as if the transaction never occurred. You have, however, gone to the trouble and expense of setting up the trust and received no benefit.

- When you transfer the residence, the beneficiaries will receive the same tax basis as you had upon the date of transfer. However, if you had held the residence until your death, they would have received a "stepped-up" cost basis based on the value at the date of death. In that case, they could have then sold the home without owing capital gains taxes.

- At the end of the term the residence may not be available for your use. Technically, the home is now the property of the remaindermen (your children) rather than your property. They must allow you to continue to live in the residence presumably under some arrangement whereby you would be paying them rent.

- If the residence is sold, the $250,000 ($500,000 for married couples) *exclusion for gain on sale of residence* is not available because it is no longer your residence.

- If there is a mortgage on the property, any payments on that mortgage are considered a gift to the remaindermen.

As you can see from the above examples, the potential tax savings through a Qualified Personal Residence Trust can be significant. If the Smiths did not die in the 16th year, but lived well beyond that, the value of the tax savings would increase because the continuing appreciation of the property has been removed from their estate. They could also make rent payments to the children in addition to their Annual Gift Tax Exclusion. This allows them to continue to move more and more assets out of their estate.

Death During the Term of the Trust

As the grantor, you can receive a larger discount by creating a **contingent reversionary interest**. With a contingent reversionary interest, you state in the trust agreement that if you die before the trust term expires, your last will and testament will determine who receives the trust property.

If the grantor dies during the term of the trust, the property is included in the grantor's estate, and at that time, receives a stepped-up cost basis based on the fair market value at the date of death. Also, any Applicable Credit Amount that was used to transfer the property to the trust will be revived to the benefit of the grantor. In other words, it is as if this deal were never done.

CASE STUDY

Let's look at a case example of how a Qualified Personal Residence Trust can reduce estate taxes for our friends John and Sue Smith. In order to simplify the case and focus on the value of QPRT, I have assumed that all assets except for the home do not increase in value and that the term of the trust was 15 years.

SCENARIO 1

The Smiths die at the beginning of the 16th year with no planning.

$1,000,000	Misc. Assets (Future growth at 0% growth rate)
+ 935,000	Residence ($450,000 current value at 5% growth rate)
$1,935,000	Estate Value in 16 years
- 751,550	Tenative Estate Tax (see Table 2-2, p. 19)
+ 345,800	Applicable Credit Amount (see Table 2-3, p. 20)
$ 405,750	Tax Due

SCENARIO 2

The Smiths transfer their residence to a Qualified Personal Residence Trust with their two children as remaindermen and die 16 years later.

$1,000,000	Misc. Assets (Future growth at 0% growth rate)
+ 0	Residence
$1,000,000	
- 345,800	Tenative Estate Tax
+ 323,400	Applicable Credit Amount *
$ 22,400	Tax Due

(Assumes the Smiths use $95,000 of their Applicable Exclusion Amount to make the initial gift to the trust.)

TAKING ADVANTAGE OF
GENERATION SKIPPING TRANSFERS (GST)

Prior to 1976, there were no laws that prevented you from leaving large amounts of assets in trust for multiple generations of family members. For example, you could place several million dollars in a trust that provided for a lifetime of income for your children and grandchildren. As long as your children did not have a "general power of appointment" the assets would not be included in their estates for estate tax purposes. Passage of the Generation Skipping Transfer Tax in 1976 significantly reduced one's ability to pass money to multiple generations without a transfer tax. While transfer opportunities have been reduced, they have not been eliminated. Therein lies the opportunity.

Let's begin with an examination of the rules surrounding generation skipping transfers (GST):

- A "skip" generation refers to family members one generation removed as would be the case of a gift from a grandparent to a grandchild. If the gift is to a non-family member, a person is considered a skip person if they are at least 37 1/2 years younger than the transferor.

- The generation skipping transfer tax that is imposed is based on the highest marginal estate and gift tax rate (currently 55 percent).

- There are three categories of transfers that can occur. The first is called a **direct skip**. Direct skips occur when you gift assets directly to a generation skip person. For example, a direct skip would occur if you gave $100,000 directly to a grandchild or if you gave $100,000 to a trust in which your grandchild was the sole beneficiary. Any GST tax due must be paid at the time of the transfer. The transferor can elect to pay the tax himself/herself or he/she can elect to have the taxes paid out of the gifted proceeds. The next category of GST occurs where there is a **taxable termination**. A taxable termination occurs when assets have been placed into a trust for multiple generations of family members and the last non-skip family member ceases to be a beneficiary of the trust. For example, you place $500,000 in a trust which will provide a lifetime income for your child. At your child's death, the trust will continue to provide a lifetime income for your grandchild. When your child dies a taxable termination has occurred and at that time your trustee would be required to pay any GST tax due out of trust assets. The final category of skip transfers relates to **taxable distributions**. A taxable distribution occurs at the time your trustee makes a distribution to a skip person. For example, you place $500,000 into a trust for the benefit of your children *and* grandchildren. If your trustee makes a distribution to a grandchild (a skip person), a taxable distribution has occurred and any taxes due must be paid out of that distribution.

So far, the GST rules do not sound very appealing. The opportunity lies in three exceptions to the GST tax rules:

1. **Deceased Child Exception.** This exception provides that if a child has predeceased you and has left children of his or her own, your gifts to that grandchild are not subject to the GST tax.

2. **$10,000 Annual GST Exclusion.** Similar to your Annual Gift Tax Exclusion, the GST exclusion provides that no GST tax is due for the first $10,000 per year of gifts to a skip person. This $10,000 per year will increase in future years due to special inflation indexing.

3. **$1 Million GST Exemption.** This important exception provides that gifts of up to $1 million (indexed for inflation) can be made to skip persons free of the GST tax. This exemption is automatically applied to direct skips. It is not automatically applied to non-direct skips and therefore care should be taken when drafting trusts that are likely to result in non-direct skips. Note that the $1 million GST exemption is available to all individuals, therefore parents' combined exemption equals $2 million.

CASE STUDY 1

Joan and Max Dole would like to make a large gift to their son and possibly their grandchildren. In our discussions, I discover that their son is likely to accumulate a large estate on his own. I explain that if the Doles make gifts to their son either directly or in trust, that substantial estate taxes will likely be due when he dies. As an alternative, I recommend that they consider a GST trust. They will use part of their (combined) lifetime Applicable Exclusion Amount to make a tax-free gift of $1,000,000 to a trust that will provide income to their son for his lifetime. At his death the assets will remain in trust for the benefit of the grandchildren. By electing the GST exemption, there will be no estate taxes due at the son's death. Using this strategy, the parents have removed the *growth* on the $1,000,000 from their estate and have avoided future estate taxes at their son's death thus preserving a much larger benefit for their grandchildren. Since each parent has a $1 million GST exemption, we structured their wills in order to take advantage of their remaining GST exemption at their death.

CASE STUDY 2

Jim and Sandra Manasco have expressed a desire to establish a gifting program to benefit their children and grandchildren. While their investments produce a large income for them, they are not comfortable making large "lump sum" gifts. They are also concerned that gifts might "spoil" their children. I recommend that they consider using their $10,000 Annual GST Exclusion to purchase a $1.5 million survivorship life insurance policy. A GST trust would be the owner and beneficiary. As a result, after the second person has died, the GST trust would be funded with $1.5 million which would benefit both their children and their grandchildren. Trust provisions would allow the trustee to make distributions to either the children or the grandchildren. In cases where life insurance is being used to "leverage" generation skipping transfers, it is important to file a gift tax return requesting that the GST exemption be applied to the gifts.

LOANS AND SALES TO FAMILY MEMBERS

There are many estate planning advantages to loaning family members money as well as sales of assets to family members. Particularly effective are installment sales and the private annuity.

Installment Sales to Family Members

Installment sales between family members are set up like any other installment sale. You determine a fair market price and then arrange repayment terms based on a market interest rate. If the sale was to include a below market price or below market interest rate, the Internal Revenue Service considers that you have made a gift for gift tax purposes. Advantages of asset sales to family members include:

- A sale of an asset to a family member removes the *appreciation* of the asset from your estate. *John owns stock in his closely held business. At some point in the future, he plans to take his company public, at which point he expects the value to appreciate dramatically. John's son, John, Jr., also works in the business but owns no stock. By selling John, Jr. stock now, John, Sr. is able to transfer the future growth out of his estate.*

- An installment sale to a family member keeps the asset in the family. *Sara Smith inherited the family farm from her parents and has a strong desire to keep the farm in the family. She sells the farm to her two children on an installment sale basis. The payments to her total $2,000 per month. Sara uses her Annual Gift Tax Exclusion to give each child $10,000 toward payment of their share of the note.*

- An installment sale prevents a family member from receiving "wealth" too quickly. *Tom Jones sells his children an apartment building that he owns. The apartment building currently produces $40,000 per year of net income. The installment note requires payments of $4,000 per month for 240 months. The children have purchased a valuable asset that will increase their net worth as it appreciates, but will receive little in the way of cash benefits for many years. Their incentive to "fend for themselves" is unhampered.*

- An installment sale provides you with a continuing income stream. Not everyone can afford to give away their assets. You may be in a situation where you do not need the asset, but you do need the income it produces. An installment sale to a family member may provide the ideal solution. You remove the appreciating asset from your estate while retaining the income for an extended period of time.

- The buyer's "cost basis" in the property is based on the price they paid, which is presumably the fair market value. If they had received the property as a gift, their basis would be the same as the donor's basis. This will likely result in less taxes upon a subsequent sale.

As with most strategies, installment sales also have some disadvantages.

- You have not entirely removed the asset from your estate. The value of the note receivable will be included in your estate.

- You have given up control of the property.

- You have accepted a "fixed" payment that will not be adjusted for inflation.

- You must recognize the gain on the sale for income tax purposes. Since it is an installment sale, taxes are due only as you receive your note payments.

- If the property is resold within two years, you may incur an acceleration of income taxes. This creates the possibility of owing income taxes without having cash to pay them.

Setting Your Interest Rate

When you are deciding what interest rate to charge your family member, you must choose a rate that is considered a "fair market rate." If you choose a below-market rate, the difference between the fair market rate and the rate you charged will be "imputed" to you for income tax purposes. Likewise, this difference in rate can be imputed as an interest deduction for the buyer. I once purchased an office building from a seller who was insistent on receiving his offering price, but was very negotiable on the terms. I offered full price but with zero interest and annual payments over nine years. He accepted. Even though according to my note, I was paying no interest, I was able to take an imputed interest payment deduction of 7 percent.

So how do you determine what a "fair" interest rate is? Fortunately, the Internal Revenue provides you with the answer under Code Section 1272 entitled "Applicable Federal Rates." These rates change from year to year but are often less than a buyer could receive if he or she sought traditional financing.

An installment sale can be combined with annual gifts to family members to magnify the power of the transaction. You sell property "A" to your son in return for a note with a market rate of interest. The note payments equal $9,500 each year for 12 years. In January of each year, you give your son $10,000 as a tax-free gift. He then uses the gift to make the note payment. You can manipulate the term of the note to make certain that the payments fall within the allowed Annual Gift Tax Exclusion. For example, if the property was valued at $100,000 and the federal interest rate was 6 percent, a 10-year term would result in payments of $13,587. By increasing the term to 16 years, you would cut the annual payments to under $10,000.

Remember that whether you give your child the money to make the note payments or simply "forgive" the note, you are still responsible for reporting and paying the income tax on the note interest. While you have not received the interest, it has been "imputed" to you.

THE PRIVATE ANNUITY

A Private Annuity is the sale of property by one family member (the annuitant), to another family member (the obligor) in exchange for an unsecured promise by the obligor to make payments to the annuitant for the rest of the annuitant's life.

Advantages

- The property and its future appreciation are removed from your estate, thus you avoid all estate taxes.
- Since this is a sale, there are no gift taxes to pay.
- You receive a lifetime income.

- The capital gains on the sale are spread over your life expectancy.

- The property is maintained within the family. This can be particularly important with closely held business interest or family land.

- If you die "prematurely" (before your life expectancy), the annuity payments end immediately and there is no remaining value in the annuity. This is unlike the installment sale in which case the note payments would continue and the present value of those payments would be included in your estate.

Disadvantages

- The note payments cannot be secured by the trust property or any other asset.

- Your children (the obligors), bear the risk that you will "outlive" the actuarial tables.

LOANS TO FAMILY MEMBERS

Unlike installment sales to family members, loans to family members offer little in the way of estate planning benefits. If you charge a below-market interest rate, you will have income imputed to you and you will have been deemed to have made a gift based on the value of the "bargain" amount. A related technique that some people use is to make a loan to a child and then use their Annual Gift Tax Exclusion to "forgive" all or a portion of the note payments each year. It should be noted that this does not relieve you of your income tax liability. One possible estate tax advantage occurs if your child is able to earn a higher rate of return on your loan than you are currently earning.

David has $200,000 in certificates of deposits earning 6 percent. David's son, James, wants to start a business that requires $100,000 of capital but James lacks the ability to borrow the money. David loans him the money, charging him 6 percent (or the Applicable Federal Rate whichever is greater). His business is successful and earns on average 15 percent per year. David has effectively helped leverage his son's net worth while earning at least as high an interest as he was earning before.

In this chapter, we discussed the various tax advantages and strategies revolving around gifts, sales, and loans to family members. There can also be substantial tax advantages to making gifts to charities. This subject will be explored in detail in our next chapter.

CHAPTER 10

Strategic Planning with Charities

I f you are inclined to leave part of your estate to charity, there are many strategies available that let you provide funds to your favorite charities while also providing estate and income tax benefits for you and your family. These strategies range from the simplicity of outright gifts to the very complex strategies which utilize specialized trusts. Tax-exempt organizations generally include traditional charities such as the Red Cross as well as qualified educational institutions and religious organizations. Before making donations to any organizations, you should confirm that the group or foundation qualifies as a tax-deductible charity. A list of qualified (non-religious) charities is available from the Internal Revenue Service Publication # 78 entitled "Cumulative List of Organizations Described in Section 170(c) of the Internal Revenue Code." Leave it to the Internal Revenue Service to come up with a "snappy" title! This is a massive publication so your best bet is to visit your local library.

Let's begin discussing the various issues involved in outright gifts to charities and then review the more complex concepts that utilize trusts.

OUTRIGHT GIFTS TO CHARITIES

By far the most common way that people donate to charities is through outright gifts. They will either write a check or donate items of clothing or other property. However, I often find that people make mistakes when donating assets to charities which result in less effective ways to reduce their estates. Once you have decided to make a donation to a charitable organization, you want to maximize the benefit to both you and the charity. Let's examine the pros and cons of various outright gifts to charities.

Gifts of Cash

Here you typically write a check or give cash. For contributions in excess of $250, you must receive and maintain a written acknowledgment from the charity. The advantages of these types of gifts include simplicity and full tax deductibility as well as the fact that you have removed the asset from your estate. One disadvantage is that you create very little leverage. You have a dollar; you give a dollar; you receive a dollar tax deduction. Depending on what type of assets you have, it may be preferable for you to donate some asset other than cash.

Gifts of Property

The types of property that you can give are as varied as the types of property you own. For example, you might own an old car that is in excellent condition but has little resale value. This can make a wonderful donation because a needy charity can benefit from use of your car.

　　If you give property such as real estate or securities, you not only remove the asset from your estate, but you also remove the future growth of that asset from your estate. The actual transfer of your property to your selected charity can take some time. If you are giving securities that are held in a brokerage account, usually the simplest way to complete the transfer is to have your charity open an account at the same brokerage firm. You can then write your broker a letter and have him or her "journal" your selected securities over to the charity's account. For real property or tangible personal property, you will have to have the deed or title transferred into the name of the charity.

Gifts of Appreciated Property

The best way to create leverage through outright gifts is by giving away appreciated property. Assume that you have made a $10,000 pledge to your church's building campaign. You are trying to decide between writing a check or giving the Coca-Cola stock that you bought 15 years ago for $1,000. You had planned to hold this stock as part of your long-term investment program. You are sentimental about your Coca-Cola stock and believe it will continue to be a good investment in the future. So what should you do?

You should give away the stock. By doing so, you create excellent leverage. If you had to sell the stock now, perhaps because of an emergency, you would incur substantial capital gains taxes. Even though you only paid $1,000 for the stock, when you give it to your church, you will receive a deduction for its full market value ($10,000). If you want to maintain the stock for your long-term investment program, you can simply buy the stock using the $10,000 cash you had planned to give your church. The result of these transactions is that you now own $10,000 worth of Coca-Cola stock with a $10,000 cost basis. Now, if you have an emergency, you could sell your Coca-Cola stock and owe no taxes on the first $10,000 of proceeds. Since your church is treated as a charity for tax purposes, when the charity sells the stock you gave them, it is a non-taxable event.

Gifts of appreciated securities and real estate are by far the most effective way to make outright gifts. For you to receive a deduction for fair market value on gifts of tangible personal property, the gift must be one that the charity can use as part of the charity's purpose. For example, the gift of a tractor to your church would likely only qualify for a deduction based on your "cost basis" in the tractor since it is not something that your church normally uses as part of its operations.

Gifts to Public Foundations

Like many people, you may have numerous charities that you would like to help. However, the transfer process described previously would be too burdensome for small contributions. Transfers would also not work if you want a deduction in this calendar year, but are undecided on the amount of your donations and to what charities to give. One excellent alternative is the **public foundation**. You are allowed to make a gift to foundations in cash, securities, or property and receive an immediate tax deduction. The foundation then holds your assets until you give them instructions on the disposition of your property to the charities you have chosen. Most of these public foundations can even provide you with information about the worthiness of charities you may be considering. For this service, you are charged a small fee that is usually based on a percentage of your contribution.

Tax Deduction Limitations on Outright Gifts

Generally, you will receive a full tax deduction for gifts totaling up to 50 percent of your adjusted gross income (AGI) during any calendar year. If your gift is to a non-public charity, your deduction is restricted to 30 percent of your adjusted gross income. Gifts in excess of these amounts can be carried forward for up to five years.

TESTAMENTARY GIFTS TO CHARITIES

Often people will make bequests to charities in their will. This is a wonderful idea and the charities are certainly delighted to receive the money. But, if you do not need the money, you can create more tax leverage by making your donation while you are alive. Say that you intend to give a certain piece of property worth $100,000 to charity. If you leave it to charity under your will, there will be no estate taxes. However, if you give it to charity while you are alive, you will not only have removed it from your estate for estate tax purposes, but you will also receive a current income tax deduction worth $30,000 to $40,000! Consider *lifetime* gifts if you do not need the asset.

GIFTS USING CHARITABLE TRUSTS

With outright gifts, you donate cash or property to a charity and receive a tax deduction. This is the only monetary benefit to you. If you are looking for additional benefits such as a continuing income stream for yourself or a portion of your assets passed to family members, you may want to consider using one or more charitable trusts. These "designer" trusts can be structured to achieve a variety of personal and charitable objectives. If you want to convert highly appreciated non-income producing property into income-producing property while avoiding large capital gains taxes, then you might consider a **Charitable Remainder Trust**. If you would like to see your favorite charity receive a stream of income from one of your assets, but want the property to remain in your family, then you should consider a **Charitable Lead Trust**. Maybe you would like to leave a lasting legacy of charitable giving for your heirs. This can be accomplished by establishing a **Private Foundation**.

Charitable Remainder Annuity Trust
The Charitable Remainder Annuity Trust (CRAT) is an ideal vehicle for taking appreciated non-income producing property and converting it into

assets that can provide you or a family member with current income. Let's say that you are age 55, and own a piece of raw land that is currently valued at $900,000. Your cost basis in the property is $90,000. You are considering an early retirement, but would need to convert assets to produce an income stream. Your first thought is to sell the property and reinvest the proceeds in income-producing assets such as government bonds. The results of the sale would be as follows:

Step 1: Determine the tax

$ 900,000	Current Value of Land
- 90,000	Cost Basis of Land
$ 810,000	Taxable Gain
× .20	Capital Gains Tax Rate
$ 162,000	Capital Gains Tax

Step 2: Determine the income

$ 900,000	Proceeds From Sale
- 162,000	Capital Gains Taxes
$ 738,000	Available to Reinvest
× .06	Expected Earnings (6%)
$ 44,280	Income Earned Annually

If you were a client, I would instead advise you to consider a Charitable Remainder Annuity Trust. Since you have a charitable interest in your alma mater, you ask me to run through the numbers with you. Here's how it would work: You can decide what interest rate you would like to receive and whom you would like to act as your trustee. In this case, you choose 6 percent and elect to serve as trustee yourself. We have your attorney draft the document formalizing the trust. Your attorney then assists you with transferring the deed from your name as an individual to your name as trustee. Once the property is transferred, as trustee you sell it for $900,000. Because it is a charitable trust, there are no taxes on the proceeds. You then place the entire sum in investments of your choosing. As trustee, you have full discretion over investment decisions. Since you elected a 6 percent payout, you will withdraw $54,000 annually for as long as you live. Not only will you increase your income, but you will receive an income tax deduction in the amount of $329,900!

You love the idea but have two concerns. First, you are worried about your spouse's continuing need for income should you predecease her. Next, you are concerned about some potentially very unhappy heirs—your children. Since at your death, the remainder goes to your alma mater, the children will receive nothing! To resolve the spousal issue, we set the trust up so that the income is paid over *both* of your lives. As long as either one of you is living, the trust will continue to pay $54,000 per year. The only thing this adjustment affects is your initial tax deduction. If your spouse were age 52, the tax deduction would be $238,900.

The issue concerning your children presents a more challenging, yet solvable problem. Perhaps the best solution would be to take your tax savings dollars and purchase a survivorship life insurance policy on the life of you and your spouse. An example of a $900,000 survivorship life policy is represented in Table 10-1. This policy should be purchased using an irrevocable insurance trust as described in Chapter 8. If your children are adults, an alternative would be to have them be the owner and beneficiary of the policy with you gifting them the cash to pay the premiums.

The Wealth Transfer Effect

Under this scenario, your goal has been to convert a non-income producing asset into one that produces income. This satisfies an income need, but what about your estate planning goals? You have removed $900,000 from your estate by way of the charitable trust and have used part of your tax savings to buy life insurance which will be received by your children income and estate tax free.

As you can see, the intelligent use of a charitable trust can create what I call the "triple win." You win because you receive more income during your lifetime. Your children win because they receive a larger inheritance. And your alma mater wins because it receives a larger sum than it would have likely received under other circumstances.

TABLE 10-1
SURVIVORSHIP LIFE INSURANCE
(MALE, AGE 55; FEMALE, AGE 52)

$900,000 (LEVEL DEATH BENEFIT)
WITH ANNUAL PREMIUM OF $5,180

Year	Cash Value	Death Benefit
1	$ 0	$ 900,000
10	$ 34,599	$ 900,000
20	$ 128,221	$ 900,000
30	$ 254,315	$ 900,000
40	$ 363,688	$ 900,000

$900,000 (INCREASING DEATH BENEFIT) WITH ANNUAL PREMIUM OF $6,950

Year	Cash Value	Death Benefit
1	$ 0	$ 903,360
10	$ 57,535	$ 963,232
20	$ 191,372	$1,091,372
30	$ 379,209	$1,279,210
40	$ 520,127	$1,420,127

One issue that might arise at this point is, that under the CRAT, what you receive is a fixed income that does not ever change. What about inflation? Inflation? Aw, CRUT! No, that's not a bad four-letter word; it stands for **Charitable Remainder Unitrust.** This type of trust addresses the issue of inflation.

Charitable Remainder Unitrust
Structurally, the CRUT is set up similarly to the CRAT. You establish the trust and transfer property into it. As trustee, you then sell the property and reinvest it as you wish. You receive an income from the trust during your

lifetime, and at your death, the remaining assets go to the charity of your choice. The income can be paid over the joint lives of you and your spouse if you desire. What is different, is how the income is figured. With a CRUT, you set an interest rate for purposes of calculating the amount of withdrawals that are due you each year. While the interest rate never changes, the amount of dollars you will receive will fluctuate based on the changing value of the account each year. For instance, in our earlier example you contributed $900,000 of real estate to your charitable trust, and from then on received $54,000 (6 percent) per year. The income amount never changed. Under a CRUT, you would receive 6 percent of the value of the account as of a certain date each year. If your account value increased to $1,000,000 in the second year, a 6 percent distribution would produce a $60,000 for you. This results in a growing income for you assuming your total account values grow. The opposite is also true. If the account values decrease, so will your distributions. Also, the federal discount tables used to calculate income tax deduction will result in a smaller deduction per dollar of contribution. Taking our same example as before and using a joint life payout for you and your spouse, your deduction under a CRUT would be $167,200 versus $238,900 for the CRAT. Since the account values of a CRUT must be determined each year, it is not an appropriate trust in which to place hard to value assets such as real estate or a closely held business interest.

USING YOUR CHARITABLE TRUST FOR RETIREMENT PLANNING

If you are a Baby Boomer, you are likely concerned about retirement planning. These are your big earning years and you will need to make the best of them. If you are fortunate enough to have an employer-provided retirement plan, then part of the job may be done for you. Many employer plans are of the 401(k) variety. These plans are very helpful, but are rarely sufficient to fully fund one's retirement. One way to supplement your retirement income is by establishing a Charitable Remainder Unitrust that contains several specialized provisions. You will need to use a CRUT, since it allows *annual* contributions whereas a CRAT does not. In this trust agreement you will include two special provisions.

- As with any CRUT, you elect to receive income each year based on a set percentage of the trust's value. In this case, you will add language that says that if the trust income is not sufficient to pay the percentage you elected, that the trustee will pay the *actual* income the trust produces. For example, you elect a 6 percent annual income distribution. The trust investments, however, only produce 1 percent income. The result is that only 1 percent is distributed to you. Note that this is a period of time in which you do not need additional income. You are still in your most productive earning years and your goal is to store up assets for your retirement.

- The next provision that you include in your trust is a "catch-up" provision. This says that any income "you were owed" but was not distributed, will be distributed to you when additional trust income is available.

Your initial trust investments will include assets that produce little or no income. This allows you to "store up" income for the future. Once you are ready to retire, you sell these investments and reinvest the proceeds in high income investments such as corporate bonds and CDs. The result is that your account achieves maximum growth during your working years and then is switched to maximum income during your retirement years. Any excess income earned by your trust can be paid out to you as part of the "catch-up" provision. Note that the sale of the appreciated securities does not result in any taxes because of the trust's tax exempt status. Let's review a Case Study to see how this might work (p. 198).

POOLED INCOME FUNDS

One disadvantage of the charitable remainder trust is the cost involved in setting up the trust. It can cost several hundred or even thousands of dollars to set one up and then you will also have annual maintenance costs. Your trustee must obtain a taxpayer ID number and file annual trust tax returns. There is also the matter of trustee duties. Your trustee (often you) is legally a fiduciary to the trust and is required to follow certain rules and procedures. Failure to do so can result in legal liability. If all of this sounds like more than you expected, then you might want to consider a **pooled income fund**.

> ### CASE STUDY
>
> Let's see how this might work for you. I will assume that you are age 40 and would like to supplement your retirement income by investing $30,000 per year. You would also like to benefit your favorite charity, the Make A Wish Foundation. We decide to establish a CRUT with a 6 percent payout and a "make-up" provision. You contribute $30,000 each January and invest in a diversified portfolio of growth stocks that pay little or no dividends. As it turns out, your portfolio earns an average rate of return of 12 percent from age 40 to your age 65. This results in your account growing to $4,480,000! You now sell all your growth stocks and invest in long-term corporate bonds with average yields of 8.5 percent. As you now begin taking income, your trust agreement allows for a 6 percent payout or $268,801. But your "make-up" provision now allows you to take the "excess" earnings as well. This extra 2.5 percent excess income amounts to an additional $112,000, bringing your total annual income to $380,801. You are allowed to continue to take the excess income distributions until all prior "deficits" have been exhausted. Remember that each time you make a contribution, you are receiving a partial tax deduction as well. You also can set the trust up so that the income is paid over both your life and the life of your spouse.

With a pooled income fund, the charity prepares all the documents and administers the fund for you (at no cost). You contribute property to the fund and receive *interest income units* during your lifetime or a specified period of time. Your deduction is calculated the same as with the charitable remainder trust. This type of trust has several advantages over the charitable remainder trust as well as some disadvantages.

Advantages

- Costs. The charity has undertaken the costs of establishing the trust and bears the ongoing costs of administration.

- Management. The charity hires professional managers to invest fund assets. This relieves you of that responsibility.

Disadvantages

- Inflexibility. Because the trust has been established by the charity, there is no opportunity to customize the document to your specific needs. You are also likely to encounter less flexibility in determining your income as well as how the investments will be structured.

- Taxation. All income from a Pooled Income Fund is considered ordinary income and is therefore taxed at your highest marginal tax rate. Income from a charitable remainder trust uses a tiered rate system that allows long-term capital gains and/or tax exempt income to flow through to you.

As a result of these disadvantages, the Pooled Income Fund is more appropriate in cases where your intended gift is relatively small (under $100,000). A perfect example would be a $25,000 gift to your alma mater. The size of this gift would make a charitable remainder trust impractical due to initial and ongoing costs. You would, however, receive the majority of the benefits of the charitable remainder trust.

CHARITABLE LEAD TRUST

With a Charitable Lead Trust, you and the charity literally switch positions. The charity receives the income from the trust for a specified period of time and the remainder interest then reverts to someone you designate (typically your child). This type of trust works well if:

1. You own income-producing property but you do not need the income or the asset.

2. You have a desire to divert the income to a charity for a period of time.

3. You would ultimately like to transfer the asset to a family member with little or no gift or estate taxes.

This trust can be set up as either an *inter vivos* (during your lifetime) trust or a *testamentary* (under your will) trust.

Advantages

- As stated earlier, the primary advantage of the charitable lead trust is that you are able to transfer a large asset to your children at significantly reduced gift tax costs.

- Not only do you remove the asset from your estate, you also re-move any *growth* on that asset from your estate.

- Contributions to a charitable lead trust are unlimited, whereas con-tributions to charitable remainder trusts limit your deduction to 50 percent of AGI (30 percent for non-public charities).

Disadvantages

- Contributions to a charitable lead trust provide you with a gift tax deduction rather than an income tax deduction unless the trust is set up as a grantor trust. The rules regarding *grantor charitable lead trust* will tend to reduce the effectiveness of wealth transfers to your children.

- Trust income is taxed to the trust to the extent that it exceeds the income paid to the charity. For example, if you set your trust up to pay 6 percent annually to the designated charity, but the trust in-come is actually 7 percent, the excess 1 percent will be taxed di-rectly to the trust. In the case of a grantor trust, excess income will be taxed to the grantor.

- Capital gains are not a tax-free event as they are with a charitable remainder trust. If the trustee sells an appreciated asset, the gain will be taxed to the trust. Therefore, you will want to contribute assets that you have no intention of selling or that are not likely to appreciate in value.

- When the trust ends and the remaining assets revert to your chil-dren, this is considered a gift of a future interest, and therefore, does not qualify for your Annual Gift Tax Exclusion. You must either pay the gift taxes or use part of your lifetime Applicable Ex-clusion Amount. Also, there are legal costs for setting up this trust; annual accounting costs for maintaining the trust; and duties that must be carried out by the trustee.

THE PRIVATE FOUNDATION

A Private Foundation can create a perpetual legacy of charitable giving for your descendants while accomplishing significant estate planning objectives for yourself. With a private foundation, you are, in effect, establishing your own tax-exempt organization for the purpose of benefiting charities, educational institutions, and/or religious organizations. Then, either during your life or at your death (under your will), you contribute money or property to your foundation. The income tax deduction during your lifetime is limited to 30 percent of your adjusted gross income. You may act as the trustee and designate family members as successor trustees. The trustees can be paid "reasonable" income from the trust for their services. Let's look at the advantages and disadvantages of this strategy.

Advantages

- Lifetime gifts to your private foundation generate an income tax deduction within certain limitations.

- Your foundation can create a lasting memorial to your family in much the same way as the Rockefellers and Kennedys have done.

- You can use your foundation to aid a specific cause such as child abuse or you can provide your trustees broad discretion in deciding how to disperse charitable contributions.

- Your lineal descendants can be the trustees. This creates a lasting legacy of charitable giving for your heirs. It places them in a position of prominence in charitable circles. As trustees, they can receive reasonable income for their services.

- Assets contributed to your private foundation are removed from your estate and thus avoid estate taxes.

Disadvantages

- A private foundation is a complex legal document. The costs of establishing one and maintaining it are relatively high. In addition to annual tax filing requirements, there are federal reporting requirements. Many states also impose reporting requirements. A private foundation is, therefore, more appropriate for large contributions.

Many advisors suggest a minimum of $500,000 is an appropriate contribution. I normally would not consider one for less than two to three million dollars.

- The people you would like to act as trustees, typically your children, may lack the investment management skills or general management skills to run the trust. They may also lack the interest. The trustees are fiduciaries and, as such, are responsible for their actions. Violations of fiduciary responsibilities can result in personal liability for a trustee.

- Private foundations are required to distribute at least 5 percent of their corpus each year. The trustee must make certain that there is sufficient liquidity for this purpose.

- The federal government imposes a 1 percent excise tax on private foundation income (increased to 2 percent in certain cases).

- Over the years, Congress has switched back and forth regarding the extent of the deduction of appreciated assets to a private foundation. Sometimes the deduction is for the full market value of the gift, and other times only your original cost is deductible. For gifts during your lifetime, check with your professional advisor to determine the deduction you will receive. This will not affect gifts under your will since all assets receive a stepped-up cost basis at death.

While the restrictions on the private foundation may sound daunting, it can deliver powerful estate planning results. Let's look at a case example:

CASE STUDY

The year is 2006. Dr. John and Mary Thompson have a *taxable* estate of $5,000,000 which places them in the 55 percent estate tax bracket. Three million of their estate is comprised of retirement plan assets and the balance is made up of family farm property which is both something they would like to keep in the family and is highly illiquid. To pay their estate taxes their heirs will need to use the money from the retirement plan. Let's look at the estate and income tax impact on the retirement plan at their death:

$5,000,000 Taxable Estate

- 1,698,000 Estate Taxes

-    408,000 Income Taxes on Retirement Plan Distributions

$2,894,000 Net to Heirs from Taxable Estate

In order to pay the taxes, the Thompsons' heirs will need to liquidate over $2,000,000 of Dr. Thompson's retirement plan.

When you use your retirement plan assets to pay estate taxes, you trigger *income taxes*. It's hard to imagine that you worked hard all your life and contributed diligently to your retirement plan only to have Uncle Sam take two thirds of it for taxes!

Now, let's assume that the Thompsons decide to establish a private foundation that they name "The John J. Thompson Family Foundation." They contribute their entire $3 million retirement plan to their foundation. They elect to have their children serve as trustees and give their children the right to elect their own successor trustees, presumably *their* children.

$ 2,000,000   Taxable Estate[1]

-            0   Estate Taxes

-            0   Income Taxes

$ 2,000,000   Net to Heirs

[1] *The taxable estate is reduced by the $3 million charitable contribution.*

There are no taxes due because John and Mary are *each* able to use their $1 million Applicable Exclusion Amount. The private foundation trust agreement allows the trustees (the children in this case) to receive reasonable management fees for their services as trustees. The children will receive some income plus the pleasure of giving money to worthy charitable causes. However, they are likely to be unhappy that they receive a reduced inheritance. After all, $894,000 is nothing to sneeze at! To put the smile back on their faces, the Thompsons' establish an irrevocable life insurance trust and place $1,000,000

of survivorship life insurance in it. As a result, when they die, the children receive $1,000,000 of life insurance, $2,000,000 of property plus management
fees for acting as trustees of their family private foundation. The family private
foundation has $3,000,000 and, if it is managed well, it will grow in size and
provide future descendants the opportunity to continue the family tradition of
charitable giving. To pay for the survivorship life policy, the Thompsons' will
make annual gifts to their children who will in turn own and pay the policy
premiums. Based on the parents' ages (both are age 53), the annual premiums
will be approximately $6,000 per year.

Our government encourages charitable giving as a social good through
the way it has structured the tax laws. There are also tax laws that allow
families to establish partnerships with other family members and transfer
assets at substantial discounts from their true values. The partnerships are
called **Family Limited Partnerships** and are perhaps the hottest estate planning technique in use today. As you might imagine, the Internal Revenue
Service is somewhat dissatisfied with their use. These partnerships will be
reviewed in detail in our next chapter.

SECTION III

Estate Transfer Strategies for Multiple Generations

CHAPTER 11

Family Limited Partnerships

The family limited partnership (FLP) is perhaps the most significant estate planning device since the irrevocable life insurance trust. Properly structured, it can serve as the centerpiece of your wealth preservation strategy.

GENERAL STRUCTURE OF THE FAMILY LIMITED PARTNERSHIP

With a family limited partnership, you establish a limited partnership agreement and then transfer title to certain property from your individual name to the name of the partnership. This transfer is a non-taxable event. Typically, you (and your spouse) are the general partner and your children and or grandchildren are limited partners. As with any partnership, only the general partners have the right to make decisions and vote. The limited partner's role is very restricted. If, as the general partner, you decide to make a partnership distribution, all partners including the limited partners must receive a pro rata distribution. Initially, when you transfer your property to the partnership, you will retain both the general partner interest and all limited partnership interests.

Assets transferred to the family limited partnership must be valued at the time of the transfer. As the general partner you may then begin to transfer limited partnership "units" to other family members through a gifting program using your annual or lifetime exclusion. Because the interests that you are transferring are limited partnership units, you are allowed to "discount" the value of the gift. For example, say you transfer farm property worth $1,000,000 to your family limited partnership with you and your spouse as the general partners. You then want to use your combined annual gift tax exclusion ($20,000 for 1998) to gift limited partnership units to your five children. You calculate that $20,000 times five equals $100,000. However, this is not the correct calculation! Because what your children will receive is a limited partnership interest in the farm land rather than the land itself, it is worth less than full value. This is because limited partners have very restricted rights. Their rights to sell and use the property are limited according to those rights granted by the general partner and the partnership agreement. In other words, the value of a 10 percent limited partnership interest in the land is worth less than ten percent of the whole value of the property. The result is a "discounting" of the value of limited partnership interests which allows you to leverage your wealth transfers. If the land being transferred into your partnership received a 50 percent discount, this would mean that your $100,000 gifts of partnership units to your children would actually transfer $200,000 of pre-partnership land value. Now that is what I call leverage! Remember, you can make gifts *every* year.

ADVANTAGES

- Control. One of the primary reasons that clients refuse to make lifetime transfers of wealth to children or other family members is loss of control. For instance, you own 100 percent of the stock in your closely held business that you estimate is worth six million dollars. You know that you should be transferring stock to your children and grandchildren in order to reduce the impact of future estate taxes. But, you're "frozen" into inaction because you do not want to risk losing control—even to your family. As a result you do nothing. The family limited partnership allows you to remain in total control of all decisions concerning your business while also letting you address your estate tax concerns. While you are the general partner, the limited partners have no voting rights or decision-making authority. You control everything except who gets which distributions. If you decide to make a partnership distribution, all partners, both general and limited, will receive a share of the distribution based on their individual partnership interest.

- Leverage. One of the primary advantages of the family limited partnership is the leverage that it creates when you gift partnership interest to your family members. Through various discounts, you are able to transfer one-dollar worth of property for substantially less than one dollar. This allows you to reduce the size of your estate much faster than would otherwise be possible. I will discuss valuation discounts in more detail later in this chapter.

- Ease of transfer. The family limited partnership allows you to take a large asset and divide it into small pieces that can be easily transferred. You can imagine how difficult—and expensive—it would be to divide a large track of land into pieces small enough to make annual gifts to children. Surveys, deed and title transfers, and court filings would make transfers impractical, particularly if you planned to make transfers each year as a part of a lifetime wealth transfer program. With your family limited partnership, you simply transfer partnership "units" which involves simple mathematics once the partnership property has been valued including the appropriate discounts.

- Asset protection. The family limited partnership provides excellent protection against creditors for the limited partners. It is possible for a creditor of a limited partner to force the partner to "assign" his or her interest to the creditor in satisfaction of a legal claim. As an assignee, the creditor's rights are limited to any distributions declared by the general partner. The creditor is also treated as a partner for income tax purposes. If the partnership has income but not distributions, the creditor is placed in the unenviable position of having "phantom income." That is, they owe taxes but received no cash to pay them with. This will serve as a deterrent to even the most persistent creditor.

- Easy to establish and simple to maintain. A family limited partnership is relatively easy to create. All you do is prepare the partnership agreement, transfer the deed or title to the partnership name, and issue partnership certificates. Even the subsequent transfers of undivided interests in real estate are easy. You simply amend the partnership agreement.

- Probate avoidance. Property held in a family limited partnership avoids probate. This is particularly useful if you have property located in more than one state. Avoiding the probate process may save your heirs time, money, and aggravation.

- Privacy. Closely related to avoiding probate, a family limited partnership provides a structure that keeps the family's business private. This is the case both during life and after your death. If you do not want the world to know what you own, how much it is worth, and who inherited it upon your death, then a family limited partnership is an excellent choice.

- Income benefits to the general partner. My clients often express the dual concerns of the continuing need for income and the need to reduce their estates to minimize taxes. They fear that if they give their income producing property away, they will be left without the income they need. The family limited partnership can address this issue effectively since the general partner can pay himself or herself an income as the manager of the partnership. This is in addition to and apart from their share of declared distributions.

- Centralized management. The family limited partnership provides the benefit of "centralizing" the management of all assets held in the partnership. There is one partnership tax return and if desired, there can be only one partnership bank account.

- Continuity of management. A significant feature of the family limited partnership is that it can provide continuity of management at your death. Your partnership agreement will list your successor manager. It is particularly important that your document include a succession plan should you become incompetent due to sickness or accident.

- Annual gifting. Your gift of a partnership interest should qualify for the Annual Gift Tax Exclusion.

Now that I have made a persuasive case for using a family limited partnership as part of your estate plan, lets look at some of the disadvantages.

DISADVANTAGES

- Valuations. In order for you to transfer portions of your partnership interest, the fair market value of these interests must be determined. For certain assets such as publicly traded securities this is no problem. On the other hand, it is far more difficult to value assets such as real estate and you will need to get qualified appraisals. A qualified appraisal does not mean that you get your friendly local real estate agent to give you an estimate of value. It means hiring an appraiser who will complete detailed research as to the partnership's value and issue a written report. The initial appraisal will need to be completed as of the date of transfer of your property into your family limited partnership. If you are making annual gifts of your partnership interests, you will need annual updates of your appraisal(s). Appraisals can be expensive, costing hundreds to several thousands of dollars. Before you decide to use the family limited partnership, you should get a sense of what the appraisal costs will be. Often you can find an appraiser who will "update" the appraisal annually for a reduced fee. One way to cut appraisal costs is to have them done every *other* year. For example, you have the partnership real estate appraised in December of one year and use that value to make gifts for that year and January of the following year. Then wait two years and repeat the process.

- Determining discounts. One of the primary advantages of the family limited partnership is that you create leverage in your gifting program. Say you want to give your son a parcel of land worth $10,000. By using the family limited partnership, the value of the transfer could be $7,000 or less. This is because you are transferring a partnership interest in the property rather than the property itself. As a partnership interest, it carries certain restrictions as to marketability and control which makes it less valuable. How much of a discount should you apply to the property? This is an important question that is best answered by an expert in discount valuations.

There are actually companies that specialize in this type of work. This is not an exact science and is subject to challenge by the Internal Revenue Service. If the IRS does challenge your discounts, the expert's report will serve as his or her testimony in most cases. You will want to choose someone who is qualified to do this type of work and who can issue a report that adequately defends his or her positions. As mentioned earlier, the costs of appraisals, discount valuations and a possible legal battle with the Internal Revenue Service can be significant.

- Retaining appreciated property. With a family limited partnership, the value of the gift of a partnership interest is based on the date of the gift. If, as the general partner, you retain a large partnership interest in appreciating property, the growth of that property is increasing the value of your estate. This can make it difficult to manage the growth of your estate which is typically one of the primary objectives. Contrast this with other strategies such as the installment sale or grantor retained annuity trust (GRAT) which effectively transfer all future growth to your donee.

- Internal Revenue Service challenge. The Internal Revenue Service is unhappy with the effectiveness of family limited partnerships in reducing and avoiding taxes. Family limited partnerships then are more likely to be subject to an Internal Revenue Service audit than some of our other techniques. This is partly due to the fact that many of your assumptions are based on estimates that are somewhat subjective rather than exact mathematics. The Internal Revenue Service will particularly focus on your assumptions as to fair market value and discount valuations. These can be easily argued since there are no exact answers. To adequately defend yourself, you will want to make sure that you employ experts in the field including attorneys, accountants, appraisers, and valuation experts.

FAMILY LIMITED PARTNERSHIP RULES

In order to be recognized as a partnership for income tax purposes, you must follow certain rules and procedures. Failure to do so may result in adverse tax consequences. Specifically, to qualify as a Family Limited Partnership you must meet the following tests:

- The partnership must have a purpose other than tax avoidance. Any of several non-tax purposes will do. These purposes might include centralized investment management; consolidation of control; business confidentiality; facilitating asset protection; facilitating future annual gifts; maintenance of family ownership; pooling of assets to maximize economic returns; and management continuity. It is vital that these "non-tax" objectives be expressed clearly and precisely in your partnership documents. Any tax avoidance objectives should either be omitted altogether or listed as secondary goals.

- The partnership must be engaged in a business or investment activity. The partnership cannot simply be a shell for holding assets until you can transfer them to the limited partners. You must show a business purpose. Capital must be a material income producing factor. The partnership will not qualify if the primary income sources are fees, commissions, or other income due to personal services. Any partner performing personal services must receive compensation that is fair and reasonable. For example, you place an apartment building in a family limited partnership with the intention of transferring interests to your three children. You obviously meet the Internal Revenue Service test—that of employing capital in the production of income. If, however, you managed the apartments yourself but received no income for those services, then you would fail the second test and the partnership income that you intended for your children to receive will be taxed to you.

- The partners must conduct their affairs in a manner that is consistent with the existence and purpose of the family limited partnership. You must run your family limited partnership as a true business. This means having periodic partnership meetings for making decisions and conducting business, periodic reports to the limited partners, filing partnership tax returns, and other activities consistent with the running of a business.

DISCOUNT PLANNING

One of the most important aspects of the family limited partnership is the ability to receive substantial discounts when transferring partnership interests. Proper planning here can make the difference of tens of thousands of dollars transferred from your estate to that of your intended heirs. Two types of discounts are potentially available under the family limited partnership:

DISCOUNTS FOR LACK OF MARKETABILITY

A limited partnership interest in a family limited partnership will normally include restrictions as to transferability. These limitations usually include a first right of refusal to the remaining partners. These restrictions as to marketability causes a limited partnership interest to be less valuable than an outright interest in an asset. For example, think of how you would determine the value of a particular piece of property you know to have a fair market value of $100,000. You have the choice of buying the entire property outright or you can buy a 10 percent interest in the property as a limited partner. As a limited partner, you have no vote or input regarding any partnership decisions. You may not even know the other partners. Would you be willing to pay $10,000 for this ten percent interest? In most cases your answer would be no. You would want to discount the purchase price, perhaps substantially, in order to be enticed to buy. Fortunately, our courts take this same view. In cases where transferability is restricted, a valuation discount is warranted even if the interest is a *majority* interest.

DISCOUNTS FOR LACK OF CONTROL

As a limited partner, you have no right to set investment policy, compel distributions, or impact any decisions regarding the partnership. The courts have consistently supported the premise that this lack of control results in your interest being less valuable and have therefore granted significant valuation discounts for holders of limited partnership interests. This is because the law looks at the value of the interest by itself rather than as a part of the whole. This is also true of *minority* interests in a partnership or corporation. Of particular importance in a partnership is the fact that taxes are passed through to the partners whether or not distributions are made to those partners. You can imagine how unhappy a partner would be if they received a tax bill for undistributed income.

CALCULATING DISCOUNTS

Calculating the various discounts is a job that should be performed by knowledgeable and qualified appraisers. Discounts for lack of control or marketability are not mutually exclusive. They can be aggregated. These discounts apply to the general partners as well as the limited partners. The fact that you transfer property from your name outright to a family limited partnership potentially creates a discount for you even if you retain the bulk of both the general and limited partnership interests. In the typical case, you would transfer property to yourself as general partner and then begin transferring partnership interests to your children as limited partners. You are entitled to a discount for your interest as a general partner. If, however, you take a limited partnership interest, you are entitled to an even greater discount. This is because a limited partnership interest is generally less valuable than a general partnership interest due to lack of control. There have been examples of discounts of as much as 85 percent being applied. Note that not all of the cases have been challenged by the Internal Revenue Service, nor will they be. The cases that have been challenged have resulted in discounts as high as 65 percent. One of the most important elements in setting up your family limited partnership is getting an appropriate discount valuation. You will want to choose someone who specializes in this field and who has experience in defending their work. Many professionals take the easy way out and apply a "safe" discount of 30 percent for virtually all of their cases. The result is lost opportunity for reducing the size of your estate and therefore estate taxes. Once you set the valuation discount, you can never argue that it should have been higher. Your goal should be an appropriate discount based on defensible evidence and facts.

MAXIMIZING YOUR DISCOUNTS

The larger your estate, the more important it will be to maximize the discounts in family limited partnership planning. This can be accomplished through several well thought out strategies.

- Consider setting up a corporation to own your general partnership interest. As the sole owner of the corporation, you give up no rights of control. Without a corporation, the death of the general partner could cause a change in tax status of the partnership. This could also be accomplished by setting up a revocable trust to hold your general partnership interest.

- If you are willing to give up control, you could receive a much larger discount by transferring your property and retaining a *limited partnership interest* versus a general partnership interest. For example, you may be willing to have your son act as the general partner knowing that he will run the family limited partnership in a manner consistent with your wishes.

- Certain states have laws that make it more difficult for partners to withdraw from the partnership or otherwise liquidate their interest. This is accomplished through a requirement that the partnership have a fixed termination date. By forming your partnership in one of these states, you will receive a larger discount.

- It is important to form *and fund* your family limited partnership *before* you make any gifts of partnership interest. People sometimes make the mistake of forming the partnership and funding it with only nominal amounts of property. They then make substantial gifts of partnership interests to family members and later transfer substantial amounts of assets to the partnership. This results in "contemporaneous" gifts to the family members and could be attacked by the Internal Revenue Service resulting in adverse tax consequences.

- Consider adding language to your partnership agreement restricting liquidation. This provision can be substantially fortified by having a non-family member limited partner, such as a charity, which must also agree to any liquidation. The inclusion of this restriction will result in a greater discount.

RECOGNITION OF GENERAL AND
LIMITED PARTNER'S RIGHTS

Care must be taken in structuring your family limited partnership so that an appropriate balance is struck between giving the general partner the desired control over decisions and income while restricting those powers sufficiently so as to not disqualify the partnership for tax purposes. This is of particular importance where the general partner is the donee rather than the donor. *You form a family limited partnership, fund it with your assets and make your son and daughter co-general partners at a 2 percent interest each. You retain a 96 percent limited partnership interest. However, you continue to make all the decisions regarding partnership business while your children act as "rubber stamps" for those decisions. As far as the public is concerned, you are still the one in control and the partnership "contact" person.* This is exactly how the Internal Revenue Service will view the arrangement and your partnership will likely not be recognized for income tax purposes.

Recognition of partnership income must be allocated in an appropriate manner. Each partner must receive their pro rata share of net of partnership expenses. For income tax reasons you may want to shift a larger portion to your children who are in a lower tax bracket than you. Some advisors will draft the partnership agreement to allow this. However, doing so means you're subject to scrutiny and possible disqualification by the Internal Revenue Service. At the same time the general partners must be compensated fairly for their management services. Often the general partner will "work for free" in order to make additional income available to the limited partners. At the opposite end of the spectrum is the general partner who desires a disproportionately higher income from the partnership and therefore pays himself or herself more compensation than the services are worth. Either extreme is subject to challenge by the Internal Revenue Service. It should be noted that what is considered "fair" compensation to the general partner can be a wide ranging dollar amount. You should consider not only what the actual services are worth but other compelling issues as well. For instance, as a general partner, you are exposed to unlimited liability.

Limited partners should receive copies of partnership tax returns and if the partnership agreement gives them any voice in management decisions, those rights should be respected. The donor should also not retain powers to unreasonably restrict a donee's right to dispose of his or her partnership interest. This is typically handled through a first right of refusal by the general partner and/or limited partners. Your agreement should not contain a "set" price for which the donor can buy back a donee's partnership interest. To do so might constitute a detrimental interest on the part of the donee which is restricted in the regulations.

MINORS' INTERESTS IN FAMILY LIMITED PARTNERSHIPS

Minors (as well as legally incompetent persons) are allowed to own interest in a family limited partnership. A minor's interest can be held by a custodian under a Uniform Gifts to Minors Account (UGMA) or Uniform Transfers to Minors Account (UTMA) or by a trustee under a trust agreement. Note that not all states have adopted the UTMA regulations and some states may not allow a minor's account to hold a partnership interest. Extra care should be taken where the donor will also act as the custodian or sole trustee. To do so could cause the minor's interest to be includable in the donor's estate. Also, the Internal Revenue Service will closely scrutinize these situations to be certain that the donor is acting solely in the interest of the minor. One excellent attribute of using family limited partnership interest for gifts to custodial accounts is that it solves the problem of transfer of control when the minor reaches legal adulthood. If you transferred securities to a custodial account, your child would legally take control of the securities based on state law (usually age 18 to 21). At that point the child could do whatever he or she pleased with the funds. However, if the asset is a limited partnership interest, their rights and control are significantly limited.

USING MULTIPLE FAMILY LIMITED PARTNERSHIPS TO MAXIMIZE BENEFITS

If you have sufficient wealth, you may benefit from establishing more than one family limited partnership. One primary advantage is to enhance asset protection by separating "safe" assets from "risky" assets. Safe assets would include assets such as marketable securities, notes receivable, or idle cash. Risky assets include real estate, closely held business interests, or general partnership interests. By separating these asset groups you insulate your safe assets from liability attributable to the risky assets. For example, say you own real estate that later becomes subject to a legal award for environmental damages. Your personal securities and cash would not be exposed to this suit or claim. Separating assets also allows you to fine-tune your gifting program by allowing you to maintain 100 percent ownership of the "safe asset" family limited partnership while gifting limited partner units of the "risky" family limited partnership. Note that it might also be appropriate to separate "risky" assets into multiple family limited partnerships for the reasons just stated. The downside to having multiple family limited partnerships is the cost of setting up and ongoing administration. While I'm suggesting that you consider setting your marketable securities and cash in a separate family limited partnership, I caution you that special rules are applicable in this situation. Care should be taken to avoid be treated as an "investment company." Be sure to consult with your professional advisor in this important area.

LIMITED LIABILITY COMPANIES

A limited liability company provides many of the same features as the family limited partnership with a few notable differences. One of the primary advantages is that *all* "members" of a limited liability company have limited liability for the debts and obligations of the company. As you remember, with the family limited partnership only the limited partners enjoy this protection. The general partner has *unlimited* liability. Whereas in a family limited partnership, the limited partners have no say in management decisions, the members in a limited liability company do participate in management decisions. As detailed in the limited liability company's documents, members' voting interest can be based on either their actual percentage interest in the limited liability company, *or* their percentage contribution to the limited liability company. The limited liability company has few ownership and operating restrictions and is treated as a partnership for income tax purposes. In all other respects, the limited liability company enjoys much of the same benefits as the family limited partnership including asset protection, valuation discounts, continuity and consolidation of management, income tax shifting and probate avoidance. There are some disadvantages to the limited liability company as compared to the family limited partnership. First, the laws governing limited liability companies are very inconsistent from state to state. You and your professional advisor will need to review your own state laws carefully. Second, in most states, a member has the right to withdraw from the company and receive the fair market value of their interest. This freedom of "transferability" can affect the size of discounts available in the limited liability company. Also, the complete withdrawal or death of a member can result in the dissolution of the company. In some states it is possible to include language in the company's operating agreement that satisfactorily deals with each of these problems.

The family limited partnership can be an ideal tool for owners of closely held business interests or family farms. Many of these people share a common goal of having family members succeed them in the family business. Succession planning is an important topic for these people. If you own your own business, Chapter 12 will provide you a thorough review of succession strategies for you to consider.

CHAPTER 12

Succession Planning for the Family Business or Farm

I f you are a business owner, healthcare practitioner, or farmer, you will face special challenges regarding preserving values for your heirs. To simplify our discussion I will refer to anyone who falls into any of these three categories as a business owner (which they are!). Most business owners are so involved in the day-to-day demands of running their business, they find little time to think about succession planning. In the back of their minds, they believe that "everything will work out all right." They may realize that they need to do something, but just never seem to find the time. The typical result? In the end, everything is not all right and the value of the business is seriously diminished. A couple of typical cases will provide us a backdrop for the importance of advance planning.

Bill Johnson, Sr., a divorcee, owns a small precision manufacturing company with an estimated value of six million dollars. He has spent his entire career building this successful company which represents the bulk of his net worth. He is grooming his son Billy to eventually take over the company when he retires. Bill, Sr. also has two daughters who are not involved in the business. Unfortunately, Bill, Sr. died suddenly, leaving his estate to the three children equally. Billy, Jr. was now "in business" with his two sisters and he was a minority stockholder. While Billy's sisters had little interest in the business, they felt they deserved an income from the business. After all, Billy was taking a nice salary. Together the two sisters owned a majority of the voting stock so they were able to successfully demand the income they felt they deserved. Since they did not work in the business, these income payments were not deductible by the business. This story does not have a happy ending. The "in-fighting" and cash flow problems eventually caused the company to fail. The sisters blamed Billy. After all, he was running the company.

There were many possible solutions in this case. One would be to make sure the daughters receive their share of Bill, Sr.'s estate from assets other than the business. This might have required Bill, Sr. to buy life insurance owned by a trust for the daughters' benefit or have the daughters own the policies individually. If insurance was not a possibility, he could have considered two classes of stock—voting and non-voting. In this way, he could give the daughters non-voting stock while giving Billy voting stock. All of the children would have equal ownership in the company, but Billy would have voting control. Another option would have been for Bill, Sr. to sell the company to Billy, Jr. for an installment note. At Bill's death the children would have an equal interest in the note.

Dr. Steve Stein's dental practice has provided him and his family a good income for 35 years. Now, at age 64, he has noticed that his number of new patients is declining significantly each month. His current patients are all in their mid to late 60s. He has also become aware that more and more current patients are moving to retirement communities out of his town, while others are dying. He seems to be surrounded by younger dentists with thriving practices. His profits are dropping month by month. He is ready to retire but cannot afford to because there is little value left in his practice. He has little choice but to continue to run an increasingly deteriorating practice. Finally, at age 75, he shuts his doors and sells his equipment for pennies on the dollar.

I have had an opportunity to work with numerous healthcare professionals over the years and one of our primary objectives is to make sure that we built value in their practices. Whether you are a dentist, doctor, chiropractor, or other healthcare specialist, your practice has value if you plan properly. Dr. Stein should have brought a younger dentist into the practice. Not only would the younger dentist have provided valuable "new blood" for the practice but he or she would have been the perfect "buyer."

Horace and Martha James own a working farm that has been in the family for two generations. It is their desire that the farm remain in the family for future generations. They have had to work hard all their lives and while the farm income has allowed them to raise and educate their two children, they have always had to pay attention to their cash flow. Consequently, they don't expect the farm to be worth very much and have not concerned themselves with any estate planning. When the parents died, their children were in for a rude awakening. The farm was rich in timber and the Internal Revenue Service valued the land at four times the Jameses' estimate. This resulted in substantial estate taxes, even though the children didn't have the cash to pay the taxes. Even with the special tax provisions for farmers, the children are unable to pay the taxes and the farm had to be sold to raise cash.

Business owners, particularly farmers, tend to underestimate the value of their businesses. This is a big mistake. For better or worse, the Internal Revenue Service seems particularly inclined to challenge business values of deceased business owners. There is a lot of money at stake and the Internal Revenue Service wins more than its share of these cases. The Jameses' best defense would have been a good offense. First, they could have reduced the value of the farm by using discounting strategies such as the family limited partnership. Next they should have considered using their Annual Gift Tax Exclusion to begin transferring undivided interests in the farm to their children at that time. Finally, they needed to monitor the value of the land and then develop a game plan that provided the liquidity to meet any potential estate tax obligation. To do this, they would have had to get aid from a qualified appraiser. The expenses incurred in planning ahead can mean the difference between meeting your objectives or not.

SPECIAL ESTATE TAX BENEFITS FOR FARMERS AND CLOSELY HELD BUSINESS OWNERS

One major problem shared by farmers and small business owners is that the farm or business typically represents the majority of the value in their estate. Under normal circumstances, estate taxes are due within nine months after the date of death. Since businesses and farms are by their nature highly illiquid enterprises, rarely is there cash to pay these estate taxes. Congress has seen fit to provide a variety of special tax provisions to make it easier for the small business owner and farmer to meet their tax obligation and thus pass the assets to family members. These special provisions include the following:

- Special estate tax deduction for Qualified Family-Owned Businesses

- Installment payment of estate taxes

- Special use valuation of certain business property

SPECIAL ESTATE TAX DEDUCTION
FOR QUALIFIED FAMILY-OWNED BUSINESSES

Recognizing the special liquidity problems associated with ownership of a small business or farm, Congress provided some estate tax relief in the Taxpayer Relief Act of 1997. The Act provides an additional deduction for deceased owners of qualified family-owned businesses, that when added to the Applicable Exclusion Amount, totals $1,300,000. For example, say you own a qualifying business valued at $2,000,000 plus have other assets of $1,000,000 bringing your total estate to $3,000,000. If you were to die in 1999, your taxable estate would be calculated as follows:

$ 3,000,000	total estate
- 650,000	Qualified Family-owned Business deduction
$ 2,350,000	taxable estate

The result is that your family received an "extra" $650,000 deduction because you own a qualified family-owned business. To qualify for this special tax benefit you must meet certain criteria:

- The business must represent more than 50 percent of the your gross estate.

- The ownership of the business must be held at least 50 percent by one family; 70 percent by two families; or 90 percent by three families as long as *your* family owns at least 30 percent.

- The business must pass a "material participation" test which requires that you or your family members must have materially participated in running the business during five of the preceding eight years.

- The business must be transferred to "qualified heirs" who must then continue to materially participate in running the business.

Qualified heirs include family members as well as certain long term employees.

- These "qualified heirs" must continue to *own* the business during the 10 years after your death.

- To qualify for this deduction, you and the "qualified heirs" must be U.S. citizens.

Failure to meet any of these requirements "nullifies" the deduction and causes a "recapture" of the estate taxes that were avoided.

While this is an important benefit if you plan to pass the family business or farm to family members, it should be noted that as the Applicable Exclusion Amount increases, the value of this benefit is reduced. For example, in 2006, the Applicable Exclusion Amount is $1,000,000, thus reducing the value of this benefit to $300,000.

INSTALLMENT PAYMENT OF ESTATE TAXES

In addition to the added exclusion for qualified family-owned businesses, the Taxpayer Relief Act of 1997 provided some "enhancements" to the estate tax installment payments rules for closely held businesses. Normally, estate taxes are due within nine months from the date of death. If the value of your closely held business or farm exceeds 35 percent of your adjusted gross estate, your executor can elect to pay your estate taxes in installments. A 100 percent deferral of taxes is allowed for the first four years based on "interest only" payments. The taxes are then paid in equal installments over ten years. As a special "bonus" the Taxpayer Relief Act of 1997 provides an interest rate of 2 percent on the first $1,000,000 of taxable value. This $1,000,00 figure is indexed for inflation.

SPECIAL USE VALUATION

Imagine that you own a working farm in an outlying area of a fast growing community. The farm has been in your family for two generations and it is your intention that it remain in the family. At your death, the Internal Revenue Service comes in and values it not under its current use, but at its "highest and best" use. Its highest and best use is for commercial development. If it were valued as farm property it would be worth $1,000,000 but as commercial property it is worth $4,000,000. The resulting estate tax is more than the worth of the entire farm! This is not an unusual circumstance. To resolve this problem, Congress passed "special use" legislation that allows your executor to elect to value the property at its *current* use rather than its fair market value. In order to qualify for this election, certain criteria must be met:

- The value of the property in question must represent at least 25 percent of your total estate. In addition, the combined value of the real estate and personal property used in the business must exceed 50 percent of your gross estate.

- You must have "materially participated" in the business five of the last eight years preceding your death.

- The property must be passed to "qualified" heirs who must then continue to "materially participate" in the business for the 10 years after your death.

- Your qualified heirs cannot sell any part of their interest for the 10 years after your death.

- The property must continue to be used in the same way as it was qualified for under the special use valuation for at least 10 years after your death.

- All qualified heirs with an interest in the property must sign an agreement which requires them to pay additional estate taxes should the land fail to continue to qualify as special use property during the 10 years preceding your death.

- The property is subject to a federal tax lien which can make it difficult for the owners to obtain traditional financing or loans using the property as collateral.

This "reduction" in value for tax purposes is limited to $750,000 except as adjusted for inflation indexing. Special use valuation is a complex area of the law. If this is likely to be an issue for you, consider involving your financial advisor early in the planning process.

VALUING YOUR BUSINESS OR FARM

Most business owners and farm owners have a poor sense of the value of their business. Farmers tend to undervalue their farm because, as a profession, farming is hard work for little profit. Our farmers deserve much more credit for what they accomplish for us and the world around us. However, the fact that farming is a hard work, low profit business has little to do with the value that the Internal Revenue Service is going to attempt to place on your property. It is important that you note that what the Internal Revenue Service thinks is *very* important. At your death it is the Internal Revenue Service that will challenge the values your executor places on the farm. The Internal Revenue Service is assuming that you are going to try to "lowball" the value. To counteract this you will need to have qualified appraisers establish the fair market value and be prepared to defend their results. Should you wait until you die to get this appraisal done? Because advance planning is so important, you should get a "ballpark" estimate now. Figure a "worse case" valuation and then develop a plan that addresses the estate tax and succession issues. In previous chapters I discussed many ways to create "discounts" for valuation purposes. Other chapters outline strategies you can use to begin transferring portions of the business or farm each year. The important thing is to develop a plan early and not wait until you die. The result then is a "crisis" management plan that often results in higher taxes and a greater burden on your heirs.

SUCCESSION OR SALE?

There are two potentially distinct issues to consider when thinking about the family business. The first one has to do with keeping the family business in the family. If there are family members who are both interested and capable of carrying on the business, you will want to make sure that you effect a transfer that gives that family member appropriate control of the business. You will also want to insure that they receive the business in a sound financial condition.

If you do not intend to pass the business to family members at your death or retirement, you will want to make sure that you structure the business in such a way in order to receive its maximum value. Your decisions here will help determine the strategy that is best for you and your family.

SUCCESSION PLANNING:
KEEPING THE FAMILY BUSINESS IN THE FAMILY

Take a long look at your business. Are there family members who are both capable and interested in continuing the business? If you have a child or children who are interested and others who are not, do you have a way of dividing your estate so that all are treated fairly? The last thing you want is to have a successful transfer of the family business only to have it divide the family. Let's assume that you do want your business to be continued by one or more of your children. Some of the planning issues to consider are as follows:

- Management training. I often find situations where children are working in the family business but the parent is still making all the key decisions without any input from the child. I am not sure how the parent thinks the child is going to gain the experience that is so critical to running a business if the child is not "in the loop" of business decision making.

- Control. If you have children who are not involved in the business, it is essential that the children who are running the business have voting control. As we saw in the case of the Johnson family, the best solution was to make sure that the children not working in the business receive their fair share of your estate from assets other than your business interest. I would encourage you to discuss these issues openly with your children so that each of them understands why you are dividing your estate the way you are.

- Financial condition. Stand back and take a clear look at the financial condition of your company. Is it financially sound or is it over-leveraged? In the hands of capable management, financial leverage is an important tool used to grow a business. Are you the key person in that management team? How would your son or daughter fare if he or she had to suddenly step in your management shoes because of your death or disability? Make sure that you have a plan for transferring the business to your children in sound financial condition. Sound financial condition should be defined in terms of *their* capabilities not yours. This may be as simple as providing adequate key person life insurance on your life and an appropriate disability plan.

- Estate taxes. For estate tax purposes, you need to determine the likely value of the business. Will there be adequate liquidity to pay estate taxes? Many succession plans have failed due to the burden of estate taxes. Consider using some of the many strategies I have discussed in this book for reducing and transferring the value of your business and other assets.

- Documentation. Remember, for your business interest to be transferred you have to have proper documentation. Do not assume that you will get around to it someday. Do it now! This can be done through your will or it can be accomplished with buy-out agreements. Consult with your tax advisor for the best method in your situation.

MAXIMIZING YOUR BUSINESS' VALUE THROUGH A SALE

If you do not plan to leave your business to a family member, you will want to take steps to maximize its value at your death or retirement. Too often, busy business owners like our friend Dr. Stein never take the time to consider the ultimate disposition of their business. To receive top dollar for your business, you have to do a lot of planning. Here are some of the issues you should consider:

- When to sell? Do you plan to sell your business while you are living or do you plan to wait until you die? This may sound like a strange question, but there are many people (myself included) who plan to work their entire life. Your strategy for selling during life might be very different from your strategy if you plan to wait until you die.

- Finding a buyer. When I ask my business owner clients what they plan to do with their business, more often than not, they shrug their shoulders and mutter something about someone selling it at their death. When I dig a little deeper they suggest that the spouse is likely the person who would end up dealing with the problem. Sometimes there is an advisor they feel they could count on to help with the sale. The truth is that none of these people are likely to be in a position to sell the business for its highest value. You are the person who intimately understands the business and it is you who is in the best position to develop a plan for selling the business. One solution is to find a buyer now and draw an agreement for sale in the event of your death. This may be easier than you think. Look around your business and see if there are any key employees who would be capable of running the business. Employees are often an excellent solution for a business sale. Not only do you have a "ready" buyer that you can "groom" to take your position one day, but knowing that they may own the business one day is a very motivating factor. These employees are not likely to leave. I recently worked on a case where the key employee purchased and paid for life insurance on the life of the business owner. They drew a buy-out agreement that "compelled" the key employee to buy controlling stock in the company at the owner's death. The agreement also required the company to sell the stock. The owner is now giving the key employee additional management responsibilities so that she could more effectively run the company in his absence. Much to his surprise, her management skills exceed his. He now has a ready buyer in the event of his death and a much more loyal and motivated employee.

What if you are not lucky enough to have a capable key employee who could buy the business at your death? Next you might consider a competitor. Are there any competitors that might be interested in your business? If they are reasonably friendly, you may be able to draw an agreement or at least a "letter of understanding" now. At a very minimum, you should sit down and write out a plan for your spouse or advisor to follow at your death. List those people who you think are the potential buyers, describe how to best determine the fair market value of the company, and detail any other matters that you feel would be useful in helping to sell your business.

- Selling during life. Perhaps the best way to receive full value for your business is to sell while you are still active in the business. This usually allows you to receive the maximum value because you are there to assist with the transition. This does not have to be an all-or-nothing deal, particularly if you have key employees. By selling a minority interest in your company to key employees, you can create a loyalty that otherwise is difficult to achieve. They are now "owners" and will likely shun offers to work for competitors. You can also prepare them, both financially and management-wise, to take over when you retire or die. Be sure to develop an appropriate "exit" strategy that will allow you to get their stock back should they cease to be employed by your business. "Minority" shareholders can cause you a lot of problems.

STRUCTURING YOUR BUY-SELL AGREEMENT

Once you have found an appropriate buyer for your business you will need to structure a formal agreement that outlines all the terms. Whether or not your buyer is a family member, buy-sell agreements offer several advantages:

- If one of your goals is to make sure the family business stays in the family, a buy-sell agreement is an appropriate tool. The agreement can be structured such that all sales must be first offered to existing stockholders (other family members) or the corporation before they can be sold or transferred to a non-family member.

- If structured properly, the buy-sell agreement can establish the value of your company for estate tax purposes. The purchase price for most buy-sell agreements is established by way of a formula, fixed price or is based on a required appraisal. What is critical is that the price is established based on an "arms-length transaction." This means that the price should be one that two unrelated parties would be willing to agree. The Internal Revenue Service looks closely at deals between family members to make sure that no "bargain" sale takes place.

- The buy-sell agreement provides a ready market for the sale of the owner's interest in his or her business. Knowing the value your family will receive for your business interest allows you to better plan your estate.

TYPES OF BUY-SELL AGREEMENTS

Buy-sell agreements are typically classified as either *entity purchase agreements* (sometimes referred to as redemption agreements), *cross-purchase agreements,* or *hybrid agreements*.

ENTITY PURCHASE AGREEMENTS

With an entity purchase agreement, the company agrees to purchase your shares of stock at the occurrence of some predetermined event such as your retirement, disability, or death. This type of buy-sell agreement has several disadvantages. First, it only makes sense where there are other co-owners. Second, if life insurance is used as the funding vehicle, it can subject your company to some rather unpleasant tax consequences (for C corporations) known as the Alternative Minimum Tax (AMT). If your facts indicate that you may be subject to this tax, you may want to consider electing S corporation status. Also, unless the agreement is carefully structured, the proceeds could be subject to ordinary income taxes. Finally, the remaining owners are deprived of a "stepped-up cost basis" which they would have received if they had purchased your shares directly. In most cases, a cross-purchase agreement is preferred.

CROSS-PURCHASE AGREEMENTS

In a business where there are multiple owners, a cross-purchase agreement is often used. In a cross-purchase agreement, each owner agrees to buy a portion of the interest of the departing owner's shares at retirement, disability, or death. The company itself is not a party to these transactions. This arrangement has the advantage of providing the buyer with a stepped-up cost basis in the business interest that he or she purchased. The primary disadvantage is the increased paperwork involved, especially if there are several owners or life insurance is being used to fund the purchases.

HYBRID AGREEMENTS

Hybrid agreements involve both the shareholders and the company in the buy-sell agreement. Typically they provide that at your death, disability, or retirement, the shareholders have the first right of refusal to buy your shares. If they do not, then the company redeems your shares. In other cases, just the opposite occurs. The company has the first right of refusal to buy your shares and if the company fails to do so then the surviving shareholders have the right to buy them. If the shareholders refuse, the company then becomes obligated to buy your shares. This is sometimes referred to as a *wait and see agreement* because the buyers wait until the "triggering" event happens before deciding how your shares will be purchased. This allows for some last-minute tax planning to take place.

FUNDING THE BUY-SELL AGREEMENT

Having a buy-sell agreement is well and good but where is the money going to come from to buy your business interest? Rarely does a family-owned business, its shareholders, or key employees have the cash to buy out the interest of a major owner. This problem is most often solved with life insurance. Premiums for "permanent" or cash value life insurance can be expensive but this is often a better solution than term life insurance. While term life insurance is inexpensive initially, it can become prohibitively expensive as you get older. Where there are several owners that need to be insured, a relatively new type of life policy should be considered. **First to die life insurance** uses one policy to cover multiple lives and pays off when the *first* insured dies.

Life insurance will not solve all your funding problems. For example if the "triggering" event is your disability, life insurance may be of little initial value as a funding vehicle. Any cash values are likely to be inadequate to fund a buy-out caused by the disability of the owner. One solution to this problem is to purchase **disability buy-out insurance**. This is a special type of disability policy that provides a lump-sum payment to buy the stock of a permanently disabled business owner. The incapacity of a business owner is a complicated issue that needs to be addressed with your professional advisor. There are certain tax issues and cash flow issues that are critical to the ongoing financial health of your company. For example, if you were to become disabled and your company continued to pay your salary, those payments *may* not be a deductible expense by your company which creates an added drain on the company. One solution is to implement a **Qualified Sick Pay Plan** which establishes a company policy for providing income to disabled employees. Another problem caused by a key person's disability is that someone will likely need to be hired to complete the duties of the disabled person. This obviously creates further cash drain where the company is paying one person who is not working and another person who is now performing their job duties.

Life insurance may also be of little value if you are selling because of your retirement. One possible solution here would be to establish a "sinking" fund whereby your company sets aside money monthly or yearly for this purpose. In the corporate world this is known as accumulated earnings and can spell tax trouble for C corporations. Accumulating corporate earnings for the purpose of buying out a majority owner's stock can cause the imposition of the 28 percent accumulated earnings surtax.

Often the best solutions are to purchase insurance where you an afford it and then plan to use financing arrangements to fund the balance. For example, your agreement may indicate that insurance will be used up to a certain dollar amount (the face of the policy) and that the balance will be paid over 5 to 10 years in monthly installments at a competitive interest rate. One danger with using installment payments is that they are made with after-tax dollars. The source of these payments is typically company salaries, bonuses, or dividends from the pockets of those people purchasing your stock. If the corporation increases salaries to cover the installment payments, the Internal Revenue Service may declare that that the owner/ stockholders are receiving "unreasonable compensation." The portion that is considered unreasonable compensation is reclassified as dividends for income tax purposes. Dividends are not deductible by the corporation which results in "double taxation." Successfully structuring the sale of a substantial business interest can be a very complicated matter. It will require the thoughtful effort of yourself as well as experienced professional advisors. Before we leave this subject, let's review one final strategy.

ONE FINAL STRATEGY—THE ESOP

Another viable alternative for selling your stock is to establish an **Employee Stock Ownership Plan (ESOP)**. An ESOP is similar to a qualified profit-sharing plan except that the company contributes company stock instead of cash. Some of the particulars regarding ESOPs include:

- Employer contributions. Just as with a profit-sharing plan, contributions to an ESOP are limited to a maximum of 15 percent of compensation. Contributions normally consist of shares of company stock rather than cash.

- Limitations regarding diversification. An ESOP does not have any limit on the amount of company stock held in the plan. This differs from a typical profit-sharing plan where diversification is a fiduciary duty. There is an exception regarding employees age 55 or older who have 10 years or more of service with the company. These employees must be offered a diversification option into any of three alternative investments. The election must be offered annually over a six-year period. During the first five years, transfers may be made up to a cumulative total of 25 percent of the employee's account balance. In the sixth year, this 25 percent limit is increased to 50 percent.

- Forfeitures. As with most retirement plans, an ESOP typically has a "vesting" schedule. In other words, contributions made on behalf of an employee are not fully vested in their names until they have been in the plan for a certain period of time. If an employee terminates employment prior to becoming fully vested, his or her non-vested portion is typically reallocated among the remaining participants.

- Financial leverage. The rules regarding ESOPs allow a company to borrow money to buy company stock in order to fund the plan's contributions. The interest on these loans is a deductible expense by the corporation.

One of the primary advantages to the ESOP is that it can provide you with a ready market for your stock. Also, under an ESOP, if the company lacks the cash flow to make a contribution, there is no requirement to do so. Since the employees ultimately will end up owning the company, the ESOP may provide additional employee motivation. Finally, using borrowed money to make stock contributions can be an effective way of raising capital for a company. One disadvantage of the ESOP as a method of selling your stock is that the stock must be sold over a number of years rather than a lump sum.

Owning and running a business can be a time-consuming and demanding proposition. You put years of your life into making your business a success. To maximize the return on your efforts, you will need to develop a plan to reap the full value of your business at your death or retirement.

One common concern that we all have is protecting our assets from legal judgments. A corporation, family limited partnership, or limited liability company can provide us with a certain level of protection from would-be creditors. For a full discussion of asset protection, read Chapter 13, *Asset Protection Strategies*.

CHAPTER 13

Asset Protection Strategies

One of the biggest threats to your wealth management plan is a potential legal judgment. Our laws allow just about anyone to sue you over just about anything. Many lawsuits are unfounded but nevertheless result in settlements as a less expensive alternative to a trial. If a case does go to trial, you have a right to a jury of your peers. But will the jury really be your peers? Almost by definition, if you are reading this book your income and/or net worth places you in the top 10 percent of wealth in this country. The typical jury is comprised of a majority of people who are not wealthy and may not sympathize with a defendant that they determine is wealthy. Remember, too, that plaintiffs—the name for the people that sue you—have nothing at risk except their time. Their attorneys typically take their cases on a "contingency" basis. This means that the attorney receives no compensation if they do not win. Thus, the attorney is in effect spending his or her own money prosecuting the case. This can cost anywhere from a few hundred dollars to tens of thousands of dollars of expenses as well as attorneys' time. Talk about an incentive to win a case! You may assume that attorneys review potential cases based on the merits of the case facts. Unfortunately, that's often not the case. Some attorneys may instead consider the probability of winning or losing a case with little regard for right or wrong. This use of our system of justice has resulted in a litigation crisis in America. It is your responsibility to make sure you and your family are protected as much as possible from this kind of litigation. In this chapter I will discuss the various strategies you can use to protect your assets from potential creditors. Some of the strategies have already been discussed briefly earlier in this book. I will now review them in more detail.

THE CONCEPT OF FRAUDULENT TRANSFERS

Many people don't think about protecting their assets until there is a threat of a lawsuit. Then they rush around shifting assets to family members, trusts, partnerships, and Swiss bank accounts. Our legal system includes the **Uniform Fraudulent Transfers Act** to prevent this from occurring. In essence, this law says that any property transferred for the purpose of avoiding creditors represents a fraudulent transfer and can be set aside. For example, you learn that you are about to be sued so you transfer your bank accounts and real estate "temporarily" to your sister, leaving you without assets. The lawsuit does take place and a substantial judgment is entered against you. You assume that since you now have no assets, you're "judgment proof." However, the law of fraudulent transfers will allow your creditor's attorney to set aside the transfer to your sister forcing her to transfer the assets back to you where they will then be available to your creditors. Don't think that you can make this transfer in secret. The attorneys will take your *deposition* which is a legal process in which your statements are made under oath. To lie under oath is a federal offense punishable by time in prison. Few people will be willing to take this risk. A better solution is to prepare now for the possibility that you may be sued later. If you implement strategies of asset protection when you have no knowledge of possible litigation, then you can avoid the fraudulent transfer laws.

State Exemptions

Each state has enacted laws that exempt certain property from the claims of creditors. For example, in the state of Florida, your personal residence is totally exempt from creditor claims no matter how much it is worth. Other states exempt certain amounts of cash, cash value of life insurance, or personal property. Check with your attorney to determine the particular laws of your state.

Insurance

One obvious answer to a lawsuit is to have insurance which will reimburse you for legal fees and any judgments entered against you. Two primary forms of this type of insurance include personal liability insurance and business liability insurance. **Personal liability insurance** is typically included in your auto and homeowner's insurance policy. If, for example, you are at fault in an accident and injure someone, resulting in a lawsuit and judgment against you, your auto insurance coverage will pay both your legal fees and claims up to your policy limits. If someone falls down the steps at your home, is injured, sues, and receives a judgment, your homeowner's policy will pay your legal costs and claims up to the policy limits. But, what if the judgment exceeds the policy limits? The excess will come from your personal assets. One way to avoid this problem is through the purchase of a **personal liability umbrella policy**. This type of policy requires that your underlying auto and homeowner's policies' liability limits be raised to a certain level (usually $300,000 to $500,000). The umbrella policy then adds an additional $1,000,000 to $5,000,000 or more of liability protection. The umbrella policy is usually purchased through your auto or homeowner's agent and is relatively inexpensive. For example, a one million dollar umbrella policy may cost as little as $100 to $300 *per year*. Note that this coverage covers only *personal* liability issues, not liability arising out of business issues. To protect you against liability when you own a business, you should consider **business liability insurance**. For healthcare professionals, this is known as malpractice insurance. For other professionals, it may be referred to as "E and O" (errors and omissions) insurance. This insurance is typically costly. Malpractice insurance for physicians can run into the tens of thousands of dollars each year. Many of these policies also have large deductibles. The deductible represents the amount of money you must pay before your insurance "kicks in." Deductibles can be $10,000, $25,000, to $50,000 or more. Furthermore, the insurance company will require that you use their attorney rather than your own. Also, the insurance company will likely want to "settle" your case even if you have done nothing wrong. Settling a case means that your insurance company will give the plaintiff money to drop the lawsuit. Unfortunately, from the public's point of view, you lost the case and maybe some of your reputation as well. You are not compensated for your time, anguish or loss of income while fighting the lawsuit. Some astute observers have even suggested that by having liability insurance, you encourage lawsuits. After all, insurance companies have been easy targets for plaintiff attorneys. Perhaps the best solution is some combination of insurance along with additional asset protection strategies.

ASSET PROTECTION FOR MARRIED COUPLES

Being married affords you some possibilities for asset protection. I have found that most couples title the bulk of their assets in their joint names. I have already discussed the many reasons for not holding title in joint names. You can now add asset protection to the list. If you are at a significantly greater risk of being sued than your spouse, you should consider transferring assets to his or her name. Let's review a simple example. *Al Hitchcock is an obstetrician and has been married to Sue, a homemaker, for 25 years. In the area they live, Al is unable to purchase malpractice insurance (a reality in certain areas of our country). To protect his assets, he transfers everything except a small checking account to Sue's name. Now if he is sued which results in a judgment against him, his assets are protected because he no longer has any assets! They are all in Sue's name!*

Is this strategy foolproof? No strategy is completely foolproof. With this strategy you must be careful of the fraudulent transfer laws. Be sure to transfer the assets *before* there is knowledge of a potential lawsuit. Next, while you are protected against lawsuit, your spouse is not. Even if he or she, as a homemaker, is not likely to be sued, the possibility that he or she will be sued remains.

When I discuss the possibility of shifting assets with a client, there is often an unspoken tension in the air. The potential transferor is thinking it but unwilling to say it—divorce. My obstetrician client is concerned about what happens if he transfers all assets to his spouse and then she files for a divorce? The results can be quite negative, but not for the reasons that you might think. First, you need to make a distinction between separate property states and community property states. If you become divorced in a separate property state, the settlement will be based upon what is called *equitable principles*. Equitable principles requires the judge to look at a number of factors including the length of the marriage, the value of the separate property brought into the marriage, the value of any inherited property, and the ability of each spouse to earn a living after the marriage. The fact that you transferred your interest in marital property to your spouse will have little effect on how property is split upon divorce. Take the case of my obstetrician client who has been married 20 years and whose wife is a homemaker. Even if all of their assets are the result of his income *and* they are all titled in his name, his wife would receive both a substantial property settlement and alimony in the event of a divorce. The issue here is not losing your assets to a divorcing spouse, it is receiving your share of the assets in a divorce. Let me explain: Assume that you have transferred the bulk of your assets to your spouse as an asset protection strategy. Sometime later you are sued, resulting in a $1,000,000 judgment against you *and* you get divorced during the same time period. As part of the divorce settlement, you receive $1,000,000 worth of property that can now be attached by your creditors. Transferring assets to your spouse as an asset protection strategy should only be used in *stable* marriages. Also, using the facts just described, if your spouse died and left you assets, those assets may become available to satisfy creditors as well.

Community property states present a unique challenge for couples interested in protecting assets through an asset shifting strategy. In community property states, all property acquired *during* the marriage is considered to be owned one half by each spouse regardless of whose name the property is in. Inherited property and property acquired prior to the marriage is considered separate property *so long as it has never been co-mingled with marital property.* Community property states include Arizona, Idaho, California, Louisiana, Nevada, New Mexico, Texas, Washington, and Wisconsin. If you live in a community property state and get a divorce, you and your spouse each keep your separate property plus one half of all community property. This sounds simple and straightforward. However, generally, a creditor can attach community property in order to settle a judgment. If you or your spouse own separate or inherited property, it is imperative that neither of you co-mingle that property with community property.

It is possible to get around the community property laws with proper planning. Each spouse can sign a *transmutation agreement* that effectively separates community property into separate property. Care must be taken not to violate the fraudulent transfer laws. The transmutation agreement takes community property and splits it into separate property. To re-title your home might read, *"John Doe, 50 percent interest as his sole and separate property; and Jane Doe, 50 percent interest as her sole and separate property."* You might separate the assets altogether by dividing the bank account into each separate name. The transmutation agreement and the re-titling of the assets are critical to a successful termination of community property.

A WORD ABOUT JOINTLY HELD PROPERTY

A quick refresher course on jointly held property may be in order. Remember that jointly held property is subject to the claims of creditors even if the claim is only against one of the joint owners. These creditors can force the sale of the property and are then entitled to up to one half of the proceeds. This joint property could be your home, and you and your family could end up in the street. Avoid jointly held property if you have concerns about asset protection.

As an alternative to joint tenancy, some states allow a form of titling called *tenancy by entireties*. This type of ownership is restricted to married couples. Property that is owned by this method cannot be attached by creditors. Let's say that you and your spouse live in a $2,000,000 home in a state that allows you to own real estate titled as tenants by entireties. Your only other asset is your pension income of $10,000 per month and you have no liabilities. You are sued and incur a $1,000,000 judgment against you. Your creditors can get nothing because they cannot attach your home unless the judgment was against *both* of you. In this situation your creditors can receive nothing until there is a divorce, the property is sold, or you die. If you die *before* your spouse, their claim is forever set aside! States that allow tenancy by entireties include:

Arkansas

Delaware

District of Columbia

Florida

Hawaii

Indiana

Maryland

Massachusetts

Michigan

Mississippi

Missouri

New York

North Carolina

Ohio

Oregon

Pennsylvania

Rhode Island

Tennessee

Vermont

Virginia

Wyoming

RETIREMENT PLANS

In 1974, Congress passed the Employee Retirement Income Security Act (ERISA) which provided many rules and regulations concerning qualified retirement plans. Some of the more widely used plans covered under this act include Profit Sharing Plans, Money Purchase Pension Plans (sometimes referred to as Defined Contribution Plans), Defined Benefit Plans, and 401(k) plans. Self-employment plans such as Keogh Plans are also covered. One of the best things to come out of this act was asset protection for retirement plan benefits. This law provides that qualified retirement plan assets are not attachable by creditors. The only exception to this rule deals with Qualified Domestic Relations Orders (QDRO). In the event that you are divorced, the court can award your departing spouse all or a portion of your retirement plan assets under a QDRO.

Typically, when people terminate employment to either take another job or retire, they will "roll over" their retirement plan to an Individual Retirement Account (IRA) in order to continue to postpone taxation on their money. If you are concerned about asset protection, this is not a good idea because IRAs are not protected under ERISA. This "rollover" has the effect of transferring a "creditor proof" asset into one that may be attachable. I say "may be" because creditor access to IRAs is governed by state law and some states do protect IRA assets. If you are changing employers, what should you do? Many employer plans will allow you to roll over your assets from a prior plan. If this is not possible, check to see if the plan of the company you are leaving will allow you to leave your assets in the plan. Some will allow you to do this. If not, you will have to roll your money over to an IRA. When you do this, you should set up a separate IRA account rather than "co-mingling" this money with other IRA money. The reason is that if you keep this money separate, you can roll the account over to a qualified plan at a *future date* should your employer establish a qualified plan that permits this. For example, assume that you have $300,000 in your 401(k) plan with your present employer. You decide to take a position with another company but find out that it has no retirement plan at all. You roll over your retirement plan to an IRA but never co-mingle it with other IRAs you own. Your new company later starts a profit-sharing plan that allows rollovers from other qualified plans. Since you have never co-mingled your retirement plan money from your previous employer's plan, it can now be rolled over to your new employer's plan.

It should be noted that qualified plans that cover an owner but no employees *may not* be protected from creditors. The Supreme Court case of *Patterson vs. Shumate* left the door open to creditors in this type of situation. If you are in this situation, consider including an employee in your plan. Using family members may not resolve this dilemma.

What are the disadvantages to maintaining your money in a qualified retirement plan rather than using an IRA? While an IRA offers little, if any, creditor protection, it does provide for maximum flexibility regarding investment options. Consider for example, mutual funds. Through an IRA you can invest in most of the more than 10,000 mutual funds available today or you can buy individual stocks, bonds, certificates of deposit, etc. Contrast this with the typical employer-provided retirement plan that offers only a few investment choices. With homework, your opportunity to earn a higher rate of return increases with the number of investment alternatives available to you. A potential lower rate of return is part of the price you pay for asset protection.

LIFE INSURANCE

Life insurance has long been considered an important tool for protecting the finances of American families. As such, our government has provided life insurance companies and their policyholders with favorable tax treatment. For example, when an insured dies, the beneficiary owes no income taxes on the proceeds. Also, there is no current taxation on the earnings or growth of the policy's cash values. Many states have carried the concept of protecting life insurance policies over to the creditor protection arena as well. For example, Alabama state law provides that no *cash value* can be attached by creditors. Other states provide similar protections while some states provide no protection. When it comes to life insurance death benefits, care should be exercised in choosing your beneficiary in order to protect the death benefits from would-be creditors. Let's say, for example, that you name your estate the beneficiary of your life insurance. At your death your estate representative is required by law to post a legal notice of your death so that creditors can file a claim against your estate. If you do have creditors, your life insurance proceeds are now available to settle their claims. You could have avoided this by having a named beneficiary. This beneficiary could be a person such as your spouse or it could be a trust. In my practice, I have a large number of physicians as clients. I am always concerned that at their death an ex-patient might present a lawsuit as a way of "treasure hunting" knowing that their doctor will not be around to defend himself or herself. You should check your state exemption laws to determine what protection they provide for your life insurance policies.

I should note that this beneficiary issue is not restricted to life insurance. When researching a client's case, I often find that they have made their estate the beneficiary of the retirement plan proceeds or their other employee benefits. Also, care should be taken regarding any annuities you own. Anything that has a beneficiary designation should be reviewed. If you want your benefits to pass according to your will but also want the benefits of asset protection, consider making your beneficiary an irrevocable trust under your will. This has the same effect as naming your estate, but will avoid both creditors and probate. Since the trust does not become irrevocable until you die, you retain the right to make changes anytime prior to your death.

Using Trusts to Protect Assets

One way to shield your life insurance from creditors is to place your policies into an **irrevocable life insurance trust**. An irrevocable trust is treated as a separate "person" for tax (and creditor) purposes. Any assets held in your trust are not subject to the claims of your creditors. This is true for both the cash values and the death benefits. A problem with building up cash values in an irrevocable life insurance trust is that you have "given away" your money *irrevocably*. Perhaps the best way to address this problem is to add a provision in your document which allows the trustee to make distributions to beneficiaries at his or her discretion. For this to work you will need both a "friendly" trustee and a friendly beneficiary. If you are married, the best choice for your beneficiary will likely be your spouse. Once this plan has been implemented, your "friendly" trustee can make distributions to your spouse should the need for cash arise. You have effectively shielded your money from potential creditors while maintaining reasonable access to your cash. For a complete explanation of irrevocable life insurance trust see Chapter 8.

For assets other than life insurance, you could consider an **irrevocable grantor trust**. This is similar to the irrevocable life insurance trust. You, as the grantor, contribute assets to the trust making yourself and one or more beneficiaries potential recipients of trust income. Because of gift and income tax issues, you will want to have the trust document give you the power to distribute trust income among "classes" of beneficiaries. If your spouse is one of your beneficiaries, you again have "access" to your money while avoiding the clutches of your potential creditors. Again, you must be careful of the fraudulent transfer rules.

Many people are reluctant to use an irrevocable trust because it is so "permanent." Once you transfer assets into an irrevocable trust, it is much more difficult to get those assets back out. These trusts can also be rather expensive to set up and maintain. Are there asset protection benefits from using a *revocable* trust? After all, this would afford you the greatest amount of flexibility. When you no longer needed the trust, you could simply "revoke" it. Having the power to revoke your trust is exactly the problem. If all of your assets are in your revocable trust and a creditor wins a legal claim against you, the judge can (and will) order you to take the assets out of your trust. This does not mean that use of a revocable trust cannot provide you with some needed asset protection. It just means that you will have to be a little more creative.

Dr. Joan Spivy and her husband John, have accumulated considerable assets. John works as a computer technician for a major corporation. Joan and John have come to me to help set up their estate plan. In addition to estate tax concerns, Joan is concerned about liability due to her anesthesiology practice. Concerning asset protection, I discussed many strategies including irrevocable trusts, family limited partnerships, and offshore trusts. However, the Spivys like to keep things simple and none of these more complex maneuvers appealed to them. I then discussed a strategy that included a revocable living trust that they loved. Here's how it worked: Since, in this case, Joan is at far greater risk of being sued, we established a revocable living trust in John's name. We then transferred all Joan's personal securities and real estate into the trust. The primary assets that Joan retained were her qualified pension plan assets and term life insurance. The combination of the assets would be enough to cover her Allowable Exclusion Amount and thus fund her Credit Shelter Trust. Even though John and Joan had a long-standing marriage, Joan had expressed concerns about giving up control of her assets. To address this issue, I made Joan and John co-trustees of John's revocable living trust. This allowed Joan to retain a measure of control over the assets that she transferred to John. Now, if Joan was the subject of a substantial lawsuit, no personal assets would be exposed because they are all in John's name. The assets that remain in her name—the qualified retirement plan and the term life insurance—are assets that are not subject to the claims of creditors. Not only did this strategy address Joan's concerns, but it also removed the assets from the probate process!

Now, before you assume that we have devised the perfect asset protection solution, let me point out its pitfalls. First, this plan does nothing to protect the Spivys from John's creditors. John's career makes him much less of a lawsuit target so we are just playing the odds. Second, making Joan a co-trustee of John's trust would not guarantee that John will not run off with the money. This trust is revocable and John could "fire" Joan as trustee or he could terminate the trust altogether. As added protection for Joan, the trust document would require 30 to 60 days notice for termination of a trustee. Also, when Joan transfers her assets to the trust, the title of the accounts would reflect both Joan and John's names as trustees. It would be highly unlikely that a bank or brokerage firm would close an account of this nature without both signatures. To make sure that John does not simply write a check for the account balance, the trust agreement provides for *dual* signatures for checks above a certain amount, say $2,000.

Using Corporations to Protect Assets

Under certain circumstances, you can limit your liability by incorporating your business. As with a trust, a corporation is considered a separate "person" in the eyes of the law. Just as you have your own Social Security number, a corporation must apply for and receive a tax identification number. Once you are incorporated, lawsuits that occur as a result of your business activities likely will be limited to corporate assets not your personal assets. I use the word "likely" because there are some important exceptions that you should be aware of.

- First, if your corporation were to fail and you have not fully paid employee withholding taxes, the federal and state government can come after you personally.

- Second, you will be personally responsible for any loans or agreements in which you give a personal guarantee. If you obtain a business loan from a bank, your bank officer will likely require that you sign both as a corporate officer and as a personal guarantor. Often, the bank will also ask that your spouse sign personally as well. In most cases you should be able to avoid having your spouse sign unless he or she is involved in the business. As your company grows in financial strength, you may be able to negotiate the removal of your personal guarantee from your business loans. Avoiding having your spouse co-sign business loans and removing your personal guarantee are prudent initiatives and are worth pursuing. One of my clients started a commercial construction company. To do so he needed to acquire bonding from a bonding company. Initially, they required his personal guarantee as well as a corporate guarantee to back up the bond. Today his company is financially strong and one of our major initiatives is to have his personal guarantee removed from the bond. The construction business can be very volatile and the future is unknown. You always want to minimize your financial exposure.

When you are transacting business for your corporation, be sure that you follow the technical procedures or you may find out that you have inadvertently given your personal guarantee. For example, when you sign an agreement, be sure to sign: *John Smith, president* and not just John Smith. Be clear with all parties that you are doing business as an officer of your corporation.

- If you establish a corporation but then run it like a sole proprietorship, it is likely that a creditor can "pierce" the corporate veil and go after your personal assets. I have reviewed many cases where people are running their corporations like a personal checkbook. They are paying their home mortgage and other personal expenses straight from their corporate checkbook. They have no "director's" meetings and no corporate "minutes." Under these circumstances, if you are ever faced with liability problems, the courts will ignore your coveted corporate status.

- If you are a professional such as a physician, dentist, accountant, architect, or attorney, a corporation is of little use in providing you with asset protection. This is because lawmakers have decided that professionals should be held liable for acts of negligence. Still, a corporation may be useful when you are in practice with other owner/ professionals. In some states, you cannot be sued personally for acts committed by other shareholder/owners. Your corporation, however, can be sued. Check with your advisor to determine if a corporation can benefit you. As a professional, you will need to employ additional strategies to protect your assets.

Use of Multiple Corporations

Under certain circumstances, it may be useful for you to have more than one corporation. Let's say that you own and operate two businesses. One is a mail-order company that sells vitamins and the other a dynamite-blasting company. Obviously the risk of a lawsuit is much greater with your blasting company than your mail-order company. By using a separate corporation for each company, you shield the assets of one company from potential judgments of the other company.

A Word of Caution to Directors

It is often considered prestigious to be a director of a corporation. You are treated very well and you may even receive compensation in the form of director's fees. However, being on a board of directors can be hazardous to your wealth. As a director, you have a responsibility to the corporate shareholders. If things go wrong, you may find yourself in the middle of a lawsuit that potentially puts your personal assets at risk. Before you join any board of directors, be sure that there is adequate liability insurance coverage and that you have a measure of control and knowledge of corporate decision making. Too often the board of directors is considered a "rubber stamp" committee for the corporation. Also, never put your spouse on your own board of directors. To do so may allow creditors to go after his or her personal assets if you have adequately shielded your own assets.

This warning is not restricted to directors of corporations. If you sit on the board of directors of your condominium association or local charity, you can have liability exposure as well. Even officers of corporations should be cautious. If a corporation fails to pay the payroll taxes, the Internal Revenue Service can trace that liability to "responsible persons." That could mean you if you are an officer in that corporation. The fact that the corporation has filed bankruptcy does not remove your liability.

Asset Protection Using Family Limited Partnerships

Chapter 11 in this book is devoted to the subject of family limited partnerships with a focus on their estate planning benefits. Here I will spend a few minutes reiterating the asset protection benefits of the family limited partnership. As an asset protection strategy, the family limited partnership receives very high ratings. To best explain the asset protection attributes of the family limited partnership, let's look at an example:

Amy Davis is a successful plastic surgeon who is concerned about protecting the family's substantial assets from lawsuits. She establishes the Davis Family Limited Partnership making her husband, Jack, the 1 percent general partner, herself a 97 percent limited partner, and their two children receive a 1 percent limited partnership interest each. Amy and Jack then placed their assets into their family limited partnership, including their bank accounts, brokerage accounts, and real estate. Unfortunately, her greatest nightmare comes true and she is sued resulting in a $5,000,000 judgment. Her malpractice insurance covers $3,000,000 of the judgment but now the creditors are coming after her personal assets for the balance. Unfortunately for them, she has no other assets except a limited partnership interest in the family limited partnership and minimal value in her professional corporation. Undeterred, the creditors move forward and receive a "charging order" against her partnership interest. The effect of this charging order is that the creditor now stands in her place with regard to any distributions from the partnership. Jack, being a very interested party, decides not to make any distributions. What can the creditor do? Nothing! Their charging order gives them no rights regarding management decisions and they have no way of causing the termination of the partnership. What is worse, undistributed partnership income is taxed to the partners even though they received no money. Since the charging order places the creditor in Amy's position, they receive the tax bill! As you might imagine, this is an uncomfortable spot for the creditor who now may be more than willing to settle for pennies on the dollar.

Limited liability companies are somewhat of the sister to the family limited partnership. One of the primary advantages of the limited liability company is that *all* of its members are protected against liability rather than just the limited partners. However the laws concerning limited liability companies lack uniformity as compared to family limited partnerships so you should determine which form of ownership is best for you based on your own state law.

FOREIGN ASSET PROTECTION TRUSTS

When you think of transferring money to a foreign bank account, most people immediately think of Switzerland. Switzerland has earned a well-deserved reputation for privacy concerning bank accounts of foreigners.

This "privacy" feature, however, is of little use as an asset protection strategy for most Americans. First, our government requires that you tell them whenever you transfer money to a foreign country. This must be disclosed on tax form 1040 Schedule B and Form TD F 90-22.1. To not do so is a federal crime punishable by fines of up to $500,000 and imprisonment for up to five years. You will find little joy knowing your assets are safe while you are enjoying free room and board in a federal prison. Assuming that you do report you have transferred money to a Swiss account, are your assets now safe from creditors? In a word, no. Switzerland, and most countries will honor judgments from a U.S. court. The result is that once you have disclosed that you have assets in a "friendly" foreign country, your creditors can get your money. The solution here is to locate a country that is "unfriendly" regarding our courts. Several countries have become havens for people that desire to protect their assets. Most noteworthy are the Cayman Islands, the Bahamas, the Isle of Man, and the Cook Islands. Each of these countries have turned foreign asset protection trusts into a major industry. They have passed special laws that protect your privacy and, most importantly, they do not recognize judgments from foreign countries. They also do not have income taxes on foreign accounts.

If you decide to enter the world of foreign asset protection trusts, you should realize that this is not an area for the timid or faint of heart. This is serious business involving hefty legal fees and a certain amount of risks.

The Basics of a Foreign Asset Protection Trust

If you are obsessed with asset protection, then you may want to consider a Foreign Asset Protection Trust. First and foremost, the single reason to establish a foreign asset protection trust is asset protection. To accomplish this goal your trust will need to contain some very special and unusual provisions:

- The trust must be irrevocable. If it were a revocable trust, a U.S. judge could require that you revoke the trust in favor of your creditors.

- In order to avoid gift tax problems, your trust must be a grantor trust. If you transfer assets to an irrevocable trust, you are subject to gift taxes starting at 37 percent on amounts above $10,000 per beneficiary. To avoid this trap you need to make your trust a grantor trust, which means that you will retain some control over the trust thus making the gift "incomplete" for gift tax purposes. Speaking of taxes, you should know that foreign asset protection trusts are tax "neutral." The income generated by the trust is taxable to you just as it would have been if you had not transferred it.

- Your trust will need at least one foreign trustee. If all the trustees are located in the United States, a judge could subpoena them to appear before him or her and compel the trustee to distribute assets in favor of your creditors. This means that your foreign trustee should not directly do business in the United States. To do so would subject them to subpoena powers.

- It will be best if you are not a trustee of your foreign asset protection trust. As a trustee, a judge can compel you to cooperate.

- It will be best if you are not a beneficiary of your foreign asset protection trust. Now wait a minute! What good is a trust if you cannot ever get your money? Again, if you must appear before a judge, you have a much stronger case if you are not a beneficiary of the trust. The best alternative is to have your spouse and children as beneficiaries. Your trustee can then distribute assets to them which can be used for their or your benefit.

- Your trust agreement should require your trustee to ignore your request to send funds to you or a creditor if such request is part of a court order. Once you have received a judgment against you and your creditor discovers that you have assets in a foreign account, the judge is likely to require that you demand release of those funds so that your creditors can be satisfied. If you refuse to do so, you can be held in contempt of court. Prison can be a lonely place so you will want to comply with the judge's request. If you do your part, but your trustee refuses to release funds, there is little else that the judge can do.

- Your trust should contain a "flight" provision. Every now and then you will run into an extremely persistent creditor. If the dollars at stake are large enough, they may be willing to pursue the matter at great length. This may include pursuing the case in the country where your assets are held or you may run into a judge who will not take "no" for an answer. A flight provision instructs your trustee to actually *move* your account to another country should the threat to your assets warrant it. Your trust agreement further instructs your trustee *not to tell you where your money has been moved*. Talk about a scary provision! The good news is that a judge cannot make you divulge information that you do not have.

- A truly foreign trust has some pretty substantial reporting requirements for our government. This can be avoided by making your trust a domestic trust until such time as your assets come under threat from creditors. One way to accomplish this is to establish a family limited partnership making yourself a 1 percent general partner and a 1 percent limited partner. The remaining 98 percent limited partnership interests will be owned by your foreign asset protection trust. You remain in control of your assets through the family limited partnership until it is obvious that you are in serious jeopardy from creditors. At that time you terminate the family limited partnership, resign as trustee of the foreign asset protection trust, and zap!—your money is moved offshore.

If all of this sounds complicated, that's because it is. There are potential tax consequences of transferring appreciated property to a foreign trust. Additionally, a foreign asset protection trust is a uniquely individual document that should be tailored to each person's specific facts and objectives. State laws concerning trusts vary widely and should be considered in drafting a foreign asset protection trust. There are numerous groups around the country promoting offshore trusts through seminars. Some of these groups are legitimate, others are not. I met with the attorney from one of these groups that was promoting offshore trusts in the country of Panama. If you invested your money with them, they guaranteed you a 14 percent annual return that they claimed was totally safe! The prevailing rate on CDs at that time was less than 6 percent. On his business card after his name he listed the initials RIA. This stands for Registered Investment Advisor and is accomplished by filing certain forms with the Securities and Exchange Commission. To use the initials in this manner is illegal because it gives the public the impression that you have somehow "qualified" or been "approved" to be a Registered Investment Advisor. When I questioned this attorney further, he admitted that he was not a Registered Investment

Advisor at all! If you are interested in pursuing this subject, you must retain a reputable attorney who specializes in this area.

DOMESTIC ASSET PROTECTION TRUSTS

If you are looking for somewhat simpler asset protection, you might want to consider a domestic asset protection trust (DAPT). Several states have passed legislation that makes it difficult for creditors to receive assets from a judgment if those assets are held in a DAPT. These states include Alaska, Delaware, Idaho, Illinois, South Dakota, and Wisconsin. While Delaware is best known for asset protection, Alaska provides the most "air tight" legislation. For instance, Delaware allows certain classes of creditors (such as divorced spouses) to invade your trust. Alaska provides no exceptions unless there is a fraudulent conveyance. Also, Alaskan trusts do not require a termination date. DAPTs in most other states require that the trust terminate within 90 years.

The Law of Fraudulent Conveyances applies to all trusts in the United States. If you feel you are a likely target for a lawsuit, you must transfer your assets into your DAPT before you have knowledge of a problem or the courts can "set aside" the transfer. Under Alaskan trust law, as the grantor, you are allowed to receive distributions from your trust. These distributions must be at the *sole discretion* of your trustee. As you might imagine, it is very important that you appoint "friendly" trustees.

In addition to asset protection benefits, these DAPTs offer important estate planning benefits. Alaska's statutes consider that transfers to a trust are a "completed gift." This means that the assets are removed from your estate for estate tax purposes. This is true even your trustee can disperse funds from your trust to you. It also means that you can use your Annual Gift Tax Exclusion and/or your lifetime Applicable Exclusion Amount to make gifts to your trust. A word of caution is appropriate regarding this issue. Let's say that you used $500,000 of your lifetime Applicable Exclusion Amount to make a tax-free gift to your DAPT. If later, your trustee distributed $250,000 of funds to you, that portion of your Applicable Exclusion Amount would be lost forever. Obviously, any distributions would also be available to creditors.

If you are a resident in a state other than one that has domestic asset protection trust laws, then a DAPT may not provide you with the creditor protection you desire. This is because our U.S Constitution requires that all states honor the judgments of other states. Be sure and check with an attorney in your state that has experience with DAPT law.

When deciding between a domestic asset protection trust versus a foreign asset protection trust you should weigh the following factors:

- Comfort zone. Most people are going to be more comfortable knowing that their assets are being held in a trust in the United States. I have found that there is something about moving large sums of money to a foreign country that makes people nervous.

- Expenses. In most cases, you can expect your legal and administrative costs to be higher with a foreign trust. Often the costs will be significantly higher.

- Level of asset protection. Most experts will agree that properly drawn foreign trusts provide a higher level of protection against creditors. Foreign countries such as the Cayman Islands do not recognize U.S. court jurisdiction or judgments. From a creditor's point of view, you can imagine how discouraging (and costly) it would be to attempt to pursue a judgment in a foreign country.

- Statute of limitations. The statute of limitations is much shorter in countries providing foreign asset protection trusts than it is in the United States. This "shorter" period means that your assets are protected faster.

Most people who have significant wealth have concerns about asset protection. Today, we live in a very litigious society in which many people are all too happy to sue you for even insignificant events. There is serious money at stake here, where even frivolous cases often end in settlements. I remember reading about a young woman who lived in Washington, DC. While she did not have a job, she did have a law degree. She managed to provide herself with quite a nice income by suing just about everyone she met. She sued her landlord. She sued her auto mechanic. She sued the local grocery store. At the time of the article, she had filed over 25 lawsuits. Most of the cases settled for less than $5,000 because the defendant (or his/her insurance company) determined that a small "nuisance" settlement would be cheaper than a trial.

Your personal level of concern regarding asset protection will determine which strategies are best for you. I encourage you to meet with your professional advisor to discuss this issue. He or she is likely to have a good sense of what strategies, if any, would be appropriate for you.

Ultimately, one of the greatest factors that will impact the effectiveness of your estate plan has to do with your attitudes toward money. In our final chapter, we will explore the psychology of money and how to remove ingrained barriers that often prevent people from implementing an effective estate plan.

CHAPTER 14

The Psychology of Money

In my 25 plus years in this business, I have become acutely aware that people's attitudes regarding money will have a material impact on what they are willing to do regarding their estate planning. Many of these attitudes have been formed over decades or even generations. If you did a quick self-examination, you would probably find that the way you think about and handle money is similar to your parents'. For most people, the subject of money ranks up there with politics and religion. Most people simply do not want to talk about it to anyone other than their financial advisors. When I'm working with a client regarding his or her estate plan, it is important that I have a sense of the size and disposition of their parents' estate. In most cases this issue has never been discussed. Why is the subject of money such a taboo? My conclusion is that money and wealth represent so much more than merely numbers on a balance sheet. Many people attribute the very deep emotions of love, happiness, self-worth, power, control, security, and/or independence to the amount of money they have. Many of these feelings are subconscious and are therefore difficult to pinpoint. As it relates to estate planning, this can lead to irrational decision making that results in less than optimal planning. Poor planning can lead to more tax dollars for Uncle Sam and correspondingly fewer dollars to the people you love.

While no one ever falls neatly into one personality type, I have found that most people's estate planning decisions are made out of the context of one of five personality types: the prudent planner, the giver, the scorekeeper, the worrier, or the controller. Let's take a closer look at each type and discuss possible solutions for breaking down any damaging money barriers.

THE PRUDENT PLANNER

I might as well start with the easiest one. Fortunately, the prudent planner represents a robust number of people with whom I have worked. These are people who want to do the right thing concerning wealth management. When I am working with a client, my number one goal is to make sure that he or she will always have enough money to maintain the same or similar lifestyle for his or her lifetime. Only after I am convinced that this goal is accomplished do I explore wealth transfer strategies. My knowledge that the client will always have enough income is only half the battle. I must also convince the client. But once the prudent planner is convinced, then he or she is able to quickly begin implementing appropriate decisions for transferring wealth to loved ones and/or charities. Thus, my job then becomes one of laying out the many options available and helping the client choose those that best accomplish specific goals.

THE GIVER

Typically my "giver" clients have received their wealth through the death of a spouse or parent. Suddenly, they have a lot of money and are delighted to have the opportunity to share it with the people they love. As with the prudent planner, the giver is a delightful person with whom to work. The trick, in these cases, is to make sure that the giver does not give away *too much* money. Often, they are perfectly willing to live with personal financial sacrifices in order to benefit their children or charities *now*. Often these people have lived frugally all their lives and they see no reason to change just because they now have substantial financial resources. While it is not my job to require that they change their standard of living, I do feel that I must make sure that they will have access to enough assets to provide for their income needs and deal with any financial emergencies.

THE SCOREKEEPER

Even though scorekeepers are challenging, I love working with them because they are most often entrepreneurs and they made their money the old-fashioned way: They earned it. Typically, they spent a lifetime building a small business into a major enterprise. In other cases, they took over the family business and made it an even bigger success. Occasionally, they started out working in a big corporation and worked their way up to a top executive position which provided them valuable stock options. The common personality trait shared by these people is that they measure their success by the size of their financial statement. It has been both stimulating and important to watch their net worth grow. The money itself has long ceased to be their motivating factor. It is "the game" that counts. When they retire (if they retire!), keeping financial score continues to provide them their "juice." What typically changes at retirement is that they focus on investment success rather than business success. When it comes to estate planning, the scorekeepers are reluctant to do the things that they know that they should do because it interferes with their score keeping. For example, take a wealthy scorekeeper who is married with four children and four grandchildren. A basic wealth transfer strategy might include annual gifts using the Annual Gift Tax Exclusion. Based on the spouse joining in the gift, these clients could give up to $160,000 (1998) free of Federal gift taxes each year. Each gift not only removes the asset from their estate, but the growth as well. So why don't they do it? The scorekeeper's net worth begins to decline, of course! Obviously, this is what we are trying to accomplish, but it is causing the client emotional fits. Our estate plan has thrown a "monkey wrench" into one of the very core reasons he or she exists. The solution here is to redefine the game for our client. Typically, I help the client make a paradigm shift from focusing on his or her own financial situation to focusing on the family as a "family unit." As we shift assets to family members, I will often continue to supervise those assets for the benefit of the children. When we are reviewing the client's net worth, I am careful to "add back" those assets that have been shifted to the children. This helps our "scorekeeper" continue to keep score in a game that is now even more exciting. The added dimension to "the game" is that the scorekeeper now has the pleasure of helping his or her children grow their own net worth and save estate taxes to boot!

THE WORRIER

An awful lot of people fall into this category. Call it a "depression mentality." Most Baby Boomers have no concept of the 1929 Depression. But for my Retiree clients, it is a different story. They either remember it vividly or have heard horror stories from their parents. Many people lost everything they owned. Jobs were hard to come by and if you had one, you barely earned enough to make ends meet. The pain of that era dies slowly. The primary lesson was that you can never be sure you have enough money. Therefore, you cannot ever afford to give any away. One of a parent's greatest nightmares is that he or she will one day be dependent on the children for income needs. Worriers will go to great lengths to make sure this does not happen to them. They are fully prepared to pay additional estate taxes to avoid this possibility. To address this important issue, I developed what I call **The Family Council**. We gather the adult children together and tell them that we are about to begin transferring assets to their names for the purpose of saving estate taxes. We make it clear, however, that if the parent ever needs the funds for any reason (they won't), we expect the children to return it to them via annual gifts. To secure the program, I typically establish segregated investment accounts and supervise the management of the money that is now in the children's names. Annually, the entire family gets together to review money issues as well as the status of the children's investment accounts that have been established by the parents.

Now, this solution is not without its potential flaws. First, once the money has been given to the child, the parents retain no legal rights to control it. They must rely on the obedient nature of their children. If their children are not the obedient types, this strategy will not work. However, the parent does carry a rather large stick. If a child were to misuse the funds, the parent would have the option of discontinuing future gifts including any final dispositions under their wills. Another potential problem is that the assets may be available to creditors of their children. This problem could be addressed by using one or more of the asset protection strategies discussed in Chapter 13. Finally, the gifted assets could be attachable by a divorcing spouse. With divorce rates in this country approaching 60 percent, this is a legitimate concern. If you are concerned with this issue, an awkward, but workable solution is a postnuptial agreement.

THE CONTROLLER

Controllers are unhappy unless they are in *full* control. To them money represents either power or a means of receiving attention or affection. Often they have little faith that their children are experienced or savvy enough to manage money properly. Often they are right—controlling parents often end up with dependent children. The solution that is most palatable to the controller is to have gifted assets go into a trust for the benefit of the children. In many cases, one of the parents will want to be the trustee during their lifetime. The trust will usually contain provisions that are fairly restrictive.

DEALING WITH PARENTS AND THEIR MONEY

In order to properly plan your estate, it is important that your professional advisor have an understanding of the size and intended disposition of your parents' estate. If their estate is large and will be left to you, the strategies employed in your own estate plan may need to be altered significantly. Likewise, if your parents' estate is small and there is a chance they may require your financial support, you need to know this. Unfortunately, discussions about money between parents and children rarely happen. If the child brings up the issue, he or she feels as if he or she is "fortune hunting." Parents rarely take the opportunity to discuss money issues with their children. As you might imagine, the result is typically a lack of multigenerational planning which causes higher estate taxes. The solution is obvious: We need to get the children and parents together to talk about money issues.

There are several ways to accomplish this. One of the best ways is to involve a professional advisor. Tell your parents that you have retained a professional advisor to help you develop your estate plan. The advisor has suggested that one of the important issues is the coordination of your parents' planning with your own planning. See if your parents would be willing to meet with your advisor. In many cases it may be best for you not to be in this meeting. Another alternative is to see if your parents will give permission for your advisor to meet with their advisor to discuss the coordination of multigenerational planning for the family. My favorite choice is for a client to give his or her parents a copy of this book for them to read. It just might be the perfect Father's Day or Mother's Day gift! Seriously, a book on the subject of estate planning can prompt a parent to rethink the appropriateness of the planning they have done. I have noticed that the estate planning seminars around the country are packed with retirees, so there is obviously interest in this subject.

If your parents are not the type to discuss money issues, make sure you do not make the same mistake. Embrace the concept of **The Family Council** and use it as a forum to discuss money matters with your own children. Once children start school they are old enough to begin learning basic money concepts. Remember, your children are eventually going to inherit large sums of money. My experience is that children who inherit money but haven't received any guidance from their parents are left to make their own choices— all too often the wrong ones—about managing their money. The money is spent on new cars, travel, or bad investments. On the other hand, if parents give their children advice regarding money, the majority of the time the children will embrace that advice. This is true even if the advice is *bad* advice! The conversation may go something like this: *"My daddy told me that I should hang on to this railroad stock because it had always been good to him and his daddy before him."* Even though the railroad stock represents 90 percent of their investment portfolio, they are reluctant to sell. Again, the family council meeting could include your financial advisor who can properly facilitate discussions about money and investments.

As you can see, estate planning is a complex subject involving a multitude of decisions and possible strategies. To do it well, you will need the assistance of one or more professional advisors who have extensive experience in estate planning matters. If you are not certain how to find a qualified advisor, review the state-by-state listings of advisors in the Appendix of this book. Each of these advisors has at least 10 years of experience in their field. If they cannot help you themselves, they can refer you to someone who can. Good luck and may God shine His glory on you, your family, and your finances!

State-by-State Listing of Top Professional Advisors

E state planning is a broad and complex subject. To do the job right, you will need the assistance of one or more professional advisors. Choosing the right advisor is vital to your financial well-being. The key elements in making the right choice include:

Experience   Each advisor you choose should have a minimum of *ten years* experience in their field. I strongly believe that *no* professional advisor should have unsupervised client responsibility until they have "apprenticed" under an experienced advisor for a minimum of five years. Experience is the foundation of all competence.

Competence   While having an advanced designation is no guarantee of competence, it is an indication of a commitment to staying on the leading edge in one's field. The following are designations worth noting. Each requires the completion of one or more competency examinations as well as ongoing continuing education.

Certified Financial Planner (CFP)   To be a CFP licensee, one must pass a rigorous national exam, complete thirty hours of continuing education every two years, agree to abide by a strict Code of Ethics, and have three years of experience in the financial planning field. If you are seeking someone to help you with your overall financial game plan, you should seek out a CFP.

Certified Public Accountant (CPA)   All CPAs must pass a series of national exams that test competency. CPAs must also complete forty hours of continuing education work each year. They must also agree to abide by a Code of Ethics. For tax planning, I recommend that you use a CPA.

Accredited Estate Planner (AEP)   This is a relatively new designation which focuses on education specifically related to the estate planning field. Five years of experience in estate planning is required to become an AEP. Designees must also complete 30 hours of continuing education during each 24 month period.

Chartered Financial Analyst (CFA)   The CFA designation is associated specifically with the securities field. To be a CFA, one must initially pass three difficult national competency exams, have three years of work experience in the field, complete continuing education each year, and abide by their Code of Ethics.

Compensation   When choosing your advisors, be sure to find out how they are compensated. Not knowing how your professional advisor is being paid can lead to misunderstandings. Most attorneys and accountants are compensated based on hourly fees. Be sure and ask what their hourly rate is and get an estimate of the amount of time they expect to have in your case. Require that they notify you immediately if they expect to spend more hours than estimated. They should also provide you with an itemized bill. Some accountants and even a few attorneys are now being compensated based on commissions from the sale of securities or other financial products. An extra measure of care should be taken on your part if your attorney or accountant recommends products to you in which they would receive a commission.

Financial planning professionals are typically compensated in one of three ways: *fee-only, fee plus commission*, or *commission only*. If you work with an advisor that receives commissions from the sale of financial products, you should insist on full disclosure of the source and dollar amount of all commissions being paid. Any reputable advisor will be happy to accommodate this request. Financial advisors that are *not* fee-only are noted with an asterisk.

Chemistry   Ideally, when you choose a professional advisor, you will have chosen someone you will work with for the rest of your life. It is not unusual to find a competent advisor that for some reason you do not "click" with. Call it a difference of personality. Most professional advisors will meet with you initially without charge. This first meeting is used to determine the scope of the work to be performed. You should also use this first meeting as an opportunity to determine if the advisor is someone you feel you would be happy working with long term.

The List   In order to assist you in locating an advisor, I have developed a list of top professional advisors across the country. Each advisor has at least ten years experience in his or her field and each has agreed to refer you to another advisor if you need help out of their field. For example, if I list an attorney in your city but you need a referral to a CPA, you can contact the attorney and he/she will refer you to a competent CPA. The list is organized alphabetically by cities within each state. Each of the attorneys listed is a member of the prestigious American College of Trust and Estate Council (ACTEC). Each of the CPAs is an Accredited Estate Planner (AEP) and member of the National Association of Estate Planners and Councils (NAEPC). The remaining financial advisors are listed among the nation's top financial advisors by *Worth* magazine. *Worth* has performed detailed background research and screening in developing their list. At the bottom of each listing, I identify each advisor's *professional category* as either: *Attorney, Accountant,* or *Financial Advisor.* Note that some of these advisors may fit into more than one category. For example, an advisor that I list as a financial advisor may also be an accountant. I have chosen the category that I felt was the best fit.

This list is obviously not an exhaustive directory of the top advisors across the United States, but it can provide you with a good starting point. As a case in point, there were so many excellent advisors in my own home state of Alabama, that I decided not to list any of them! If you want a referral to an Alabama-based advisor, give me a call and I will be happy to refer you to one.

About THE WELCH GROUP   My company provides "fee-only" wealth management services to high–net worth individuals throughout the United States. I began my career in the financial services field in 1973 and formed my own company in 1984. If you would like additional information about the services offered by my company, my contact information is the first listed.

ALABAMA
Birmingham
Stewart H. Welch, III, CFP, AEP
The Welch Group, LLC
3940 Montclair Road, Fifth Floor
Birmingham, Alabama
800-709-7100
205-879-5001
www.welchgroup.com
Financial Advisor

ALASKA
Anchorage
Ronald Greisen, CPA, AEP
Thomas, Head & Greisen
907-272-1571
Accountant

Robert L. Manley
Hughes, Thorsness *et al.*
907-274-7522
Attorney

ARIZONA
Phoenix
Ira Feldman, CPA
Toback CPAs, PC
602-264-9011
Accountant

Thomas J. Shumard
Law Office of Thomas J. Shumard
602-224-9706
Attorney

Tucson
Thomas Rooney, CPA, AEP
Bratt, Girvin & DeVries, PC
520-298-6200
Accountant

Paul D. Slosser
Slosser, Hudgins & Struse
520-529-3280
Attorney

Bert Whitehead
Cambridge Connection
520-531-1310
Financial Advisor

ARKANSAS
Little Rock
Larry Waschka
Waschka Capital Investments
501-664-8036
Financial Advisor

CALIFORNIA
Campbell
Rodney Wade, CFP
Wade Financial Advisory
408-369-7399
Financial Advisor

Del Mar
Carolyn Person Taylor
Weatherly Asset Management
619-259-4507
Financial Advisor

Fullerton
Carl Camp, CFP
Eclectic Associates, Inc.
714-738-0220
Financial Advisor

Irvine
Victoria Collins, CFP
Keller, Collins, Hakopian &
Leisure, Investment Counsel, Inc.
949-476-0300
Financial Advisor

Rick Keiler, CFP
Keller, Collins, Hakopian &
Leisure, Investment Counsel, Inc.
949-476-0300
Financial Advisor

Los Angeles
Jon J. Gallo
Greenburg, Glusker *et al.*
310-553-3610
Attorney

Paul Gordon Hoffman
Hoffman, Sabban & Watenmaker
310-470-6010
Attorney

Margie Mullen, CFP
Mullen Advisory
213-469-0919
Financial Advisor

Newport Beach
Laura Tarbox, CFP
Tarbox Equity, Inc.
800-482-7269
Financial Advisor

Orinda
Peggy S. Cabaniss, CFP
HC Financial Advisors
925-254-1023
Financial Advisor

Palo Alto
Karen Goodfriend, CPA
Moorman & Co.
650-327-9000
Financial Advisor

San Diego
George E. Olmstead
Olmstead, Hughes & Garrett
619-239-6188
Attorney

Dale Yahnke, CFP, CFA
Dowling & Yahnke, Inc.
619-554-0090
Financial Advisor

San Francisco
Timothy Kochis, CFP
Kochis Fitz
415-394-6668
Financial Advisor

Linda L. McCall
Law Offices of Linda L. McCall
415-835-6730
Attorney

Thomas Tracy, CFP, CFA
Kochis Fitz
415-394-6671
Financial Advisor

San Luis Obispo
Robert Wacker, CFP
R. E. Wacker Assoc.
805-541-1308
Financial Advisor

San Rafael
Richard Stone, CFP
Salient Financial Group
415-456-8839
Financial Advisor*

Sherman Oaks
Mitchell Freedman, CPA
Mitchell Freedman Accountacy
Corp.
818-905-0321
Financial Advisor

Torrance
Richard P. Moran, CFP
Financial Network Investment
Corp.
800-998-3642
Financial Advisor*

COLORADO
Aurora
Mark J. Smith, CFP, CPA
M. J. Smith & Associates, Inc.
303-695-1098
Financial Advisor*

Boulder
Myra Salzer, CFP
The Wealth Conservancy, Inc.
303-444-1919
Financial Advisor

Colorado Springs
Colin B. Coombs, CFP
Petra Financial Advisors, Inc.
888-636-6300
Financial Advisor

Dave Forbes, CFP, CFA
Petra Financial Advisors, Inc.
719-636-9000
Financial Advisor

Denver
Patricia Clowdus
Attorney at Law
303-321-6872
Attorney

James F. Ingraham
Zisman & Ingraham, PC
303-320-0023
Attorney

Thomas E. Zanecchia, CPA
Wealth Management Consultants,
Inc.
303-296-3586
Financial Advisor

Englewood
Judith A. Shine, CFP
Shine Investment Advisory Services
303-740-8600
Financial Advisor

CONNECTICUT
Hartford
Suzanne Bocchini
Reid & Riege
860-240-1030
Attorney

Norwalk
Ann D. Jevne, CFP, CPA
Schwartz & Hofflich, LLP
203-847-4068
Financial Advisor

Simsbury
John W. Eckel, CFP, CFA
Pinnacle Investment Management,
Inc.
860-651-1716
Financial Advisor

Woodbridge
Alan P. Weiss, CFP
Regent Retirement Planning, Inc.
800-443-3101
Financial Advisor*

DELAWARE
Wilmington
Judith W. Lau, CFP
Lau & Associates, Ltd.
302-792-5955
Financial Advisor

F. Edmund Lynch
Ament, Lynch & Carr
302-655-2599
Attorney

Joanna Reiver
Schlusser & Reiver
302-655-8181
Attorney

Ann Taylor Tansey, CPA
Tansey Tabeling & Co., PA
302-425-3523
Accountant

DISTRICT OF COLUMBIA
Washington
Julian E. Markham, Jr.
Thompson, O'Donnell *et al.*
202-289-1133
Attorney

Carol Rhees
Steptoe & Johnson, LLP
202-429-6220
Attorney

Margaret Welch, CFP
Armstrong, Welch & MacIntyre
202-887-8135
Financial Advisor*

Doris Blazek-White
Covington & Burling
202-662-5490
Attorney

FLORIDA
Boca Raton
Robert Levitt, CFP, CFA
Evensky, Brown, Katz & Levitt
561-498-0905
Financial Advisor

Clearwater
George Bollenback, CPA, AEP
Bollenback & Forret
727-446-5858
Accountant

Coral Gables
Harold Evensky, CFP
Evensky, Brown, Katz & Levitt
305-448-8882
Financial Advisor

Coral Springs
Frank Pugliese
Personal Financial Profiles
954-755-8647
Financial Advisor*

Jacksonville
Richard Camp, CPA
Richard Camp, CPA, PA
904-281-9924
Accountant

Clay B. Tousey, Jr.
Fisher, Tousey *et al.*
904-356-2600
Attorney

Lighthouse Point
Jay L. Shein, CFP
Compass Financial Group, Inc.
954-946-8501
Financial Advisor*

Miami
Linda Lubitz, CFP
Lubitz and Associates
305-670-4440
Financial Advisor*

Paul M. Stokes
Kelley, Drye & Warren, LLP
305-372-2400
Attorney

Orlando
John Prizer, CFP, CFA
Resource Consulting Group
407-422-0252
Financial Advisor

Palm Beach Gardens
Charles Lamn, CPA
Lamn, Krielow, Dytrych & Co.,
CPAs
561-694-1040
Accountant

Plantation
Benjamin Tobias, CFP, CPA
Tobias Financial Advisors
954-424-1660
Financial Advisor

Tampa
Leslie J. Barnett
Barnett, Bolt, Kirkwood & Long
813-253-2020
Attorney

Thomas Ellwanger
Fowler, White *et al.*
813-228-7411
Attorney

GEORGIA
Atlanta
Andrew Berg, CFP, CPA
Homrich & Berg
404-264-1400
Financial Advisor

Franklin H. Butterfield, CFP, CFA, CPA
Homrich & Berg
404-264-1400
Financial Advisor

David E. Homrich, CFP, CPA
Homrich & Berg
404-264-1400
Financial Advisor

James Howard, CPA
Smith & Howard
404-874-6244
Accountant

Frank S. McGaughey, III
Powell, Goldstein *et al.*
404-572-6651
Attorney

Wayne Vason
Troutman Sanders, LLP
404-885-3232
Attorney

Columbus
E. Lowry Reid, Jr.
Page, Scrantom, Sprous, Tucker & Ford, PC
706-324-0251
Attorney

HAWAII
Honolulu
Harry G. Kasanow, CFP
Kasanow & Associates: Wealth Management
808-988-1311
Financial Advisor

David Larsen
Cades, Schutte *et al.*
808-521-9200
Attorney

John Lockwood
Ashford & Wriston
808-539-0400
Attorney

Thomas Rulon
Attorney at Law
808-537-5311
Attorney

IDAHO
Boise
P. LaVern Gentry, CPA
Deloitte & Touche, LLP
208-422-1867
Accountant

John McGown
Hawley Troxell Ennis & Hawley LLP
208-344-6000
Attorney

ILLINOIS
Chicago
R. Mark Bell, CFP
Mark Bell & Assoc.
312-840-8265
Financial Advisor

Gary Bowyer, CFP
Gary N. Bowyer & Assoc.
773-631-8070
Financial Advisor

Timothy G. Carroll
Carroll, Kline & Wall
312-214-9000
Attorney

Tim Emmitt
Lewis, Overbeck & Furman
312-580-1240
Attorney

John Marshall
Mayer, Brown & Platt
312-701-7129
Attorney

Oak Brook
Armond Dinverno, CFP, CPA
Dinverno & Foltz Financial Group
630-954-4740
Financial Advisor

Palatine
Carol C. Pankros, CFP
CCP, Inc.
847-303-1220
Financial Advisor

Rockford
Brent Brodeski, CFP, CFA, CPA
Savant Capital Management
815-227-0300
Financial Advisor

Schaumburg
Mark Balasa, CFP, CPA
Balasa & Hoffman, Inc.
847-925-9400
Financial Advisor

Springfield
Robert M. Bellatti
Bellatti & Barton
217-793-9300
Attorney

Winnetka
Janet Tussing, CFP
Albanese Hemsley & Tussing, Ltd.
847-446-3636
Financial Advisor*

INDIANA
Columbus
Larry Nunn, CPA
Larry Nunn & Associates CPAs,
LLC
812-376-3061
Accountant

Ft. Wayne
Gregory Galecki, CFP
Galecki Financial Management
219-436-8525
Financial Advisor

Indianapolis
Elaine E. Bedel, CFP
Bedel Financial Consulting, Inc.
317-843-1358
Financial Advisor

Kristin Fruehwald
Barnes & Thornburg
317-231-7245
Attorney

South Bend
Carolyn Metzger, CPA
Metzger, Mancini & Lackner
219-232-9973
Accountant

IOWA
Des Moines
Steven Zumbach
Belin Lamson McCormick
Zumbach Fly
515-243-7100
Attorney

W. De Moines
Jerry Foster, CFP
Foster Capital Management, Inc.
515-226-9000
Financial Advisor*

Phil M. Kruzan, Sr, CFP
Foster Capital Management, Inc.
515-226-9000
Financial Advisor*

Mark Stadtlander, CFP
Foster Capital Management, Inc.
515-226-9000
Financial Advisor*

KANSAS
Overland Park
Howard Rothwell
Stepp & Rothwell, Inc.
913-649-3311
Financial Advisor

Kathleen Stepp, CFP, CPA
Stepp & Rothwell, Inc.
913-649-3311
Financial Advisor

Wichita
Linda K. Constable
Fleeson, Gooing *et al.*
316-267-7361
Attorney

KENTUCKY
Bowling Green
John Grider, CPA, AEP
Baird, Kurtz & Dobson
502-781-0111
Accountant

Lexington
Glen S. Bagby
Brock, Brock & Bagby
606-255-7000
Attorney

Louisville
John Cummins
Greenebaum, Doll & McDonald,
PLLC
502-587-3602
Attorney

LOUISIANA
Covington
Robert J. Reed, Jr., CFP
Personal Financial Advisors
504-898-0450
Financial Advisor

Metairie
Michael Zabalaoui, CFP, CPA
Resource Management, Inc.
504-833-5378
Financial Advisor

New Orleans
Deke G. Carbo, CPA
KPMG Peat Marwick, LLP
504-584-1050
Financial Advisor

J.Grant Coleman
Nesser, King & LeBlanc
504-582-3800
Attorney

Joel Mendler
Baldwin & Haspel, LLC
504-585-7711
Attorney

Robert Perez, CPA
KPMG Peat Marwick, LLP
504-584-1016
Accountant

Shreveport
J. Edgerton Pierson, Jr.
Blanchard, Walker *et al.*
318-221-6858
Attorney

MAINE
Portland
Judith Coburn
Verrill & Dana
207-774-4000
Attorney

MARYLAND
Annapolis
Steven Ames, CFP
Ames Fee-Only Financial Planning
410-280-2390
Financial Advisor

Baltimore
John Abosch, CPA, CFP, AEP
KAWG&F CPAs
410-828-6432
Accountant

Lyle Benson, Jr., CFP, CPA
L. K. Benson & Co, PC
410-494-6680
Financial Advisor

Max Blumenthall
Stewart, Plant & Blumenthall
410-347-0512
Attorney

J. Darby Bowman
Attorney at Law
410-821-0074
Attorney

Donald Mering
Ober, Kaler *et al.*
410-347-7688
Attorney

Bethesda
Marvin Burt, CFP
Burt Associates, Inc.
301-652-2405
Financial Advisor

Clinton
Thomas J.(Tim) Murphy, CFP,
CPA, AEP
T.J. Murphy, PA
301-856-4100
Accountant

Columbia
J. Michael Martin, CFP
Financial Advantage, Inc.
410-715-9200
Financial Advisor

Ellicott City
Kevin Condon, CFP
Baltimore-Washington Financial
Advisors
888-461-3900
Financial Advisor

Silver Spring
Peg Downey, CFP
Money Plans
301-439-8687
Financial Advisor

Towson
Timothy Chase, CFP, CPA
Wealth Management Services
410-337-7575
Financial Advisor

MASSACHUSETTS
Boston
Katherine L. Babson, Jr.
Hutchins, Wheeler & Dittmar
617-951-6600
Attorney

Winifred I. Li
Hill & Barlow
617-428-3352
Attorney

Jon E. Steffensen
Steffensen, Herman, McOster &
Daggett, LLC
617-523-7935
Attorney

Richard Vitale, CPA
Vitale, Caturano & Co.
617-912-9000
Financial Advisor

Cambridge
Cary P. Geller, CFP, CPA
Tofias Fleishman Shapiro & Co.
617-761-0600
Financial Advisor

Robert Glovsky, CFP
Tofias Fleishman Shapiro & Co.
617-761-0600
Financial Advisor

Canton
Judith Ludwig, CFP, CPA, AEP
Tandem Financial Services, Inc.
781-821-4890
Accountant

Lexington
William Baldwin
Pillar Financial Advisors
781-863-2200
Financial Advisor

Beth Gamel, CPA
Pillar Financial Advisors
781-863-2200
Financial Advisor

Lincoln
Alice Finn, CFP
Ballentine, Finn & Company, Inc.
781-259-8126
Financial Advisor

Norfolk
Spring Bixby Leonard, CFP
SBL Financial Enetrprise
508-520-1144
Financial Advisor*

Tewksbury
Arthur Ford, CFP, CPA, AEP
Sullivan Bille, PC
978-970-2900
Accountant

Wellesley
Susan Kaplan, CFP
Kaplan Financial Services
781-237-4022
Financial Advisor

MICHIGAN
Bloomfield Hills
Marilyn Capelli Dimitroff, CFP
Capelli Financial Services, Inc.
248-594-9282
Financial Advisor

Detroit
Harvey B. Wallace, II
Joslyn Keydel & Wallace
313-964-4181
Attorney

Farmington Hills
Richard Bloom, CPA
Bloom Asset Management
248-932-5200
Financial Advisor

Grand Rapids
Thomas W. Czerney, CPA, AEP
Beene Garter, LLP
616-235-5200
Accountant

Iron Mountain
Jerry Picucci, CPA, AEP
Fluery, Singler & Co
906-774-0833
Accountant

Southfield
Ronald M. Yolles, CFA
Yolles Investment Management
248-356-3232
Financial Advisor

MINNESOTA
Minneapolis
Robert Klosterman, CFP
White Oaks Wealth Advisors, Inc.
612-542-8128
Financial Advisor

MISSISSIPPI
Jackson
David B. Grishman
Watkins, Ludlam, Winter &
Stennis, PA
601-949-4770
Attorney

Tim Medley, CFP
Medley & Co.
601-982-4123
Financial Advisor

R. James Young
Young & Marchetti, PLLC
601-969-7007
Attorney

MISSOURI
Chesterfield
Jeffrey Buckner, CFP
Plancorp, Inc.
314-878-3778
Financial Advisor

Kansas City
Peter W. Brown
Husch & Eppenberger, LLC
816-421-4800
Attorney

St. Louis
Joan Malloy, CFP, CPA, CFA
Arthur Andersen
314-425-9228
Financial Advisor

MONTANA
Billings
Larry Petersen
Dorsey & Whitney, LLC
406-252-3800
Attorney

NEBRASKA
Lincoln
M. Douglas Deitchler
Baylor, Evnen *et al.*
402-475-1075
Attorney

Thomas Haase
Perry, Guthery *et al.*
402-476-9200
Attorney

Omaha
Ronald C. Carson, Jr, CFP
Carson Feltz Retirement Planning
402-333-5448
Financial Advisor*

NEW HAMPSHIRE
Exeter
Henri Richard, CPA, AEP
Henneberry & Richard
603-772-9341
Accountant

Manchester
Brian Grodman, CFP
Grodman Financial Group
603-647-9999
Financial Advisor*

Portsmouth
Kathryn Bickford, CFP
Bickford Financial & Investment
Services, Inc.
603-431-1156
Financial Advisor*

Wolfeboro
Roy Ballentine, CFP
Ballentine, Finn & Company, Inc.
603-569-1717
Financial Advisor

Susan John, CFP
Financial Focus
603-569-1994
Financial Advisor

NEW JERSEY
Cherry Hill
Harry Scheyer, CFP, CPA
Practitioners' Financial Advisors
609-424-3318
Financial Advisor

Clinton
James J. Chesterton, Jr, CFP
Brighton Financial Planning, Inc.
908-730-7000
Financial Advisor

Flemington
Albert Zdenek, CPA
Zdenek Financial Planning, Inc.
908-782-1600
Financial Advisor

Florham Park
Pat Hamel, CPA
Hamel Associates, Inc.
973-822-3477
Financial Advisor

Morristown
Bernard M. Kiely, CFP, CPA
Kiely Capital Management, Inc.
973-455-1894
Financial Advisor

New Providence
Diahann W. Lassus, CFP, CPA
Lassus Wherley & Assoc., PC
908-464-0102
Financial Advisor

Oradell
Gary Greenbaum, CFP, CFA
Greenbaum & Associates, Inc.
201-261-1900
Financial Advisor

Princeton
Marsha Beidler
Drinker, Biddle & Reath
609-716-6516
Attorney

Constance Herrstrom, CFP
Premier Financial Planning, Inc.
609-924-2424
Financial Advisor

Trenton
Clive Klatzkin, CFP, CPA, AEP
Klatzkin & Co
609-890-9189
Accountant

NEW MEXICO
Albuquerque
Roberta Cooper Ramo
Modrall, Sperling *et al.*
505-848-1800
Attorney

James M. Parker
Modrall, Sperling *et al.*
505-848-1800
Attorney

Santa Fe
David Johnson
Hickey & Johnson
505-988-4300
Attorney

Robert Rikoon
Rikoon Investment Advisors
505-989-3581
Financial Advisor

Robert Worcester
Worcester & McKay
505-820-2244
Attorney

NEW YORK
Albany
James Ayers
DeGraff, Foy *et al.*
518-462-5300
Attorney

Timothy B. Thornton
McNamee, Lochner, Titus &
Williams, PC
518-447-3200
Attorney

Bay Shore
Charles Hughes, CFP
C.G. Hughes Company
516-665-7881
Financial Advisor

Buffalo
Steve M. Newman
Hodgson, Russ *et al.*
716-856-4000
Attorney

Elmsford
Barry Steinfink, CPA
Steinfink & Napolean, LLP
914-347-4700
Accountant

Garden City
Henry Graber, CPA
Graber & Co
516-742-0100
Accountant

Medford
Mark J. Snyder
Mark J. Snyder Financial Services, Inc.
800-543-5283
Financial Advisor*

New York
Karen Altfest, CFP
L.J. Altfest & Co, Inc.
212-406-0850
Financial Advisor

Lewis J. Altfest, CFP, CFA, CPA
L.J. Altfest & Co, Inc.
212-406-0850
Financial Advisor

Warren Bergstein, CPA
Straus & Comas, PC
212-268-1800
Accountant

Brit Geiger
Rubin, Baum *et al.*
212-698-7700
Attorney

Al Lingelbach
Jackson & Nash
212-370-8129
Attorney

Sandra S. Weiksner
Cleary, Gottlieb, Steen & Hamilton
212-225-2290
Attorney

Roslyn
Larry Marchisotta, CPA
Satty, Hollis & Ciacco, CPA, PC
516-621-6600
Accountant

White Plains
Andrew S. Kenward, CPA
Andrew S. Kenward, CPA, PC
914-592-4343
Accountant

Williamsville
Anthony Ogorek, CFP
Ogorek Capital Management
716-626-5000
Financial Advisor

Williston Park
David A. Black, CPA
David A. Black, CPA
516-294-6638
Accountant

NEVADA
Las Vegas
Layne Rushforth
The Busch Firm
702-892-3789
Attorney

Reno
Vicki P. Schultz, CFP
Schultz & Schultz, Inc.
702-828-1400
Financial Advisor

NORTH CAROLINA
Asheville
W. Barton Boyer, CFP
Parsec Financial Management
828-255-0271
Financial Advisor

Greensboro
Keith Hiatt, CPA
Breslow, Starling, Frost *et al.*
336-292-6872
Accountant

Thomas Sinks
Carruthers & Roth
336-379-8651
Attorney

NORTH DAKOTA
Fargo
Harris Widmer, CPA
Widmer, Roel & Co
701-237-6062
Accountant

OHIO
Centerville
G. Mike Crawford, CFP
LifePlan Financial Group, Inc.
937-438-8000
Financial Advisor*

Cincinnati
Gilbert C. Bernhardt, CPA
Franz CPAs
513-489-4848
Accountant

J. Michael Cooney
Dinsmore & Shohl
513-977-8236
Attorney

David Foster, CFP, CPA
Foster & Motley, Inc.
513-792-6640
Financial Advisor

Ruth Longenecker
Frost & Jacobs, LLP
513-651-6800
Attorney

Cleveland
Robert Ford
Thompson Hine & Flory
216-566-5500
Attorney

Karen Spero, CFP
Spero-Smith Investment Advisers
216-464-6266
Financial Advisor

Columbus
Peggy Ruhlin, CFP, CPA
Budros & Ruhlin, Inc.
614-481-6900
Financial Advisor

Toledo
John R. Duncan, CPA, AEP
Lublin, Sussman, Rosenberg &
Damrauer
419-841-2848
Accountant

OKLAHOMA
Oklahoma City
Joe W. Bowie, CFP
Retirement Investment Advisors
405-842-3443
Financial Advisor

Randy Thurman, CFP, CPA
Retirement Investment Advisors,
Inc.
405-942-1234
Financial Advisor*

Tulsa
Bill Brumley, Jr.
Brumley & Bishop
918-582-0043
Attorney

Jana L. Shoulders, CPA
Adams Hall Investment Mgmt,
LLC
918-665-2446
Accountant

John Turner
Stuart, Biolchini *et al.*
918-582-3311
Attorney

OREGON
Portland
Marilyn R. Bergen, CFP
Capital Management Consulting
503-227-5284
Financial Advisor

Charles Mauritz
Davis Wright Tremaine LLP
503-778-5320
Attorney

PENNSYLVANIA
Easton
Alan S. Abraham, CPA
Abraham, Borda & Co, PC
610-258-5666
Accountant

Media
Thomas D. Smedile, CPA
Swarthmore Financial Advisors
610-892-9922
Financial Advisor

Philadelphia
Roy Diliberto, CFP
RTD Financial Advisors
215-557-3800
Financial Advisor

Morey Rosenbloom
Blank, Rome *et al.*
215-569-5599
Attorney

Spencer D. Sherman, CFP
Sherman Financial, Inc.
215-656-4280
Financial Advisor

B. Michael Watkins, CPA, AEP
KPMG Peat Marwick, LLP
215-299-3943
Accountant

Pittsburgh
Roger Gibson, CFP, CFA
Gibson Capital Management, Ltd.
412-369-9925
Financial Advisor

Kenneth Lewis
Kabala & Geeseman
412-391-1334
Attorney

Louis Stanasolovich, CFP
Legend Financial Advisors, Inc.
412-635-9210
Financial Advisor

Yardley
George Luciani, CFP
Capital Planning Advisory Group
215-579-5760
Financial Advisor

RHODE ISLAND
Providence
Nathan W. Chace
Chace, Ruttenberg & Freedman
401-453-6400
Attorney

Westerly
Malcolm Makin, CFP
Professional Planning Group
401-596-2800
Financial Planner*

SOUTH CAROLINA
Charleston
John von Lehe
Young, Clement *et al.*
803-724-6676
Attorney

Columbia
Cheryl Holland, CFP
Abacus Planning Group
803-933-0054
Financial Advisor

Greenville
William Dennis
Leatherwood, Walker *et al.*
864-242-6440
Attorney

Mt. Pleasant
Kyra Hollowell Morris, CFP
Morris Financial Concepts
843-884-6192
Financial Advisor

SOUTH DAKOTA
Rapid City
Casey C. Peterson, CPA
Casey Peterson & Associates, Ltd.
605-348-1930
Accountant

Sioux Falls
Sarah Richardson Larson
Davenport, Evans *et al.*
605-336-2880
Attorney

TENNESSEE
Brentwood
Richard Hammel, CFP
Hammel, Hari & Kendall, LLC
615-371-5222
Financial Advisor

Chattanooga
Marion G. Fryar, CPA
Joseph Decosimo & Co
423-756-7100
Accountant

Memphis
Joseph B. Walker
Armstrong, Allen *et al.*
901-523-8211
Attorney

Christopher J. Ward, CPA, AEP
Rhea & Ivy, PLC
901-761-3000
Accountant

Robert Winfield, CFP
Legacy Wealth Management
901-758-9006
Financial Advisor

Nashville
James Gooch
Bass, Berry & Sims, PLC
615-742-6247
Attorney

Michael G. Kaplan
Sherrard & Roe, PLC
615-742-4572
Attorney

Howard Safer, CPA
Bradford Trust Company
800-522-7037
Financial Advisor

TEXAS
Austin
John Henry McDonald, CFP
Austin Asset Management Company
512-453-6622
Financial Advisor

Bryan
Janet Briaud, CFP
Briaud Financial Planning
409-260-9771
Financial Advisor

Dallas
Barbara McComas Anderson
Law Office of Barbara McComas Anderson
214-367-8090
Attorney

Santo Bisignano, Jr.
Bisignano & Harrison, LLP
214-360-9777
Attorney

Allen Burgess, CPA
Burgess Co.
214-828-0114
Accountant

Barbara B. Ferguson
Thompson & Knight
214-969-1481
Attorney

Kathryn G. Henkel
Hughes & Luce, LLP
214-939-5500
Attorney

J. Richard Joyner, CFP, CPA
Ernst & Young, LLP
214-969-8482
Financial Advisor

El Paso
Brainerd Parrish
Studdard & Melby
915-533-5938
Attorney

Fort Worth
David Diesslin, CFP
Diesslin & Associates, Inc.
817-332-6122
Financial Advisor

Houston
Don Fizer
Fizer, Beck *et al.*
713-840-7710
Attorney

Carol Warley, CPA
KPMG Peat Marwick, LLP
713-319-2180
Financial Advisor

UTAH
Salt Lake City
Herbert Livsey
Ray, Quinney & Nebeker
801-532-1500
Attorney

Carol Wilson, CFP
Wilson Financial Advisors
801-355-5210
Financial Advisor

VIRGINIA
Annandale
Glen J. Buco, CFP
West Financial Services
703-354-1661
Financial Advisor

Fairfax
Lynn Hopewell, CFP
The Monitor Group, Inc.
703-968-3002
Financial Advisor

Falls Church

Marjorie L. Fox, CFP
Rembert, D'Orazio & Fox
703-821-6655
Financial Advisor

McLean

Eleanor Blayney, CFP
Sullivan, Bruyette, Speros &
Blayney
703-734-9300
Financial Advisor

James Bruyette, CFP, CPA
Sullivan, Bruyette, Speros &
Blayney
703-724-9300
Financial Advisor

Gregory Sullivan, CFP, CPA
Sullivan, Bruyette, Speros &
Blayney
703-734-9300
Financial Advisor

Richmond

Michael Joyce, CFP, CFA
Michael Joyce & Associates, PC
800-784-6771
Financial Advisor

Thomas McN. Millhiser
Hunton & Williams
804-788-8732
Attorney

Roanoke

Roger Anglin, CPA
Brown, Edwards & Company, LLP
540-345-0936
Accountant

Andrew M. Hudick, CFP
Fee-Only Financial Planning
540-342-7102
Financial Advisor

Salem

Ronald Salyer, CPA, AEP
Salyer, Garbee & Co
540-387-0229
Accountant

WASHINGTON
Lynnwood

Kathleen L. Cotton, CFP
Cotton Financial Advisors
425-672-6050
Financial Advisor

Seattle

Edward Ahrens
Ahrens & DeAngeli
206-652-0101
Attorney

Kaycee Krysty, CFP, CPA
Tyee Asset Strategies, Inc.
206-343-8900
Financial Advisor

Spokane
Donald K. Querna
Randall & Danskin
509-747-2052
Attorney

Vancouver
Charles Bishop
First Pacific Associates/KMS
Financial Services, Inc.
360-254-2585
Financial Advisor*

WEST VIRGINIA
Charleston
Thomas Freeman, II
Jackson & Kelly
304-340-1235
Attorney

Robert Galloway, CPA, AEP
Simpson & Osborne
304-343-0168
Accountant

WISCONSIN
Madison
Thomas Hoffner
LaFollette & Sinykin
608-257-3911
Attorney

Richard Langer
Michael, Best & Friedrich
608-283-2248
Attorney

Milwaukee
Keith Christiansen
Foley & Lardner
414-297-5746
Attorney

WYOMING
Casper
John Warnick
Brown & Drew
307-234-1000
Attorney

Estate Planning Terms

Abatement   The reduction of bequests when the assets of an estate are insufficient to pay all taxes, expenses, and bequests in full.

Ademption   When property listed in a will is subsequently disposed of prior to death, thus preventing the beneficiary from inheriting the property.

Administrator (male); **Administratrix** (female)   The person or institution appointed by the court to administer or settle the estate of a deceased person who dies intestate.

Alternate Valuation Date   The date six months after your death. Your estate representative has the option of valuing your assets as of the date of death or *alternate valuation date*, if certain criteria are met.

Annual Gift Tax Exclusion   Every individual can give away assets or cash up to the annual gift tax exclusion amount to as many people as they desire each year free of gift taxes. For 1998 the annual gift tax exclusion amount is $10,000. For subsequent years the amount is indexed for inflation.

Applicable Credit Amount   A tax credit allowed by the federal government against taxes due on gifts or transfers from your estate.

Applicable Exclusion Amount   The dollar value of assets that you can give to a non-spouse either during your lifetime or at your death free of estate or gift taxes. For 1998, the dollar value is $625,000. The dollar amount is scheduled to increase to $1 million by 2006.

Beneficiary   A person who is designated to receive benefits under a will, trust or insurance policy.

Bequest   Property left to a person or organization under a will or trust.

Bypass Trust   See *Credit Shelter Trust*.

Codicil An amendment to a previous will. A codicil is executed with the same formalities as a will.

Community Property Nine states have community property laws which, in general, state that all property acquired by either partner in a marriage, is considered owned one half by each partner.

Contingent Beneficiary A person or organization that is a beneficiary only upon the occurrence of some "contingent" event. For example, "I give Jean Daily the sum of $5,000 only if she is married to my brother John Daily at the time of my death."

Credit Shelter Trust (or *Bypass Trust*) A trust established under your will to take advantage of the *Applicable Exclusion Amount*. The *Applicable Exclusion Amount* is the dollar value of assets that can be left to someone other than a spouse free of estate taxes.

Curtesy See *Dower* and *Curtesy*.

Custodian A person or trust company responsible for the care and management of property for a minor. The relationship is a *fiduciary* relationship.

Decedent The person who died.

Disclaimer When a person disclaims benefits received from a decedent. If the disclaimer is timely (usually within nine months of receiving the rights to the property); irrevocable; and the person never received any benefits from the property, then there will be no tax consequences to the disclaiming person.

Domicile The state in which you have your permanent residence.

Donee A person receiving a gift.

Donor A person making a gift.

Dower (female); **Curtesy** (male) Some states have laws that give your spouse the right to receive a certain portion of your estate (usually one-third to one-half) even if he or she is left out of your will. Also referred to as an *elective share*.

Escheat If you die without a will and without heirs, your estate will revert to your primary state of residence.

Estate All of the property you own at your death (your *gross estate*).

Estate Taxes   Transfer taxes imposed by our federal government (and our states in some cases) for the privilege of giving your property to your heirs.

Executor (male); **Executrix** (female)   The person (or institution) you name in your will who will be responsible for settling your estate at your death.

Fiduciary   A person or institution occupying a position of trust. Fiduciaries are held to high standards of accountability by our courts.

Five and Five Power   A provision common in a trust agreement giving a surviving spouse the non-cumulative right to withdraw annually the greater of (a) 5 percent of the trust corpus or (b) $5,000. The exercising of such right does not cause inclusion of the trust assets in the estate of the surviving spouse.

Generation Skipping Transfer Tax (GSTT)   A tax imposed on transfers of assets (either through gifts or your will) to a "skip" generation (a grandchild for example). Currently the first $1 million (adjusted for inflation) of transfers are not subject to the tax. The current tax rate is 55 percent.

Gifts   The transfer of property to another person or organization without receiving anything of value in return.

Gift Tax   A tax imposed on the transfer of assets made during a person's lifetime. Note that the tax is due on gifts in excess of certain limits.

Grantor   A person who establishes and transfers property to a trust. Also called a *settlor*.

Guardian   A person responsible for the care of a minor (called *guardian of the person*) or a minor's property (called the *property guardian*).

Heir   A person entitled under state law to receive assets of another person who died without a will.

Holographic Will   A will that is completely handwritten. Many states recognize holographic wills only under certain circumstances.

Incompetent   Someone who has been judged by a court of law to be incapable of managing his or her financial affairs.

Inheritance Tax   A tax imposed by some states on heirs who receive an inheritance.

Inter Vivos Trust   A trust created during your lifetime rather that under your will. Also called a *living trust*.

Intestacy Laws   The laws of each state which determine who will receive the assets of a person who dies without a will.

Intestate   To die without a will.

Irrevocable Trust   A type of trust that cannot be revoked, changed, or amended. This type of trust is often used to remove assets from one's estate.

Issue   Your direct descendants such as children, grandchildren, and great grandchildren.

Joint Tenancy   A way of titling property whereby at the death of one joint tenant, the remaining joint tenant(s) automatically receives the deceased person's interest.

Joint Will   A single document that serves as the will for two people (usually a married couple).

Legacy   A gift of property under a will. The recipient of such property is called a *legatee*.

Life Estate   The right to use property during one's lifetime. At death, that person's rights terminate.

Living Trusts   See *inter vivos trust*.

Living Will   A document that declares the level of care you desire should you become medically incapacitated. Generally, it states that you do not wish to be kept alive by artificial means.

Marital Deduction   The law provides that a married person may leave (or gift) an unlimited amount of assets to his or her spouse free of estate and gift taxes. This typically results in a "postponement" (rather than elimination) of the estate or gift taxes.

Marital Trust   A trust set up to receive assets that qualify for the *marital deduction*. This is more appropriately called a *power of appointment trust*.

Minor   A person who is not legally considered an adult (age 18 to 21 in most states). Minors cannot legally enter into binding contracts.

Non-contest Clause   A provision in a will that provides that any person contesting the will shall have no rights to any assets under the will. Also known as the *In-terrorem clause*.

Nuncupative Will   An oral will. Many states do not allow oral wills at all; other states allow them only in extreme circumstances such as emanate death.

Per Capita   A distribution that is divided "equally" among the named persons (or their descendants) who have survived the testator. For example, you leave $100,000 to be divided "per capita" among your two sons and two daughters ($25,000 each). If one of your daughters predeceased you but had two children, your surviving children and two grandchildren would each receive $20,000.

Personal Property   All property other than real estate.

Per Stirpes   A distribution that is divided among named persons *or their descendants* should they predecease the testator. For example, you leave $100,000 to be divided among your two sons and two daughters ($25,000 each). If one of your daughters predeceased you but had two children, your surviving children would each receive $25,000 and your deceased daughter's children would each receive $12,500.

Power of Appointment   A right given to a person allowing them to designate to whom someone else's assets will go at the occurrence of a specified event.

Power of Attorney   A document executed by you which gives another person (your *agent*) the right to act on your behalf. A power of attorney can be written to include very broad powers or very limited powers.

Primary Beneficiary   The person (or persons) who will receive property under a will, trust, or insurance policy.

Probate   The court-supervised process of transferring one's property at death to his or her rightful heirs.

Probate Property   All property of a deceased person that is subject to probate. Certain property such as joint tenancy property is not subject to probate.

QDOT Trust   Legally referred to as a Qualified Domestic Trust. This is a spousal trust which allows non-U.S. citizen spouses to receive assets qualifying under the *unlimited marital deduction*.

QTIP Trust   Legally referred to as a Qualified Terminable Interest Property Trust. This spousal trust allows you to control the ultimate disposition of the assets in the trust. Your spouse receives all income from the trust during his or her lifetime. This trust can qualify for the *unlimited marital deduction*.

Real Property   Land and fixed improvements such as buildings, trees, and fences.

Residue   The portion of your estate that remains after all specific distributions have been made. Also known as the *Residuary Estate*.

Revocable Trust   A type of trust that can be changed, modified, amended, or terminated at any time by the grantor during his or her lifetime.

Rule Against Perpetuities   A complicated section of the law that prohibits leaving assets in trust indefinitely while avoiding taxes. Basically, the law states that funds can be left in trust for the lifetime plus 21 years of any beneficiary living at the time the grantor establishes the trust. Beyond that time a severe penalty is imposed.

Settlor   A person who establishes and transfers property to a trust. Also called a *grantor*.

Spendthrift Provision   A provision in a trust that prevents trust assets from being pledged, assigned, or otherwise used as collateral for a loan. The purpose is to protect the assets from the beneficiary's creditors.

Sprinkle Provision   A provision in a trust that allows the trustee the discretion to distribute trust income among the beneficiaries as the trustee deems appropriate. The distributions can be "uneven" (excluding some beneficiaries in favor of others) or the trust income can be accumulated.

Stepped-Up Cost Basis   The tax basis of appreciated property "steps up" to fair market value on the date of death. For example, if you own a stock that is worth $40,000 for which you paid $10,000 (your tax basis), you have a taxable gain of $30,000. If you died, the tax basis "steps up" to the fair market value of $40,000 and an immediate sale would result in no taxable gain.

Taxable Estate   The portion of your estate that is subject to federal and/or state taxes. From the gross estate you subtract funeral and administrative expenses; debts (including certain unpaid taxes); charitable contributions; and the marital deduction (if applicable).

Testamentary Trust   A trust that is created under your will which will take effect at your death.

Testator   One who dies having made a valid will.

Trust   A legal arrangement whereby one person (the *trustor, grantor,* or *settlor*), places assets under the management or supervision of another person or institution (the *trustee*) for the benefit of a third person (the *beneficiary*).

Trustee   A person or institution that manages and administers a trust.

Unified Credit   See *Applicable Credit Amount.*

Unified Gifts/Transfers to Minors Act   State laws that provide a method of holding assets for minors.

Unlimited Marital Deduction   A provision in the law that allows a married person to give or leave an unlimited amount of assets to his or her spouse free of gift or estate taxes.

Will   A legal document that details how your estate is to be distributed upon your death.

Index